WEST BY
WEST

Also by Jonathan Coleman

Long Way to Go: Black and White in America

Exit the Rainmaker

At Mother's Request: A True Story of Money, Murder, and Betrayal

WEST BY
WEST

MY CHARMED,
TORMENTED LIFE

Jerry West
and Jonathan Coleman

Little, Brown and Company

New York   Boston   London

Little, Brown and Company
Hachette Book Group
237 Park Avenue, New York, NY 10017
www.hachettebookgroup.com

First Edition: October 2011

Little, Brown and Company is a division of Hachette Book Group, Inc.
The Little, Brown name and logo are trademarks of Hachette Book Group, Inc.

The publisher is not responsible for websites (or their content) that are not owned by the publisher.

Photo credits: frontispiece, NBAE/Getty Images; chapters 1–3, author's collection; chapter 4, *Los Angeles Times*/Art Rogers; chapter 5, Andrew D. Bernstein/NBAE/Getty Images; chapter 6, David Sherman/NBAE/Getty Images; chapter 7, Melchior DiGiacomo/*Sports Illustrated*/Getty Images; chapter 8, Todd Warshaw/Getty Images; chapter 9, Joe Murphy/NBAE/Getty Images; chapter 10, The Pete Newell Challenge; chapter 11, Wen Roberts/Photography Ink; chapter 12, © Gail Mooney/CORBIS; chapter 13, Karen West; epilogue, John W. McDonough/*Sports Illustrated*/Getty Images. Excerpt from *Darkness Visible: A Memoir of Madness* copyright © 1990 by William Styron. Used by permission of Random House, Inc.

Library of Congress Cataloging-in-Publication Data
West, Jerry
   West by West : my charmed, tormented life / Jerry West and Jonathan Coleman.
      p. cm.
   Includes index.
   ISBN 978-0-316-05349-5 (hc) / 978-0-316-19616-1 (large print)
  1. West, Jerry.   2. Basketball players—United States—Biography.
3. Basketball coaches—United States—Biography.   4. Basketball managers—United States—Biography.   5. Los Angeles Lakers (Basketball team)   I. Coleman, Jonathan.   II. Title.
   GV884.W4W48 2011
   796.323092—dc23
   [B]   2011019736

10 9 8 7 6 5 4 3 2 1

RRD-C

Printed in the United States of America

For the West family,
my siblings Patricia, Charlie, Hannah, Barbara,
and, especially, my brother David,
who never had an opportunity to live his life;
to my five sons,
David, Michael, Mark, Ryan, and Jonnie,
all so uniquely different yet loved equally;
and my wife, Karen,
who loves, cares for, and nurtures a very complicated man

Contents

Prologue

Early morning in the City of Angels and I began my day as
I always do: poring over the *Los Angeles Times* and *USA
Today*, eating a banana and a bowl of cereal, working out.
Heading south on the 405 at a little past eight and listening to the
Eagles sing about a peaceful, easy feeling, I couldn't help thinking
the opposite—of how much Los Angeles had been roiled and
affected by different incidents during the early 1990s. The beating
of Rodney King in March of 1991; the announcement in November of that year that Earvin "Magic" Johnson, a beloved Southern
California treasure, was HIV positive; the riots that ensued the
following spring in response to the not-guilty verdict by an all-
white jury in the trial of the officers accused of beating King; and
then, not long after that, the Northridge earthquake, which—
along with autumnal Santa Ana winds and encompassing fire—
Californians always expect, but never quite get used to. But in the
wake of such things—the trial of O. J. Simpson was still in the
distance—there was always the prospect of rebuilding, of renewal,
not just in Los Angeles as a whole but in the specific domain that
I, ever the pessimistic optimist, was an integral part of—the dramatic, often operatic, world of the Los Angeles Lakers.

I am a creature of fastidious routine, of habit—an everyday guy who relishes nothing more than creating things and solving problems. *Complacency* is not in my vocabulary; neither is *serenity*. They make me nervous. I don't trust them. Trust is something I place and have in people, not in soft notions and vague concepts. As I arrived at my office at the Forum in Inglewood—a white-columned building where I had been coming to work since 1967 and where I had been robbed at gunpoint two years earlier—traveling a superstitious route to Manchester Boulevard that caused great amusement to others but made perfect sense to me, I saw someone waiting outside my door; someone whom I had known and admired for more years than I could even remember. It was Bill Bertka, a longtime assistant coach and basketball aficionado, and he didn't look happy.

"Every day, Jerry, every single fucking day when I wake up in the morning and look in the mirror, I know what *I* see," he said, his legendary cologne wafting through the air. "What the hell do *you* see?" he demanded to know.

Good question. Even though he was asking about himself, about why we weren't likely to make him the next head coach of the Lakers, what follows will be an unflinchingly honest, painful, soul-searching attempt to answer that question about a very flawed individual—me. To reveal who I am.

While this book is my autobiography—a book that I have been urged to write by some and vehemently discouraged to do by others, including members of my family—the approach that I have taken, in close collaboration with Jonathan Coleman, is one that is built on deep reportage. It represents nothing less than a full-scale attempt to bring forth the truth, to rely not just on my recollection of things, but to do something more ambitious: investigate myself, speak with others, and come to grips with what I find. Nothing you read here will be gratuitous or a cheap shot or an attempt to elevate myself at the expense of anyone else. This book is not meant to be comprehensive in the way that a biography might be, and it is not meant to glorify my athletic accomplishments, as many books of this kind do. It is a memoir and it is selective, choosing to focus on the things that explore and illuminate the mind-set—give, I hope, the reader deeper understanding—of someone who, many feel, has been aloof and inscrutable and unpredictable. What is here is here because it advances the complex, tangled narrative of my life—certain strands of which I have learned for the first time, odd as that may seem—that I am so determined to convey. I am not a conventional person or thinker, not someone who walks a straightforward line. I am too rebellious and defiant for that, always have been. I am, if I may say so, an enigma (even to myself, *especially* to myself) and an obsessive, someone whose mind ranges far and wide and returns to the things that, for better or worse, hold me in their thrall. The way I have chosen to unfold my story at this most reflective time of my life is consistent with that.

We tell ourselves stories in order to live. That line, from Joan Didion's essay "The White Album," perhaps comes closest to what I feel I have done, in my own peculiar way, over these many years in order to protect myself. Until now.

I have been the silhouetted figure of the NBA logo since 1969. This book is my effort to unravel the mystery of that person with the deceptively simple name, to explain myself, to share my story and my improbable journey with those who have perhaps had similar thoughts and who have struggled to overcome the many challenges and obstacles that life has put squarely in their paths. More than anything else, I am someone who takes enormous pleasure in seeing others succeed. My hope is that this book will be both a help and an inspiration to those who read it as they strive to realize their dreams.

Nothing happens unless first a dream.

 —CARL SANDBURG

I played with an angry, emotional chip on my shoulder and a hole in my heart.

My worst personal trait, by far, is that I expect everyone to care as much as I do, about everything, *and it is both terrible and unfair.*

My life has been about trying to figure out my limitations and I know them quite well. Once you find out what they are, it really gives you a chance to find your niche.

 —JERRY WEST

My dad? He's weird.

 —RYAN WEST

WEST BY
WEST

1
Climbing Up from the Abyss

Age seven

Come with me, come to the flinty, hardscrabble world of West Virginia where I grew up: a world of Methodist church bingo, Red Ryder BB guns, and coal tipples; of mean dogs (one in particular—Bear—used to chase my ass) and sneaky cats and heated political discussion among edgy union men; of one big river—the mighty Kanawha—and many black, coal-darkened creeks. The place where I engaged in the most intricate of jigsaw puzzles, mainly of paintings; the harder they were to complete (because of the dark floral colors) the more I liked them (though when I worked on these puzzles with my siblings, I employed some methods that Karen, my wife, disapproves of). I cherished my solitude—did I ever—because I lived in a home where I did not want to be for much of the time, and there were reasons for that. As a result, winter was always the season I dreaded most. I never liked being cooped up. Still don't. I like to be free, free to roam, free to be alone with my fertile and wide-ranging imagination, my closest friend and soul mate as a child. I quickly came to know where the nearest exit was and, long ago, became a Houdini of sorts.

I have the easy-to-remember name of Jerry West, the boy next door. I was born on May 28, 1938, in Chelyan, West Virginia, right next to Cabin Creek—two hollows (burgs, I call them) nestled in the Upper Kanawha Valley, fourteen miles from Charleston, well-defended fortresses against the world. And with the exception of a brief, disastrous period spent in Mineral Wells, near Parkersburg, where we were forced to move because of some union activities my father was engaged in that caused him to lose his job, that was where you could find me, if you cared to look, until the summer of 1956.

My parents were Howard and Cecile West (though she gave it the manly pronunciation of "Cecil"), and I am the fifth of six children, raised in a home, a series of them actually, that was spotless but where I never learned what love was, and am still not entirely sure I know today. What I do know is that I harbored murderous thoughts, and they, along with anger, sadness, and a weird sort of emptiness, are, in part, what drove and fueled and carried me a long way, traveling a path to the future that, even with the depth of my crazy imagination, I never had the self-confidence to allow myself to fully envision, not really.

When I left the state of West Virginia in 1960—a year of transformation in which my name was used without my permission by the campaign of John F. Kennedy (whom, as it turned out, I was in favor of) to lure voters during our Democratic primary; a year in which I married and became a father far too young; went to Rome and wore the uniform of my country in the Olympics and brought back a Gold Medal and then headed west to play professional basketball for the Los Angeles Lakers—I thought I was leaving home for good. But it didn't take long to realize that that would never be the case, at least not for me.

West Virginia, you see, is far more than the place where I was born. And this whole notion of "home," I have come to discover, is not an easy thing to define or explain, but bear with me.

In late August of 2008, Jonathan and I drove from White Sulphur Springs, where I live for three or so months out of the year, to Chelyan, still just a dot on the map. It had been a while since I had visited and on this particular day I was going to see two of my sisters, Patricia and Hannah, who still lived in the area. I am not very good, not very good at all, in reaching out to my siblings, in simply picking up the phone and asking how they are. I don't entirely know why this is, but I do know it has caused tension and disappointment and, at times, considerable resentment toward me. I can't think of much I wouldn't do — or haven't done — for any one of them if they asked me, but the mere act of initiating contact appears to be beyond me. This is not something I am proud of.

I can be an extremely willful person — *defiant* might very well be my favorite word; it has such a perfect, competitive ring to it — but I have not always been this way, far from it. Jack Nicholson thinks of me as "fierce, frank, but *very* fragile," and he is right, but it is the last word — *fragile* — that best characterized me as a child, along with *painfully shy* and *almost backward*.

On the way to Chelyan that morning, the sky was a clear, West Virginia blue. I love driving, hitting the open road, losing myself in thought. Much as I enjoy people, I never mind being alone. Not at all. As we rolled west on Interstate 64 in a white Lincoln SUV, Jonathan asked what I saw in my mind's eye. Well, on this particular day, I saw mountains and landscapes and various configurations of clouds and sky that I have always wished I had the talent to paint. In my imagination, I am a French Impressionist, a Monet, who can, with a masterly stroke of my brush, create a dreamlike state of shimmering color, a world of such natural richness and nuance that *richness* and *nuance* might actually be inadequate for what I am trying to express. I know it when I see it, and yet I have always wondered, *What are the things, what are the elements, what are the revealing clues that set a Monet, or even a Picasso, apart?* I think you can almost read the personalities of these people. I am no art connoisseur, but if you look at paintings that were painted at different periods of their lives, I find myself wanting to know what happened to their lives in between great works to make them change like this?

As a young kid growing up there were distinct changes in my

life, points at which if I could have put that change on canvas, it might have been startling for someone else to see the difference. And yet the truth is, most people can't see that because they don't know what is going on inside you.

I constantly hear people talk about me in terms of legacies. Forget legacies. The legacies that true geniuses leave in this world are the things that can be put on canvas, written on a piece of paper, in a song, or in a speech—creations that will stay there for years. I saw Stevie Wonder in concert a month or so before this trip. An absolutely incredible genius. Somebody who is blind and does what he does? That's just amazing to me. What if he hadn't used that gift? We would never have had Stevie Wonder. I think about someone like Albert Einstein. Could I, could anybody, carry on a conversation with him? Because he was so far beyond our intellect, the way his mind was wired, my best guess is no, you couldn't (though I would have loved to try, especially about his belief that "imagination is more important than knowledge"). Einstein and these other figures are the true geniuses, not basketball players.

And yet I feel pretty sure that a Monet or a Picasso (or even a writer whom I admire, like Malcolm Gladwell) has felt things very similar to what I have felt. Basketball is, and always has been, a huge, huge part of me, the canvas I tried to paint each time I stepped on the court and never stopped trying to perfect. It's been my life. It's been my love. I've hated it. Been frustrated with it— and delighted with it—beyond tears. There's always been the allure of that damn basketball (though I am convinced it chose me, not the other way around). And there has always been a constant battle for me to try to find the satisfaction that I should have got by now (*should* being one of the trickiest, most dangerous words imaginable). It was really hard to find, and even harder to hold on to. It was almost like I was tormented.

When I think even more carefully about it, the art of creating something is not that different from what I did for so many years as the general manager of the Lakers: judge talent, try to determine not only what made a particular player good but whether he might have the potential to be great (or to be a great role player), and have a sense of all the mysterious intangibles that made up the chemistry of a winning team and organization. It was like putting on a Broadway play and hoping you had cast it perfectly; there was hardly any room for error. At season's end, you knew that only one team was going to be truly happy and everyone else was going to be different degrees of miserable. That's part of the reason I tried to instill a family atmosphere, to create something in my professional life that I didn't have growing up. To say that I was mildly obsessed with doing all of this—including pleasing our fans and pleasing the owner—is, frankly, an understatement, a joke, a half-truth. It was far more than that; it consumed me, and often made me ill. Trusting my instinct has always served me well. I haven't always been right, far from it, but I seem to have been right far more than I have been wrong. When Gladwell's *Blink* was published, a book that underscored the importance of not doubting your first impulse and going with your gut, I read it with great interest. He was able to explain and articulate in writing what I had always hoped was true.

When I would wake early in the mornings and didn't have to trudge off to school, where I was an indifferent student, I couldn't wait to climb the steep Alleghenies (part of the Appalachian range) and hike around the woods like an explorer, some sort of modern-day Daniel Boone (who spent a lot of time in West Virginia) or Davy Crockett. With my Daisy Red Ryder BB gun in hand, then later a Remington .410 single-shot shotgun, I loved the fact that I had no idea what the heck I was going to see (though secretly I was both excited and terrified by the idea of running into a bear). I wanted to go places where no one else would be, or even think to venture. To me, the woods held the possibility of finding a magic elixir, a perfect-world Magic Kingdom where every animal I ever wanted to see—or have an opportunity to shoot—would be; they'd be there but hiding, watching me, as I would be on the lookout for them: squirrels, rabbits, and, if I was lucky, ruffed grouse. It became a competition, one of the first of many in my life, and in retrospect, I viewed it as one way to climb up from the abyss.

I had a sense of wonderment, a tingling feeling that would wash over me when I found spots high up where I could get a vast overview of what lay below (a feeling that has endured all these years, be it on a golf course at the top of a ridge or in an upper-level suite at an arena or from the window of an airplane). If I could have afforded binoculars or a telescope at the time, it would have been even better. The way I see it, we all have a different idea of what's beautiful, what's attractive to look at, what captures the eye. I am, more than anything else, a visual person. I love vibrant colors (if you ever saw my collection of patterned Missoni sweaters, which I take a lot of kidding about, you would see why). And I love to observe people practice their crafts.

Every August I could hardly wait to go to the State Fair, near Lewisburg, or the Kanawha County Fair, in Charleston. But instead of marveling at the largest cucumber or the largest tomato (though I have put in and tended a number of gardens in my life and can talk about the finer points of heirloom tomatoes with anyone), I most enjoyed watching the amateur sketch artists, trying to figure out how they could draw a person so quickly and make him or her so lifelike. That fascinated me, in part because I couldn't. And yet I wanted to know more. That's how I have always been. If I don't know something, I will strive to find out about it, and I will often drive everyone around me—including myself—crazy in the process.

In this case, I wanted to know, to figure out, which of these people might go on to become professional artists and make a real living and perhaps paint masterpieces and which would not, maybe in part because they were merely content and comfortable to do what they were doing. What I came to realize, to sense even then, is that it is one thing to have a vague vision and quite another to be able to bring that vision into sharp focus and have the drive and will to go beyond it. So much depends on finding out what's inside a person that, eventually, will enable him to achieve on a larger scale.

Take someone like Abraham Lincoln, for instance. Last time I checked, there had been nearly five thousand books written about him. *Five thousand.* I am a voracious reader, particularly of history, and I have always found it interesting that Lincoln was viewed as a failure at this, that, or the other, and yet he became one of our greatest presidents. I don't know for sure if Lincoln was considered a great intellect, but even if he wasn't, it didn't prevent him from achieving greatness. He was able to find that one little niche in himself that allowed his greatness to surface.

This is what happens when I drive back into my past. All sorts of things come crashing down, some of which I would just as soon forget.

As we get near the exit for Chelyan and Cedar Grove, there is a sign that reads:

HOME OF
JERRY WEST
NBA BASKETBALL
GREAT

I have always, all my life, experienced an odd sensation whenever I am singled out. I am embarrassed by the attention, uncomfortable with it. When I was younger, my face would get red and I would look away and down and want to be somewhere else, anywhere but there. You might think I am kidding, but trust me, I am not. When you had a father who beat you, as mine did, for reasons I am still trying to fathom, it is hard to think of yourself as very special, as deserving of acclaim.

The sign on the highway I expected to see. What I didn't expect (and was distressed to see) once we got into the burg of Chelyan was a sign written in Magic Marker on a bedsheet attached to a chain-link fence at the Appalachian Power Plant (where I worked one summer) and billowing in the wind. It informed everyone when the Class of 1960 from my alma mater, East Bank High School, was holding its reunion, but it also told me that things had gotten worse, not better, since I had last been there, a few years before. The lawns were not as well kept, and there were more trailers. The old, gray wood-frame home I'd lived in, on Little Lane, had burned down in 1962, two years after I left for Los Angeles. But the smaller brick home across the way, in which my mother, father, and youngest sister, Barbara, lived after the fire, is still there. Brown's Theater has gone, and so has Wade's Pool Hall, where one window or another was always broken, often because someone had gotten thrown through it, someone who had almost certainly been drinking moonshine well into a Friday night, the day the miners got paid. It didn't take much for people to get crossways around these parts.

It might have been 2008, but for me it was like being transported in a time machine back to the years between World War II and the Korean War, which was the war that forever altered the life of the West family.

*   *   *

We came into the world in this order: Patricia, Charlie, David, Hannah, me, and Barbara. Patricia is fourteen years older than me, and Barbara (whose name within the family was Cookie) is nine years younger. Owing to the wide age range, and for other reasons that I will get into, it sometimes seemed as if there were two separate households. David was our glue. He was nine years older than me and he epitomized goodness. Our shining light. I always felt he was looking out for me, even though he threw a basketball at me once and told me that I was too small to join in the game he was playing with his friends and that I should scram. "You're going to be sorry that you didn't let me play," I yelled, "because one day I am going to be a great player, you wait and find out." I am not exactly sure where the confidence to say that came from, but the incident only made me more determined. I *was* small—my growth spurt didn't occur until high school, when I grew six inches in one summer—and I was skinny, so much so that I couldn't play football in school, which was a great disappointment to me. Football and baseball, you see, were king in my part of West Virginia when I was growing up, not basketball. On Friday nights, people would come from far and wide to see the East Bank Pioneers play. (And kids would come from a radius of twenty-two miles to go to school there.)

I wish I could say with absolute certainty when I started to shoot baskets, or why. I do know that there was a makeshift basket in a neighbor's dirt yard (two poles, a hoop, and a wooden backboard) and that at first I summoned all my strength to get the ball up there, underhand. And I do know that I attached a wire basket with no net to the side of a bridge, and if the ball didn't go in, it would roll down an embankment and I would have to chase it a long way, and because of that, I learned the practical importance of following my shot and following through. And as much as I hated winter, I would be out there in all seasons and in all weather, because I did not want to be at home. I can hear my mother's voice still, bellowing that it was time for dinner and promising me a whipping if I didn't come on the double (a whipping I often got).

I had neighbors I liked—especially the Kirks, whose family was so large (thirteen or fourteen kids) I could never figure out how everyone got fed; and a man named Francis Hoyt, the safety director at the power plant, who sort of adopted me as his son, taking me fishing and doing things with me that my own father apparently had no interest in doing.

But there were other neighbors—one couple in particular—I will never forget. It was summer, and as I was walking by this couple's house on my way to shoot baskets, they were outside on their porch, fanning themselves, and one of them said, in a voice loud enough for me to hear: "There goes that West kid again, goin' nowhere in a hurry. He's not goin' to amount to nothin'." Strangely enough, I have always been grateful to them for their resolute belief in me.

When I talked earlier about the world I grew up in, I should have added this: I was surrounded by diminished expectations. It was like a thick cloud layer that perpetually hung above me. But instead of letting this weigh me down, it only stoked my anger and determination, something I kept in my back pocket the way another kid might carry a rabbit's foot, something that always stayed lit, like the eternal flame at Arlington. If, as I already noted, the words *serenity* and *complacency* are not to be found in my personal dictionary, neither is *no*.

For my particular psyche, *no* is the best—and the worst—word there is.

My sense of competition revealed itself in all sorts of ways. As Jonathan and I continued to drive around that morning, one look at the railroad tracks of the Chesapeake and Ohio—the C & O—reminded me of some of the rare occasions when I did things with others. My friends and I would sit on the tracks and count the number of Fords and Chevrolets we saw pass by; each one you saw was good for one point. If you spotted the rare Cadillac, which I had the good fortune to do (out of the corner of my eye, far off in the distance) more than once, you got extra points and were sure to win. I have often wondered if my ability to see the whole basketball court when I played—even, it seemed, what was going on behind my head—to see and anticipate things before they actually happened, was honed way back then, one Cadillac at a time.

I can also remember walking along those tracks with a broom handle, throwing rocks up in the air and hitting them with all my might, imagining that one day I could play center field for the New York Yankees. And the times I would head out to go fishing, pole and plastic bait box in hand, and challenge myself by walking on a pipeline moist with morning dew. If I slipped, I would fall into the grass or dirt.

My great fear of water has a lot to do with the fact that I almost drowned once. Later, when I took a required swimming class in college, I panicked when I had to go to the bottom of the pool and come back up. Even though I modeled a lot of swimsuits in the 1960s for Jantzen, I never told anyone I could barely swim (and still have no desire to), and yet I am deeply fascinated by water all the same. I love being near it, and I love looking out onto it and fishing from it, and I love all the different sounds it makes. I just don't want to be paddling around in it.

Speaking of fishing, if someone told me the fish weren't biting, that he and his buddies hadn't caught anything all day, I was never deterred—I was intent on catching the biggest damn fish in the river, and I would never give up. Never. After all, I had gone to a lot of trouble to prepare, carefully making some dough balls and sprinkling them with cinnamon — my own scented concoction — and I wasn't about to go home empty-handed.

Someone has to be the last one standing, the last lone figure at day's end.

On the few occasions my sons have visited my hometown with me, they shake their heads, trying to figure out what I could possibly have done to occupy my time, telling me how bored they would be, how they couldn't have stood it. "How could you grow up here?" they'd ask. "There's nothing to do." Instead of being irritated, though, I would be amused and come right back at them. "What? You've got to be kidding me. I had plenty to do." How different their lives might have been, I often think to myself, if they could have appreciated having their minds as their best friends instead of some damn cell phone or video game.

Patricia was so happy I was coming to visit she had baked an apple pie, a gene she had inherited from our mother, who could bake anything. My nephew Billy, who was Patricia's son and possibly loves West Virginia University more than life itself, who practically bleeds Mountaineer Blue and Gold, was there to greet us as well. Patricia had had a terribly unhappy marriage to Jack Noel, who fought in World War II, but as a boy I didn't really know that. I just knew that they would take me places from time to time, even as far as Morgantown for a WVU basketball game once. Back in those days, the trip could take nearly five hours, over pretty rough road. Anytime I went somewhere away from Chelyan and Cabin Creek was an adventure, and I often imagined I was an astronaut, traveling to another planet. Even a bus trip to Charleston, the state capital, was a big deal, and I was sometimes afraid I would get lost or miss the last bus home. But as I got a bit older, it was in Charleston, as a matter of fact, where I learned about women, when I worked there for a few summers during college and played ball in the Charleston Summer League.

Patricia had been the postmistress at Cabin Creek for a number of years, as had Aunt Katherine, my mother's sister, and that was the reason our family's mail went there instead of to Chelyan and why to this day people think I am from there, which gained me the nickname I have never liked — "Zeke from Cabin Creek." I know it might seem like a distinction without a difference, but it mattered to me. In any case, it was my job to go and fetch the mail, and I would always run up there to do so. The truth is, I ran *everywhere*, not just to collect mail or escape mean dogs. If I were an actor, I could have played the lead role in *The Fugitive*. I have a reservoir of restless energy that accelerates and intensifies everything I do. If you come out to eat with me, I might be done before you have your second bite; one of my closest friends, Gary Colson, who has had a thousand meals with me, maybe more, advises others to order their food to go, and he is not kidding. If you play golf with me, I can be so impatient it's a joke. You can ask Michael Jordan or, better yet, the irritated foursomes who have played in front of me over all the years. I do everything fast. Shaquille O'Neal says that whatever I had to say to him, whether I was praising him or bawling his ass out, I could say it in less than a minute. That's who I am, and I am unlikely to change. But I do want to say this, and it is true: I am good company and know how to crack wise and cut up as well as anyone. For some strange, inexplicable reason, I will sometimes be the first one to playfully put on a wig or a mask or some other form of disguise. A sense of mystery has always appealed to me.

On the matter of eating quickly, I would like to explain further. Aside from Sunday dinners, which were a noonday, after-church meal, we tended to eat buffet style in the West house, and there was no sitting around the table for long discussions. In that respect, it was more like families in America today, where nearly everyone is rushing around, coming and going, separate entities almost. And when I see all the fast-food restaurants everywhere I look, I think of one thing: they are the main reason most American families don't sit down together for dinner on a daily basis. We have lost something, something I never really had growing up (though Karen always made sure that we ate dinner together as a family).

Thanksgiving was a big exception, my favorite day of the year. Everyone was together and in a good mood, my mother's hot rolls and buttermilk pie and cake with apricot filling were in abundance, and the weather was as it should be — cold and crisp. When I moved to California, Thanksgiving lost a certain bit of its appeal to me because of the mild climate. Now some might say that that is a peculiar notion, but there you have it.

I am often painfully awkward or detached when I greet someone, including family, and today was no exception. I am not very demonstrative. I hardly ever hug. I rarely do it with my own children, or with Karen. It doesn't mean I am not glad to see them; it doesn't mean I don't care. It's the same as not easily picking up the phone to call someone; it's just how I am. And much of that, I am convinced, has to do with the almost complete lack of nurturing I received as a child. Cookie refers to the home we grew up in as "the ice house," but that isn't even the half of it.

Patricia had pulled together a lot of photographs and letters and various newspaper clippings in anticipation of our visit, and one of the first things we looked at were pictures of my father and the farm he had grown up on in Roane County, which is about fifty miles north of Charleston. He had been ten when his mother died, in 1910, and he and his eight siblings were sent to live with second cousins, the Starchers. (I later learned that nearly everyone in Roane County is named Starcher. It's as if you went to Korea and said you were looking for a Lee; there's millions of Lees there, and your chances of finding the person you want are pretty slim. West Virginia has lots of enclaves of families like this.) My father's father, my grandfather Max, had been a ladies' man and was not a presence in his life or, later, in mine.

I do know that my father was in the navy for a brief period during World War I. He came to Cabin Creek to work for Pure Oil ("Where the oil is pure as gold" went the company slogan) and he met my mother, but he did not stay faithful to her, something I did not learn until recently and that helps me understand why there was such distance between them, why I never saw them be affectionate toward each other in any way.

My father was very bright, very, but he was uneducated in any formal sense, and very unfulfilled. He read the paper every day, as I do now and have always done; he read it "cover to cover," as he liked to say, and he often fell asleep on the couch with the paper covering his face. He put in twenty-seven years at Pure Oil as a machine operator, but eventually the wells ran dry. He was also involved in union activity—he had a passion for all things political, really—and, rightly or not, it was easy to be branded a troublemaker. When he moved us to Mineral Wells, not long after World War II, it was not just because he wanted to be his own man—there is nothing wrong with that—but because he was having trouble finding work. That was a fact. The other fact was this: he bought a gas station and he didn't know a damn thing about cars because we didn't own one.

I am a firm believer in doing things for others; I well know the deep satisfaction that comes with that, with doing something that you can't put a price on and not caring one bit if anyone knows about it. But I believe, equally strongly, that you have to put your family and its needs first. And my father didn't do that, and I came to resent the hell out of him for it.

I thought I was a good boy, the sort of kid any father would have been proud to call his son. But my father, it would appear, didn't see it that way. You couldn't disagree with him, you couldn't cross him. I had no idea what my siblings would say on the subject of my father; in fact, I was pretty certain they were in denial about the kind of person he was, and that was one of the reasons they worried what I might write. After all, I couldn't say for sure what did or didn't happen to any of them (except for Hannah), just as they, because of our age differences, couldn't say with any certainty what had happened to me.

And yet here I was at Patricia's home, and while I was in the kitchen speaking with Billy about the prospects for the Mountaineer football season and his certainty that there is something lurking under the ground in the Amazon rain forest, my sister was telling Jonathan about the way things were in our household, about the corporal punishment our father would mete out if you stepped out of line.

I know that *incarcerated* is a strong word, but that is how I felt; it is also how I felt in the locker room before a game, like a caged animal that needed to break out; and it is why I still, today, look to escape from places and keep moving, a man on the run. That's why the Sunday family dinners were such façades, really, cover-ups for the atrocities that occurred far too often.

Not long after we moved back to the Cabin Creek area, in 1947, two things happened: there was a strike in the mines (my father had caught on as an electrical worker for one of the coal companies, Oglebay Norton) and my brother David went off to serve his country in Korea.

During one particularly hard stretch, we ate the same soup out of the same pot for six days until I told my mother I simply couldn't do it any longer. Well, let me tell you, I took the most god-awful beating that day from my father and it made me into a tough, nasty kid and it turned me even more inward than I already was. I never forgave him for it. Still haven't. But I promised myself that I would do everything I could to make sure that never happened to me again. I screwed up my courage and told him so, told him that he'd better never lay another hand on me and reminded him that I had a shotgun under my bed and would damn well use it if I had to.

Where, you might ask, was my mother during all this? Did she even try to intervene? No, she did not, at least not that I remember. She was dealing with her own deep unhappiness.

I was ten when David enlisted and went overseas, and it was as if the sun, hardly bright to begin with, stopped shining altogether in our house. I can't honestly say that David was my protector, but he did look out for me as best he could; he was the one I tried to emulate, that's for sure, and I missed him terribly when he left. If I could be as perfect and well liked by everybody as he was, then maybe, just maybe, my father would stop picking on me, stop jumping all over my ass.

One of the things I most loved doing at home was listening to the radio in my room, listening to boxing matches and to WVU basketball games. I inherited David's radio when he left to go to war, and I came to love Ray Robinson and Joe Louis, who incidentally became two of my three favorite sports heroes (the other being Jim Brown, the football player) and whom I later had the chance to meet. I will never forget seeing Sugar Ray on the cover of *Life*, leaning against his pink 1950 Cadillac in front of two businesses he owned in Harlem with an adoring crowd milling about. My love for boxing has been lifelong and has never waned. Whenever there is a big match, if I can possibly get there, I do, or I will watch it on television. When I went to Rome for the 1960 Olympics, in the midst of the Cold War, I was as excited to watch a young Cassius Clay box as I was to do what I had gone there for—play basketball. Playing in the Olympics was the single greatest thrill of my athletic career. I will never forget the indelible moment when, as the American flag was raised and "The Star-Spangled Banner" reverberated throughout the Palazzetto dello Sport, co-captain Oscar Robertson and I, my knees shaking, stepped up to the top rung of the podium and accepted the Gold Medal. To this day, it is my most cherished possession.

Listening to boxing and to Mountaineer games on the radio was great for another reason: it reassured me that indeed there was a wider world out there. What wasn't great about the radio was the reception; it would fade in and out and I would fall asleep, and I hardly ever knew the outcome until the next day. That might be one of the main reasons I love suspense novels.

When you are used to seeing someone in your house day after day and then, suddenly, he is not there, it is a strange, unsettling feeling. So when a letter from David arrived, it was a relief and a gift. I didn't read them at the time, but my mother would occasionally read parts aloud to me. I would watch her reading them and get a pretty good idea of their contents just by seeing how she reacted. I wanted to know, yet I didn't want to know.

Holding them in my hands now, all these years later, causes me to tremble, brings emotions to the surface that I can barely contain. He left for Korea in January of 1949.

On American Red Cross stationery, a year later, January 9, 1950:

Dear Mom,

Don't worry if you don't hear too often from me, as the mail is slow and it might not be going out.... How is the New Year treating you, fine I hope.... If I don't write to everybody regular tell them not to get mad at me and just keep writing as usual.... The days are okay but the nights are not so good. I guess the Chinese are feeling pretty happy. They have kicked us around pretty bad. But someday it will be our turn....

Hope Jerry is doing okay and also Hannah and Cookie. Keep up the morale at home. The article that you sent me about prayer was very good. Mom, hope you attend church regular. Still wish you would join the Church and make God your Saviour and the family guide.

Love,
Dave

I knew that religion was important to David—everyone expected him to become a minister when he returned—but I never heard him speak so directly about it. (Another thing I didn't know was that people called him "Deac"—as in Deacon.) Six weeks later, on February 23, 1950, he wrote to say that his unit had

lost two guys but two new guys were coming in...I think we will get hit again hard, but I don't think they will drive us out....I wish this war would get over but I don't have any idea about it....

I got another blood test today....I will send you this paper on hepatitis, maybe you can get something out of it....I hope I can go to Church this Sunday as I need to very much. May God Bless you and protect all the family.

Love,
Dave

Seven months later, in September, a full month after the event had happened, we received the following piece of information:

Private First Class DAVID L. WEST, RA15288301, Infantry, Heavy Mortar Company, 35th Infantry, United States Army. On 5 August 1950 and 6 August 1950, the 1st Platoon of Heavy Mortar Company was supporting Company F when enemy forces launched an attack in the vicinity of Haman, Korea. Working under artillery, mortar and small arms fire Private First Class West remained in his position receiving instructions from the forward observer, making computations and relaying the firing data to the gun positions. Private First Class West's courage and skill enabled his company to repulse the enemy attack and are in keeping with the highest traditions of the military service. Entered the military service from West Virginia.

BY COMMAND OF MAJOR GENERAL KEAN

Less than two weeks later, on August 17, David pulled a fellow soldier who had been seriously wounded in the leg to safety. We didn't find out about this from David, nor did we learn from him that in October he was awarded the Bronze Star for meritorious service. In fact, it wasn't until shortly before Christmas that we found out. The young man whose life he had saved, Corporal Don Woody, from the town of Institute, West Virginia, was interviewed by the *Charleston Daily Mail* and mentioned how a David West of East Bank had dragged him from a rice paddy after he was hit.

In a series of letters in November, David said, over and over again, that we shouldn't get our hopes up that he would be home for Christmas. He asked our mother not to worry about him because it would only get her upset and said he hoped "Dad will work six days a week" in order to get the family out of debt; he also wanted to make sure she had received the money he'd sent so that he could feel he was helping with Christmas presents in his absence. The main reason he was fighting, he reminded her, was so that "Jerry and Hannah and Barbara can grow up in a free world," and that with God's help and grace all good things would occur, hallowed be His name.

He hoped that I would make the basketball team that year and do better than he had, that I would pay attention to my studies, and that, all in all, I would be "a good Joe." He wrote that the reason they didn't use the A-bomb was that it would kill too many women and children. In a letter to the *Kanawha Citizen* just before Christmas, he wrote: "I hope that people are praying for peace all over the world." And to his pastor, Rev. H. E. Chowder of Chelyan Methodist, he said, "The innocent are really suffering over here. We feel very sorrowful, but what can we do about it? We need more Christians at home and in the army."

I did make the team that year at Chelyan Junior High, where I played for Duke Shaver, who was obsessed with having us do the duck walk as a way to get fit (and *not* because everyone wanted to imitate Elvis Presley). Besides being small and skinny (I suffered from a vitamin deficiency for a time, mainly because I hardly ate), I had long, gangly arms, and ears that stuck straight out; I could easily have been a stand-in for Ichabod Crane. I wasn't much to look at, and I was self-conscious, and the fact that I lacked a real support system at home certainly didn't help matters.

As it turned out, I didn't play very much in seventh grade; I may have gotten in one or two games. I tried to pay attention to my studies, but I wanted to be away from the house as much as possible.

I wish I could say these letters from my brother surprise me, but they don't. Every person he could possibly be concerned with, he expresses concern for. The concern is never for himself.

Or was.

On June 8, 1951, Sergeant David West was killed in action. David, whom I looked up to and who looked out for me. David, the model of goodness, who'd planned to become a Methodist minister, a man of God, the person people would turn to for solace. Now he was gone.

Bad news, it seems, always travels fast. I was on my way home from I can't even remember where, probably school or the store, running as usual, minding my own business, and somebody yelled out to me that he'd heard my brother had died. What the hell was this guy talking about? Why would somebody feel it was okay to say something like that to me? I had just turned thirteen years old. I shouldn't have to deal with things like that. It didn't seem right.

David was supposed to have come home the previous January, but he had been "frozen in service," whatever the hell that meant. Well, let me tell you, that day is frozen in my memory. It is a day that changed me and has never stopped haunting me. Or any member of my family, except for Barbara, perhaps, because she was only four. You can't say the name General Douglas MacArthur (who was in charge of the forces in Korea) around me today without getting a reaction. When David Halberstam's *The Coldest Winter* was published in 2007, I tore through it looking for something, *anything*, that would explain to me what the Korean War—"the forgotten war"—had been about. I found that Halberstam shared my low opinion of MacArthur, and I finally understood what an egomaniac MacArthur was. I will always love Harry Truman for finally throwing his sorry ass under the bus, which was long overdue. I don't like people who are deceitful, and MacArthur wasn't straight with the president about what was happening over there. MacArthur had that line about old soldiers never dying, just fading away. Well, my brother had his whole life ahead of him. When someone dies young, as he did, another kind of freezing takes place: David West was cut down at twenty-one and he will be twenty-one forever. Some things I just see in black and white, see them for what they are.

Anytime I speak of David, I choke up and become morose.

Word of David's death reached us by telegram, and I believe my brother Charlie, who worked for the post office, Patricia's husband, Jack, who worked for the railroad, and Aunt Kate, the postmistress of Cabin Creek, were the first to know. To this day, I will never forget my mother's reaction to the news. She began pounding her fists on the walls—sounds of heartbreak I could hear in the distance, well before I got home—pounding with such fury that I thought her fists would go straight through.

She didn't stop there. She went outside and began doing the same thing to the ground, raging at the utter unfairness and randomness of it all.

My mother was never the same after David's death. David was her favorite; everyone knew that. She was there, but not there. A large part of her died with him. Though I didn't know it for what it was at the time, she had a breakdown. *Life changes in the instant. The ordinary instant.* I have been reading a good bit of Joan Didion recently and those words, from *The Year of Magical Thinking*, really resonate with me. She was talking about the death of her husband, how she was fixing dinner and he was having a drink, and then, suddenly, he had a heart attack and was gone, just like that. I often tell people that, at this point in my life, I am really just sitting in God's waiting room (even though my actual belief in God is a complicated matter). I don't do it to upset them, and I don't do it to be morbid. But Karen, who is fifteen years younger than me, absolutely hates when I say this, though it is true.

When we left Patricia's house we slowly made our way to the cemetery in London, on the other side of the river. In order to get there, I headed down Highway 61, going past my old high school, East Bank, which had merged with another school in 1999 and was no more. For some odd reason, it is still hard for me to come to terms with that. Anyone who knows me, though, knows that I am deeply sentimental.

I saw all the old homes along the road and it saddened me. Those rundown places had been there forever. So many people just merely exist, and that is what kills me about West Virginia. What I don't understand is that some of these coal miners make sixty to a hundred thousand dollars a year and yet their first impulse is often to get a new car. I am loath to tell other people how to live, but I feel strongly that if their first instinct would be to embrace the enduring importance of education, their children would be better off. Every kid has some hidden talent which needs to be nurtured. If people doubt or don't fully accept how important education is, all you have to do is come to this state. The coal industry and its lobbyists and special interest groups have run West Virginia for years, and it depresses me that education is not the first priority. Back when I was going to school, things were more vibrant, if you can believe it. But when I visit there now, not a day goes by that I don't think how lucky I was to get out. Some people might take that the wrong way, but I love West Virginia and that is why I am saying this.

Eventually we reached Montgomery, where there is a small college, West Virginia Institute of Technology, that did not offer David one of six basketball scholarships it had available when he graduated East Bank in 1947. Without it, he couldn't afford to go to college, and he wound up going to work at Kroger and then enlisting. Maybe if my father had been able to go further in school and make a better living for his family, David would have found a way to go to school and would still be alive now. I know that sounds harsh, and I know that my father is not here to defend himself and that some reading this might feel it is very unfair to speak ill of the dead, but that's how I feel.

I crossed over the Kanawha and entered the gates of Montgomery Memorial Park. By now, shortly after noon, it was sweltering. It had been a while since I had been here to visit the graves of my parents and David. I believe I had some of my children with me then, but I can't say for sure. I stared at each foot marker and what was written there:

HOWARD STUART WEST
WEST VIRGINIA
F2 USNR
WORLD WAR I
FEB 26, 1900–FEB 28, 1967

CECILE S. WEST
BELOVED MOTHER
MAY 17, 1905–APR 10, 1991

DAVID LEE WEST
WEST VIRGINIA
SGT 35 INF 25 INF DIV
KOREA
NOV 21, 1929–JUNE 8, 1951

I acknowledged my parents' markers, but the one I really focused on was David's, and my mind went back in time. Flowers arrived at the house until I couldn't stand the smell any longer. People dropped off food, no one knowing quite what to say. I fished and I hunted and I shot baskets over and over again, from different angles; the more I made, I thought, and the more perfect I could be, the more chance there was of David's coming back— my own form of magical thinking.

David's death, I see now, truly resulted in the basketball court's becoming my sanctuary and my refuge, the place where I felt most alive, where I was most in control. The sweet beauty of being by myself out there—a boy from deep inside West Virginia with a ball and barely concealed anger and a burning desire, a fierce longing, for more than what I had—is that I was in charge of everything and I was everything: coach, scorekeeper, referee, timekeeper, the opposing player trying to stop me *and* pushing me to do my best, the fans, and, of course, the guy with the ball with the game on the line, hungry to take the last shot and decide the outcome. Oh, how I loved hearing the clock tick down, *five, four, three, two, one,* and then letting it go, following the arc as the ball dropped cleanly through the basket. I lived for that, for the inimitable swish, one of the sweetest sounds I know.

I would run these scenarios over and over and over again, then shoot some more. Sometimes I'd let my imaginary team lose so I would have greater incentive the next time. Sometimes I would make the buzzer go off early and foil myself. Other times I would add an extra second (just as I sometimes managed to come up with the final dark piece of the jigsaw puzzle that I had "discovered" hiding in the carpet or under my chair). It was peaceful out there—dawn and dusk in West Virginia, let me tell you, are something to behold—and I was content, striving for my own form of perfection. In the years since, I have often wondered if I was trying to be like David or to separate myself from him; if playing as well as I could was meant to honor him or to fill the considerable void that his death had left. As I stood before his grave that day, I was reminded once again of the thing I will never be able to change: He never got a chance to see me play, to see me *really* play.

The summer of 1951 came and went, and Senator Joe McCarthy was seeing Communists everywhere he looked. Autumn arrived and, with it, Bobby Thompson's monumental, pennant-winning home run against the Brooklyn Dodgers, "the Shot Heard 'Round the World," and still we waited for David's body. In the end, we had to wait six long, cruel months for him to come back to us. In the beginning, letters he'd sent kept arriving at the post office and I was there to get them; it was almost as if someone were deliberately mocking us, rubbing it in. Letters that continued to ask how all of us were doing, to ask if his money to help out the family had been received, and to stress the enduring importance of God in our lives.

Everyone told me to be a big boy, and that was it. That was the extent of the advice I was given on how to cope, and I had no idea how to do it, not really. The gloom in the house was oppressive. I'd shared a room with David, and his bed was empty, as it had been for more than two and a half years and would likely remain. Thanksgiving was nothing like it had been before. I would occasionally go to church, thinking it would please David if I did what he'd asked us to do, draw closer to God, but the truth is what I most enjoyed was going up there to play bingo. It was another form of competition for me, and I figured out rather quickly that, along with luck, quickness was key, quickness in being able to shout out what so many had shouted out before me in churches everywhere. Though when I did it, the word *Bingo!* came forth in a meek voice.

*   *   *

David's flag-draped casket came home to us by train on December 14, and two soldiers from the army accompanied it. It was first taken to Pryor Funeral Home, and then, at my father's insistence, out of some crazy notion he had that it was the right and proper thing to do, it was brought to the house, where it stayed in the living room for a day or so, the soldiers watching over it. I can see it there still, and I can remember how strange and weird that was, especially with our meager Christmas tree right next to it.

On December 16, 1951, a cold, dreary day, the kind of day some people call godforsaken, my brother was laid to rest. The sound of "Taps" coming from the bugler at the top of the hill never sounded so beautiful, or so awful. And every time I have heard it since, the sharp pain and sorrow of that day come flooding back to me.

As I drove away from the cemetery and headed to St. Albans to see my sister Hannah, I was thinking about war, a subject I think about a lot. I wonder, *How many of us know the number of people who were killed in World War II? Specifically, on the beaches at Normandy?* Very few people know, I think; very few even have a clue. The night before this trip, I was reading a review of Dexter Filkins's *The Forever War,* about our going into Iraq, and was reminded that it was because of journalists like David Halberstam and Neil Sheehan, men who dared to question the strategy of the military during Vietnam, that the American people learned as much as we did. If more pressure had been brought to bear on MacArthur, maybe things would have been different.

Driving along I saw something I hadn't noticed before: a number of houses along the road and in the distance had stars on them, and I didn't know why. I later found out that a blue star symbolized that the family had a loved one in the military overseas, and a gold star symbolized that the family had lost a loved one in battle. This sent a chill down my spine.

I looked to my left as I continued on and recalled that a beautiful girl in high school lived there, in Glasgow. Her name was Carol Dunfee. She and another girl, Janet Kitchen, had been interested in me, and I went out with each of them a few times. But because I was shy, I always worried about what we would talk about, and because I had very few clothes, I worried about what I would wear.

Christmas was always disappointing, and it was even worse after David died. I remember one time I prayed for Santa to bring me a bike, and when he did, I immediately noticed that it wasn't brand-new. Each of us would get one thing for Christmas. I saw other kids getting more, and I couldn't figure out why I didn't. It gave me the feeling of being left out of the good things in life. I know how trite this might sound, but what you don't know is how awful I felt, always wishing for something special. (Still, even though I was embarrassed to get a used bike, I rode that thing everywhere.) This mixture of envy and jealousy did something to me, and it is one of the main reasons I dread Christmas and am almost always depressed around the holidays. Karen pours her heart into Christmas in our house—weeks of preparation, a huge tree covered with ornaments, a display of some sort or another everywhere you look—and yet somehow it is those West family Christmases back in West Virginia that haunt me. To this day, I don't want people to give me presents. I would much rather give things to them, surprise them with something, buy their lunches or dinners. Perhaps I was Santa Claus in another life. Perhaps I am Santa Claus. I like to keep people guessing.

*   *   *

I stare at the DuPont chemical plant in Belle, and it reminds me how awfully unhealthy life must be for the people who live here. Between the frequent reports of leaks and the ever-present dangers of the coal mines and the power plant, is it any wonder that West Virginians are such gritty people? My father used to come home from work, black from head to toe, and have to remove all his clothes before my mother would allow him to come inside the house, where he would frequently just sink into his chair, barely speak to her or to me, and fall fast asleep. What energy he had he seemed to save for Cookie, his favorite.

She might have been his favorite, but I didn't trust him or his temper, so I tried to watch over her, be the best older brother I could, the way David had been for me. Things have been strained between us for quite some time now (frankly, it burns me up that she thinks of me as an elitist), but we used to have a lot of fun together, sitting on the couch and raising our legs in the air and forming a temple and seeing who could force the other off. I was older and stronger and could have won all the time, of course, but I didn't. Cookie adored me and would often watch from a secret spot inside the house as I shot baskets; apparently, she was certain that I would make a name for myself. (Hindsight, you could say, is a wonderful thing.) And speaking of Santa Claus, I know she wondered if he and I were one and the same. One time I brought in a bike and told her that Santa had asked me to take it inside and give it to her because he was behind schedule and too busy to stop. But when she looked outside, she didn't see him through the lightly falling snow.

2

Venturing Forth

Senior year in high school, 1956

I hadn't been to my sister Hannah's home in St. Albans for nearly twenty years, something she gently scolded me for not long after I arrived. Hannah was three and a half years older than I, and she was happily living there with her third husband, Tom Bowman, a classmate whom she had reconnected with at an East Bank reunion.

Her life had been tragic in many respects. Her first marriage ended when she was only twenty-one, leaving her with little money and a small daughter to raise; and her second husband (with whom she had three children, including a Down syndrome baby who died at the age of two) suffered a slow, horrible death from cancer.

She asked how my visit with Patricia went and I told her that she apparently was still battling with her neighbors next door— "It's almost like the Hatfields and the McCoys, for Christ's sake"—and that she was just as cantankerous as ever. Even though Patricia's home had been a source of misery to her—her late husband's infidelity made her think of the place as a hotel that he checked into and out of whenever he wished—she had no interest in moving to assisted living, and her family was concerned. We spoke of our brother Charlie, who had lived in St. Albans himself for many years and was now living in Burlington, North Carolina, close to his daughter (who was the first Karen West). Charlie had become hard of hearing, and he talks and talks. He is still sharp as hell, but I usually try to have a buffer between us when he visits so I can disappear. I always worry that he will talk me to death. Charlie and my wife, Karen, communicate a lot, mostly by e-mail, but I don't really communicate with anyone, I told Hannah. (This is not entirely true, of course, and it's ironic I would say this to Hannah because in my professional life I've always stressed the importance of communication, though I don't always subscribe to that belief in my personal one. I have reached a point now where I won't do anything I don't want to do.)

Like me, Hannah named her first (and only) son David. Just as Patricia had, Hannah brought out pictures for us to look at. We both stared at a handsome one of our deceased brother, a photo she keeps on her refrigerator because, she said, that way "he's with me every day." The pictures of our parents reveal how much bigger our mother was than our father; she was rangy and had broad shoulders and was strong enough to do nearly anything a man could do. She was like a mule, whose back could easily have supported the building of this country. My height came from her.

I told Hannah that the last time I had seen our mother, which was not long before she died, in April of 1991, she had called me David, and I'd said to myself, *Holy Christ*. When I left, I remember thinking that if I ever got to the point where I had something really wrong with me, if I couldn't recall a member of my family, I would call Dr. Jack Kevorkian. I would not subject my loved ones to that. No way. I don't think it's fair.

I actually do have something wrong with me and have been dealing with it for quite some time, as far back as my playing days. At first I didn't know what it was; I would just start hyperventilating and have to breathe into a paper bag. I struggle with atrial fibrillation, a medical condition fairly common to athletes in which my heart rate is irregular and gets out of whack and skips beats. I take Coumadin and Xanax for it, and I have to be checked on a monthly basis to see if my blood-clotting levels are correct. Several years ago, I went to the Cleveland Clinic for a procedure called an ablation, which was not successful. When these incidents occur, they are unsettling, *very,* and I become even more restless than usual, and depressed, something else I have long struggled with and that I take Prozac for. But none of this affects my ability to remember who people are—yet.

Hannah and I both admired our high school principal, Dana Ervin, and a particular English teacher named Betty Underwood. It's funny that I liked her, because my first experience with English was not good; it was boring and mundane, and I had no talent for it (same with mechanical drawing). Then I had an English teacher who absolutely loved me. She was beautiful, and she showed more than a normal amount of interest, which I was flattered by but which also made me uneasy.

But Betty Underwood was something else. She was perhaps the first true eccentric I ever knew. She was brilliant but crazy. She often wore two different shoes, and her hair was rumpled, but she instilled in me a love of reading that remains to this day. I had always thought teachers were supposed to look a certain way, but not her. She was different, and I realize now that my love of people who are different and odd and quirky started with her. When I left her class, I felt better in a way that almost defies description, which of course is what a great teacher should make you feel. I remember, as if it were yesterday, coming out of her class and saying, "Holy cow." She wound up leaving her brain to West Virginia University, and I have often wondered what the research revealed.

As with Patricia, I didn't know what Hannah would or would not want to say about our family life. I knew that she was worried about how much I might reveal, in the interests of candor and unburdening myself.

Hannah talked about how many relatives we had in the area and how she'd liked going over to Aunt Lena's because Lena didn't have any children and would spoil her. "That was something I didn't get at home," she said.

"I don't think any of us got that," I said.

"You were the only one Mother rocked," she said.

"That didn't happen," I shot back. If it did, I was too young to recall.

"Well, then, Dad may have done so, because he was the rocker."

"Are you kidding me?"

"Well," she said, giving the true picture, "there was certainly no affection, and that's one thing Karen couldn't understand. I said, 'Remember, Karen, there were no birthday presents.' Mom made us an angel food cake but there were no presents. A birthday was just another day."

I'd told my kids and Karen the same thing, that birthdays weren't important, though I am not so sure that's how I really felt.

Hannah talked about how she had contributed to the family's finances by handing over her paycheck when she worked as a legal secretary, a job she had even while she was still in school. She recalled how our father was only working two or three days a week.

I brought up the incident with the vegetable soup and how my father beat the hell out of me when I complained and how I told him that if he ever touched me again, I would kill him. "And there's one other incident I wasn't going to bring up, Hannah, and it involved you, but I feel as if I should."

There was silence for a minute in the room, a minute that seemed like five. Hannah's grandson Hunter had come over after school, and she didn't want to say anything in his presence. Her husband, Tom, sat there, motionless. I didn't know if he knew about it or not, and I didn't care.

Finally, she said, choosing her words carefully, "That was the only run-in we ever had. Because I knew to stay—"

"That's when I told him," I said, "if you ever do anything again—"

"Actually I left home for a little while," she jumped in. "I went up to my uncle's. Dad had an irrational temper. But most of the time he would tell you when you were getting in trouble. He would warn you, 'You are about to go too far.'"

"I was always trying to figure out what I did to get in trouble," I said.

"I can remember three bad incidents if you really want to talk about it," she said. "I don't remember what perpetrated the third one, but the first one was over food. Remember you had that vitamin deficiency and you had to go take those shots and you were going off with a neighbor and helping this guy do some farming. You were always interested in growing things.

"Anyway, you didn't take any lunch and you were gone all day. Well, when you got back, your fingernails began to look strange and you got this gooseflesh. And you refused to eat that night, and I don't remember what we were having, but Dad tried to force you and that was a bad incident, it really was.

"The other one was you asked Dad for money and he said, 'I don't have any,' and you said, 'You're a liar,' and you just did not do that, and that was a terrible one. You remember that big old oak dining room table? You ran from him and he pinned you between it and the buffet."

She couldn't remember the third incident, but it didn't matter. "I had a fear of going home," I said, "and when you're little, it's a helpless feeling. But I remember the day I told him, 'If you ever do this again, something ugly is going to happen.' I became absolutely defiant. It was like facing up to the bully, that's what it was. He was a bully. And I will never forget when my life changed, because I could do something that maybe some other people couldn't do."

"He was very proud of you," Hannah said.

"Yeah, he was," I said, "but I told Mother, 'Never *ever* let him see me play basketball again. I don't want him ever to come to the games, *ever.*'"

"Well, I know you got on him one time because he got in an argument with somebody up at East Bank. Somebody said something negative about you and he turned around and said something like 'How'd you like to take on his old gray-haired pappy?' Do you remember that?"

It wasn't something I was likely to forget. I remember telling him to never embarrass me at a game again. I barely talked to anyone during a game (the most I might say to a ref was "I think you missed that one"), and I never heard *anything* when I played except the stirring sound of "The Star-Spangled Banner."

Again and again, our conversation circled back to our family's brief but ill-fated move to Mineral Wells, the return to Chelyan, and another thing we could both agree upon: that even though our father's union activities hurt us as a family, we grudgingly admired the fact that he stood up for the things he believed in. Though it is exceedingly hard, if not impossible, for me to either forgive or forget the things my father did to me, the truth is that we were brought up by both our parents to believe in the importance of fair play, of being a good citizen, of being honest and hard working and always humble, of having little or no ego, of never bragging on yourself or holding too high an opinion of yourself. I have always embraced these things in my life, particularly humility. I think you would be hard-pressed to find someone who would disagree, who would say that was not the case. I've never placed myself above anyone else. Ever. I wouldn't do that. There were times when I wanted to say I was pretty darn good. I tried not to do that. In those moments when I have slipped, I haven't felt good about myself, and I've taken the words back as quickly as they came out.

Everything I did, I tried to do perfectly. Not just well, but perfectly. In the summer, I would cut people's grass. You couldn't find a weed when I was done. I was meticulous because I knew that was my way of being able to make some money if I wanted to buy a fishing pole, or a basketball, or shotgun shells. If someone wanted me to dig a perfect ditch, I dug a perfect ditch. But it was more than about making money, and all this striving for perfection, I would soon discover, took a tremendous toll on me, and on others around me.

The discussion of politics was a constant in our house, and we would sit around listening to the conventions on the radio; once we got a television, we would watch the news. The Democratic convention took place in Denver that very week I was visiting my sisters, and as soon as I returned home to White Sulphur Springs, I turned on the television to watch. The possibility of America electing a black man president was incredible, something I hadn't thought I would see in my lifetime, even though Bobby Kennedy had predicted it would happen at some point. I had been following Barack Obama with great interest and had decided months earlier that I was going to vote for him—a decision that did not sit well with many of the guys I play gin with at Bel-Air Country Club in Los Angeles. Every chance they got, they chided me about this, reminding me that I would be paying a lot more in taxes. I didn't care; I liked the cool, graceful way he conducted himself, and I had a sense that he could be a unifying figure, a brilliant leader.

My playing career with the Lakers had spanned the era of the civil rights movement and beyond; I had witnessed the indignities visited upon my black teammates and admired the way players like Elgin Baylor, Oscar Robertson, and other black athletes had spoken out. I was not one to speak out at that time. It's not who I was. Even though I had grown up in a household in which I had learned to be prejudiced toward things but not people, I was no crusader. I believed that everyone deserved fair and equal treatment and opportunity, but I wasn't going to make any noise about it.

I remember when Villanova came to Mountaineer Field House to play West Virginia in 1960, my senior year. Both teams were highly ranked, and Villanova had two black players—George Raveling and Hubie White—and I instinctively knew that they were probably a bit fearful coming to play in Morgantown. Before the opening tip, I went over to George, who has since become a close friend of mine and one of the most beloved men in the sport, and shook his hand. I wanted him to feel welcome, and then I wanted to do everything I could to destroy him and his team. During the game, there was a tense moment when he and I went after a loose ball and George knocked me down. It was a fair play and as soon as I got up I patted him on the rear. I was not about to give the raucous hometown crowd a chance to harass him. Three years later, I found out recently, Martin Luther King Jr. handed the typewritten version of his "I Have a Dream" speech to George right after he delivered it on the Mall in Washington. And then three years after that, in 1966, I remember watching the University of Kentucky play Texas Western for the national championship, a game that was featured years later in the movie *Glory Road*. Texas Western made history by starting five black players, and I rooted for them to win, but I never told anybody that. Not even Pat Riley, who played on that Kentucky team and later became a close friend and teammate of mine on the Lakers and was the team's coach when I was general manager. His coach at Kentucky, the fabled Adolph Rupp, had called me the greatest college player he had ever seen, but Rupp was widely considered to be a racist. It was thrilling to see that team from El Paso take home the championship—and to see the pained, shocked look on Rupp's face—and it was great for basketball. One player from that team, Jim "Bad News" Barnes, became a teammate of mine on the Lakers, but he never experienced anything close to the success and thrill of that one night in College Park, Maryland.

To my mind, in one way or another, this all comes back to politics and the making of laws. I understand all too well that you can make legislation but you can't legislate how people feel toward one another. One of my biggest regrets is that I never found the wherewithal, emotionally and mentally, to go back to West Virginia and run for governor, something I had been encouraged and was sorely tempted to do on a few occasions once my playing days were over.

It was getting late, and I was eager to leave Hannah's and return home. But before I did, we talked of the awful place we had lived when we returned from Mineral Wells (in fact, it was so awful I didn't want Jonathan to see it; I told him I couldn't remember precisely where it was, but that wasn't true). Hannah and I laughed as we recalled the old woman who dressed like a witch and owned a farm nearby with apple trees, which we helped ourselves to. Hannah saw it as stealing, but I did not. "Well, they didn't belong to us," she said. "No, they didn't, but it wasn't stealing because she just let them rot anyway." I can be like this, always finding a way to rationalize something.

The old lady also had a bull that used to chase me all the time, and I did the same thing to the bull that I'd done to that mean dog Bear: I shot him in the butt with my Red Ryder BB gun. And then there were the crazy guinea hens who wouldn't leave me the hell alone. I am not sure why all these animals decided to chase me at different times—I don't recall doing anything to provoke them, I really don't—but they kept me fit because I could run like a deer and I knew how to scurry up a tree. I can also see why anyone reading this now, even me, would find the whole thing hilarious. It was another form of competition and it was fun.

What wasn't fun was the fire that destroyed our two-story home in 1962, a topic that was bound to come up during my visit, a subject of great sadness in our family because of all that was lost. It was late March, and my father had had a heart attack and was in the hospital in Charleston. According to Cookie, right around suppertime, while my mother and she were watching *American Bandstand* in the living room, a neighbor came by to ask how my father was doing. Suddenly, they all saw flames in the kitchen (apparently the hot oil in the pan on the stove had flashed up and set fire to the nearby curtains). The old house went up like tinder. Since Chelyan was so small it didn't have a volunteer fire department, and so it took forever for help—and hoses—to arrive. Whether that would have mattered is unclear.

Nearly everything burned up in that fire, including all of my trophies, stuff from East Bank, a huge Olympic flag I had proudly brought back from the Rome Olympics, and the thing that bothered me the most: a green trunk that contained so many items that had belonged to David. Even though I had moved away, I still felt as if a part of my life had been wiped out. But given some of the awful memories I had associated with that house, I didn't necessarily see its loss in negative terms. Miraculously enough, no one was badly hurt (my mother did suffer some burns), and the two things that survived were my Olympic Gold Medal and my Olympic uniform (though it was singed)—my two most important possessions.

My mother was distraught. Her relationship with my father was as strained as ever, and now the house and all its contents, especially David's green trunk, were lost. I know full well how cruel and awful life can be, and sometimes the bad news never stops coming. Even though she struggled with how to be a mother—her own mother was cold and distant—she was still my mother, and one of the best feelings I ever had was when I paid off the house that she and Cookie and my father moved into across the way. It's not as if I was making a significant amount of money at that time, but I was able to finally afford to do something for my family. Five years after the fire, in 1967, my father died, and I flew home from New York, where we had been playing the Knicks, for the funeral.

Looking back, the worst thing, though, is that I didn't feel as if I knew either of my parents. Or what I knew, I wanted to forget.

On the way back home, it was clear to me that Hannah was still sad, all these years later, that she hadn't been able to afford to go to college, which is a crime. Her IQ was very high, 136. I decided to tell Jonathan what it was she had alluded to.

"My dad hit her with the handle of a hammer, and this really set me off. I witnessed it and it was awful. 'You son of a bitch, you,' I said to him. 'You leave her alone.' He was a vicious man. I don't even remember what it was about. He had a violent temper and it was an ugly way to live a life."

Hannah was perhaps the sanest one of all of us and yet she had all these things happen to her, but she has somehow endured. She's still the same calm, easygoing person she always has been and she is a great mother. Not just good, but great. I am grateful that she understands me, even if she is not always happy with me. When I'd reiterated what she already knew, that I was the one person in the family who didn't communicate, she'd said there was a reason why, and the reason was my father. We are all aware of it, even if my brother Charlie wishes it were otherwise. I know that it is wrong to constantly blame others for things that happen in your life. But I think most people would agree on this: there are certain events that are important in your life and can do damage to it. Life-changing events. And I've had some of those, and, unfortunately, they happened to me when I was young. But they, perhaps more than anything else, formed much of the crucible of who I am, and almost certainly made me into the determined person and sick competitor that I became. A tormented, defiant figure who carries an angry, emotional chip on his shoulder and has a hole in his heart that nothing can ultimately fill.

Even now, all these years later, I would still like to know what it is I did. I can say I don't seek the approval of others, but nothing could be further from the truth. People can say that I am overly sensitive and too easily hurt, but there are reasons for that. I can say I don't give a damn about something when in fact I do, a lot. I can say I wasn't trying to fill the void that David's passing had left, but I can see now that I was.

3

Willie, Ann, and the Clamor for "Heroes"

Willie and me at WVU, 1958

When I think back to my steal of the inbounds pass that led to the winning basket in Game Three of the 1962 NBA Finals against the Boston Celtics, and think back to my ever-present desire to take the last and deciding shot in a game, and think of all the people over all the years who have told me that they consider me a hero, someone they grew up wanting to emulate, it makes me terribly uncomfortable. And yet I still wonder: *Was this something I sought for myself, or was this something that was thrust upon me?*

When my East Bank High School team won the state championship in 1956 in Morgantown (over two games, the semifinal and final, I averaged forty-one points), it was the proudest day of my life up to that point. The celebration the next day in front of the school brought two thousand people from miles around. You would have thought someone had discovered a cure for cancer. I look back at the black-and-white photographs from that Sunday—it was cold as hell and all the people were huddled in their overcoats—and I still struggle to believe it. A decision was made that every year after that, on March 24, the day we'd won, the town's name would be changed to West Bank. I was overwhelmed by all this clamor and attention. People began to look at me differently, and it embarrassed me, but I didn't let it change me. I was still the same kid who not that long before had been teased for his big ears and long arms and funny head and ill-fitting clothes. We had won that tournament as a team, yet everyone was determined to put the focus on me. (In one of the photographs, I am holding the trophy, and someone later remarked I looked like James Dean.)

Rod Hundley, West Virginia's All-American, sat on our team's bench because he had been assigned by Fred Schaus, his coach, to show me around the campus and persuade me to come to school there the following year. (Little did I know that we would become lifelong friends and teammates on the Lakers and that our numbers would eventually be retired at WVU. I had originally been given Rod's number 33 to wear, which I did for a bit, but then I told Fred I wanted to be my own man and wear number 44.) I have been around sports long enough by now to partly understand why this hero worship exists, why the fans — a whole community, really — need to have something or someone to look up to and be proud of, to live through vicariously and perhaps fill a void they feel in themselves, but I know the negative side of that as well, the side in which the hero turns out to have clay feet. The whole glorifying of athletes is, in the end, not healthy, not healthy at all, and dangerous, often leading to terrible disillusionment. One minute fans can love and be for you, and be ugly toward you the next.

What happened with Tiger Woods around Thanksgiving of 2009 is a pretty good example of that, but there are many others. The public persona everyone saw as the epitome of cool and control and perfection turned out to be a man with a different private life. When Tiger was a teenager growing up in Southern California, his father asked me to speak to him about the celebrity he was sure would come Tiger's way and to advise him on how to deal with the pitfalls he was likely to experience. I told Tiger very much the same thing I would tell players on the Lakers: Know who your friends truly are and be very careful both whom you associate with and with your money; your good character and reputation are *everything*. Be mindful of how you deal with the press and how important those interactions can be. I played at a time — the Stone Age,

I like to call it—when there was a lot less money, when there was no Internet and no twenty-four-hour news cycle, and when sports-writers looked the other way at athletes' indiscretions. Golf is a very conservative sport that has always had a certain decorum about it; the difference between it and the far sexier world of professional basketball couldn't be larger. There is a good reason why Michael Jordan was uncomfortable being anyone's role model. I personally admire and like Michael very much, and we get together whenever we can—in my opinion, he is the greatest, most competitive player to ever play the game (though I always beat him in golf when we first started playing, but not now)—but he is flawed and he is human, just as I am, and he would be the first to tell you that.

I decided to reach out to Tiger because my sense was that very few people were. I sent him a letter and a copy of *The Noticer,* a little inspirational book that urges one to keep a larger perspective no matter what kind of crisis is being faced. In my letter, I expressed my concern for him and my hope and belief that he would eventually weather this and resume his quest to become the greatest golfer who ever played the game. Sometimes you have to fall, and fall hard, in order to gain the personal wisdom that Andy Andrews's book speaks about. To this day, I don't know if Tiger ever received the book, but if he did, I hope he read it.

Speaking of heroes, I went to visit one of my three athletic ones not long ago—Jim Brown, the Michael Jordan of football, the greatest running back of all time, who played for the Cleveland Browns. He wore number 44 at Syracuse—he graduated from there three years before I graduated from West Virginia—and that is the main reason I wanted to wear it. He lives high above Sunset, not far from me, in Los Angeles. He had the courage to walk away from the game long before anyone expected him to, and shortly afterward he moved to California. When I learned that he worked out in the mornings at Sports Club/LA, where I was also a member, I would try to go there around the same time so I could work out near him and perhaps draw him into a conversation. I was always very curious, but I was also in awe of him, so the most we ever did was bullshit. When I told him all this, he said, "Jerry, I wish I would have known that. We could have had some great conversations." (These days, I would probably be called a stalker.)

What Jim had to say startled me and embarrassed me and touched me greatly. For as long as I can remember, Jim has been trying to solve the gang problems in California. When he and Bill Russell of the Celtics (they were close friends and, coincidentally, had just had dinner together the night before) were still playing (and had a lot to lose), they spoke out about race and injustice and were vilified in many respects for doing so. (I always sensed how difficult it was for Bill to play in a fiercely segregated city like Boston, but I did not know his house was broken into and that feces were smeared on his bed until Jim told me.) In any case, Jim brought up something I had practically forgotten—that I had phoned him and offered to help in any way that I could but that I was not seeking any recognition for doing so, and in fact made it very clear I not receive any. This was not because I didn't want to be publicly tied to what Jim was doing but because I feel the best and purest way to help is simply by giving, be it of your time or of your money. Jim never took me up on my offer, and I told him how disappointed I was that he hadn't.

"Jerry, it was very clear to me," Jim said that day, "that you were sincere in wanting to help and not wanting anything from it—no instant gratification, as so many people do, no recognition, nothing. You would always say something that set your shit apart, that made me know you were a thinker, that you were smart and conscientious. I can't even begin to tell you what that phone call meant to me. How could I have known that you knew what I was trying to do with these gangs and the prison population? But you had clearly done your homework before you made that call to me. The reason I didn't take you up on it is that I wanted to wait until your help could have the most impact. I didn't want to waste it." In Jim's mind (and this still both amuses and baffles me), he had put me on some sort of pedestal, perhaps for no other reason than that I'd made a call that I didn't need to make.

"Now that we have a black president in the White House," he said, "I am hopeful that more attention can be focused on what I am trying to do."

In terms of people who wanted to help mainly to further their own image, we both agreed that Jesse Jackson fit into that category. I knew Jesse and didn't trust him emotionally, thought of him, negatively, as "the greatest politician of all time," and it still irked Jim that Jesse had smeared Martin Luther King Jr.'s blood on his shirt on that night in 1968 that King was cut down in Memphis. For me, when I watched Jesse crying on television the night of Obama's election celebration in Grant Park in Chicago, I found his tears of joy oddly unconvincing, especially since he had tried to throw Obama's ass under a bus during the campaign. (In 2010 I became upset with Jesse all over again. When Dan Gilbert, the owner of the Cleveland Cavaliers, reacted angrily to LeBron James's leaving for the Miami Heat, Jesse injected race into it by suggesting that Gilbert was acting like a slave owner who was furious that one of his slaves had been ungrateful and disloyal and run off for a better life. I understood Gilbert's frustration, shock, and disappointment, and I do think LeBron should have informed him of his decision before going on national television to announce it.

I didn't agree with many of the things Dan said, because LeBron James had earned the right to do what he did. But I also thought Jesse did what he always does — pop up out of nowhere and take things way too far.)

Jim then brought up O. J. Simpson, a subject that still disturbs me. His kids went to the same preschool as mine in Brentwood, and he was always gracious to me whenever we ran into each other. He would occasionally come to Lakers games, and he would always enter late so that people would notice him, which always amused me, but other celebrities did that too. I was shocked, frankly, that he was acquitted of murder, but I was also saddened to see how quickly his life and his reputation spiraled downward.

Not long after my trip to see my two sisters, I was sitting on my back porch in West Virginia in the late afternoon, reading a book that had been published nearly fifty years before: Joseph Campbell's *The Hero with a Thousand Faces*. When I am curious about something, as I have already noted, there is little I won't do to learn more. I can be like a federal marshal, tenaciously on the case until I find whatever, or whomever, I am seeking. The question I asked myself at the beginning of this chapter — whether I'd sought to be a hero or had that role thrust upon me — as well as Bill Bertka's question about what I saw when I looked in the mirror prompted me to read this. I vaguely recalled seeing Campbell on public television in a series of interviews with Bill Moyers and hearing him advise people to "follow their bliss" — a truly foreign concept to me. But if by *bliss* he meant "passion" — now, that I can relate to.

I like how it is arranged in stages, with essentially three sections: "Departure" (or Separation), which shows the hero setting out on his quest; "Initiation," which recounts his adventures and mishaps and missteps; and "Return," which portrays the hero's coming home with the knowledge and, perhaps, power he acquired while away. I am not sure how much of this relates specifically to me and my convoluted life, but I can see that it could be a good way to understand the development — the journey — of someone who has left some sort of mark that people are curious about. A way to understand what goes on in that person's mind, what drives him. A writer, a painter, someone who has the vision to create a Microsoft, someone who excels in sports. I learned that the book had a great influence on Bob Dylan, Stanley Kubrick, and Jerry Garcia, and that George Lucas drew great inspiration from it in making the *Star Wars* movies.

"What I think," Campbell wrote in a different book, *Pathways to Bliss,* "is that a good life is one hero journey after another. Over and over again, you are called to the realm of adventure, you are called to new horizons. Each time, there is the same problem: do I dare? And then, if you do dare, the dangers are there, and the help also, and the fulfillment or the fiasco. There's always the possibility of a fiasco.

"But there's also the possibility of bliss."

I am well acquainted with the first possibility. In fact, I seem to thrive when there is a fiasco, when there is a crisis that I can try to resolve. Bliss, on the other hand, I am not sure I will ever find — or could easily embrace, day after day, even if I did. As the novelist Bernard Malamud said, "Life is a tragedy full of joy." I deeply believe the first part, and frequently struggle with the second.

Not only do I not think of myself as a hero, I actually think of myself as someone who had come in second more times than he cared to remember, someone who was a prince far more often than a king.

Three years after East Bank won the state championship, my West Virginia University team lost the 1959 national championship by one point to the University of California. The final that the country apparently wanted to see was WVU against Cincinnati, me against Oscar Robertson, who was Player of the Year. But the wily, defensive genius of Cal's coach, Pete Newell, interfered with all that. His team found a way to stop Oscar in the semifinal. We had beaten Louisville, the hometown team, in the other semifinal by a score of 94 to 79 before a raucous crowd at Freedom Hall. It was one of the best games we played all year, and I finished with thirty-eight points and fifteen rebounds. But the next night was a different story. We got off to a terribly slow start, which wasn't unusual, and put ourselves in a difficult position. Cal was cautious and conservative in the way they played, choosing to possess the ball as long as possible, whereas we played much more of a fast-break game. Anyway, we started pressing all over the court and began whittling down the deficit, but we were never able to get the lead. Near the end of the game, their center, Darrall Imhoff, who was bigger than anyone we had (and who became a close friend and teammate of mine), made a play that I continue to see in my sleep; he was left-handed yet he somehow knocked in a basket with his right hand, probably the ugliest play you could ever imagine. It didn't matter. The game ended at 71–70, with me having the ball at midcourt and unable to get off a shot.

I scored twenty-eight points and had eleven rebounds and overall had 160 points over five games, tying the NCAA record up to that point. I was named MVP of the tournament—the first of two times in my life I would be accorded such a dubious honor in a losing cause. As I did then, and would continue to do, I agonized as to what more I could have done to help us win, always felt that I had let the team down.

But it was more than the team, I reluctantly came to realize, that I had let down. We, as a team, had let down an entire state. Not long ago, a car dealer from Wheeling, who was twelve years old when we lost that game, told me he had listened to every second of it on the radio. When it was over, he said, sounding as if it were yesterday, he cried for the state of West Virginia, he cried for himself, and he cried for me. But he wasn't through. He insisted that the sting of that defeat — not just for him, but for the entire state — didn't lessen until Mary Lou Retton (whose father, Ronnie, was on that team) won a Gold Medal at the 1984 Olympics twenty-five years later.

Not only did that comment not upset me, but I fully understood and empathized with it. In West Virginia, everything revolves around the Mountaineers. There are no professional teams to root for. That is not to say that Marshall University doesn't have its followers or that it hasn't had, in people like Hal Greer and Randy Moss, its share of great athletes. But the overall mood of the state is so tied to West Virginia University basketball and football that it borders on the fanatical.

To this day, I have never gotten over that defeat to Cal, and I never will. I knew that at the time, believe it or not. But there is something else, something I didn't know. I didn't know that that one defeat, on a March night in Louisville before nineteen thousand people, would become a blueprint, a road map, an omen of sorts, for what lay ahead.

But, as I often do, I digress, and I get ahead of myself. My back porch has a view of the mountains. And when I look at those mountains, their trees beginning to change colors in the state where I was born, I think, *If I were on top of that mountain up there, what would I see on the other side?* If you're young, those are the things that are going to define who you are. Are you going to take the time and make the effort, and do you have the interest to do that? Some kids would say, "No, it's too hard," or "It's going to look the same on the other side." But I would say just the opposite: "What am I going to see going up the mountain *and* on the other side?" I always wondered if I would get lost or, when it was dark, what I might run into. Every time I heard a noise, I would freeze, worrying that a red fox might come my way, trying to figure out what was scratching in the leaves. Whatever it was, I always expected to see something I wasn't likely to see in my neighborhood below. So there was a fear factor. Adding to it, strangely enough, was my fear of heights and still I went. A lot of places I would go there would be these big rocks and I might stand on one and look out and worry that it would fall over. But I was still curious enough to do it, because along with the fear was the utter excitement. And there was a feeling of security: that was the place I felt really safe, away from my home below, where I did not.

For a variety of reasons, my son Ryan apparently thinks I am weird. I prefer the word *different*. To this day, he can't believe that I didn't go to Game Seven of the Portland–Los Angeles series in 2000, and that when he and my son Jonnie and Karen eventually came home after it, they found me asleep, even though I knew the Lakers had rallied to win. I always know the score. To this day, for personal reasons, I prefer not to go to Boston. When the NBA honored the Top 50 players in its history to mark its fiftieth anniversary, at the 1997 All-Star Game in Cleveland, I didn't go. When I retired as Lakers' head of basketball operations in 2000, I didn't attend the press conference.

Even today, when I watch television, I spend as much time watching the Discovery and National Geographic channels as I do watching basketball. Why is that? Why at my age do I still have that curiosity about animals? Why do I sit here wondering who would win a fight between a coyote and a pit bull, or whether a tiger or a lion is bigger? (I thought they would be similar, but tigers are bigger.) I love zoos, particularly when they are natural looking, not when it seems an animal is caged in there. It reminds me of how I felt in the locker room before games, like a caged animal, sweat just dripping off me, occasionally throwing up, ready to get out there and do battle the minute the door flew open. Ready to go out there and compete. It probably wasn't until the Lakers moved to the Forum on New Year's Eve of 1967 that I truly began to think of myself as a gladiator—it was partly the Roman architecture, I am sure, and the fact that Lakers' owner, Jack Kent Cooke, insisted the ushers wear togas and so forth—but, come to think of it, it probably went back to Rome, when I went there for the Olympics, and even before that, when I played at Mountaineer Field House and the sixty-eight hundred fans were so close to you they felt like a mob. I have always been interested in the fact that basketball players were originally known as cagers because they played within the confines of one.

My adult life took me away from those mountains for the most part, and I regret it. I often think how much more meaningful my life would have been if I could have continued to climb around up there.

Something else has occurred to me as well. If my home life had been the kind of world Norman Rockwell would have painted, perhaps it wouldn't have been as interesting. If I had grown up in a big city, I would have missed out, I feel pretty sure, on many of the things I am describing. I didn't have a father who wanted to do these things with me. So I did them alone. And even today, there is a solitary side to me that is not seen, but that, really, is the essence of who I am. The mountains I ascended were not just mountains.

They were my sanctuary, just as the basketball court became; they were also my cave, but one that wasn't always dark. They were shelter from the coming storm, and I never knew when the storm was going to come.

I am well aware, because I feel this myself at times, that when people read a book, there is a certain amount of skepticism some of them might have about what they are reading because they don't have a good feeling about the writer, or because they are envious or jealous. In my case, it has taken a lot of courage for me to even talk about these things because I have hidden them for so long. Still, there will be people who will say, "Oh, this didn't happen, and that couldn't have happened."

Well, they didn't live my life. They don't know what my life was like.

The ordinary world of the "hero," according to Campbell, consists of suffering, boredom, and neurotic anguish, but I would say that *suffering* and *anger* are the most accurate words to describe what I experienced and how I felt growing up. I was always trying to figure out what might trigger an outburst from my father, always walking on eggshells hoping that I wouldn't be confronted with an ugly situation—one of the reasons, no doubt, that I hate confrontation to this day. If I have something critical to say to someone—usually to my sons, or even to Karen—I often ask Gary Colson or others to say it for me. I am not saying that this is a positive attribute (and I am sure it is one of the reasons Ryan thinks I am weird). I am stating it as a fact, something that has caused me a great deal of anguish at times. I can be, and often am, maddening, a master of indirection.

In my house growing up, you didn't hear the words *I love you*, which I am sure plays a large part in why I find it so difficult to say the same thing, or fully understand what it is. Three goddamn words, and I struggle like hell with them.

In terms of the neurotic anguish Campbell writes about, I don't think *neurotic* applies to me, I really don't. *Superstitious,* yes. *Odd,* no doubt. *Experiences and suffers anguish,* most definitely. But neurotic? No. I'm not Woody Allen, for Christ's sake. But what I have always been is incredibly excitable, something I do my best to hide but that I'm generally unable to. For me, everything has always been about anticipation and instinct. It is certainly true of the way I played. As far back as high school, I sensed that maybe I was a little bit better because I could move my feet and see how a play should develop long before it unfolded; I could read eyes and body movements and knew what players were going to do, what directions they liked to go in and which they didn't, and see *everything.* It enabled me to steal balls and block shots. It also made me keenly aware of the players who possessed that same ability—guys like Bill Russell and Wilt Chamberlain and Oscar Robertson come to mind. After I had my shots blocked a few times—one block by Russell still embarrasses me even now, partly because anyone, including my kids, can see it on YouTube, day or night—I learned how to make adjustments, do things a little bit differently in order to get a different outcome. I might still have gotten my shot blocked and had the ball stolen, but it happened far less.

It was this same combination of anticipation and instinct that helped me enormously in running the Lakers. Anticipating what the team needed before it was readily apparent. Knowing that even if a particular player was having a terrific year, he probably was unlikely to do as well the following one. Knowing who could possibly help us, be that missing piece of the jigsaw. Anticipating criticism and a shaking of heads but sticking with my conviction.

Throughout my life, the key has been having a vision, a good work ethic, and goals; taking my work, but never myself, seriously; treating people the way I would want to be treated and never placing myself above anyone; saying hello to everyone, saying thank you, trying to help others if they need assistance. And, as much as possible, doing all this with a smile, because a smile is more disarming than most people ever realize.

Unfortunately, another life lesson I have learned is that fairness and trustworthiness are not always a given; in today's world, trust must be earned. A person's good word and a handshake should mean something, but often it doesn't. My biggest objective as an executive was to put the players' welfare first. The one period when I feel I really didn't do that was during the three years I coached, a time of extreme turmoil in my life.

What Campbell describes as a call to adventure was, in my case, really more of a call to action. I am a fatalist. I think our lives are meant to travel certain paths, that we are all pigeonholed to a certain degree, and that where that path takes us is our journey. I've always felt there's a place for everyone regardless of what a person's skills might be or what arena they might be in. That place for me could have been in Africa, living among the animals and experiencing their incredible will to survive. I used to think about going to Africa all the time when I was a little boy because of my fascination with animals. As a child, you dream and you put yourself in places you don't tell anyone else about for fear you'll be told it is ridiculous and asked why you would even think of something like that. But Africa, it turned out, was *not* where I was supposed to end up. I was supposed to end up doing what I did.

Just recently, I was up at the library at WVU for a meeting and the people there had a photo of me on the computer, a photo of me taking a jump shot when I played there. I stared at the photo and I asked myself, *Have you ever seen anyone with a prettier jump shot?* and I had to answer no. It would be disingenuous of me to say anything other than that my jump shot was sweet and it was quick and it was effective.

Now, why would that one picture lead me to that question? Because if you looked at my body and you looked at how I held the ball in my right hand and the way my left hand protected it before I shot, looked at all the things I think are important in shooting, you would wonder—should wonder—how in the hell did someone learn that on his own unless it was a gift? I had no one to copy. There was no one who shot like that. Over and over again, I tell anyone who asks that I did it this way—my way—in order not to be bothered or distracted; I did not want to allow anything or anybody to make me lose my focus. Preparing to take my shot, I would first dribble two or three times to my right and then, on the final dribble, I would bounce it extra hard so the ball would come up to exactly where I wanted it, and I would then jump and extend myself as high and far as I could. As I got older, I learned that this last part wasn't as necessary, that I had better control when I didn't jump so high. But knowing that I had that extra jump was important if I needed to make a particularly difficult shot.

I remember being at Ed Macauley's camp in Missouri (Ed played for the Celtics) in 1961 and showing all of this to a young man named Bill Bradley. (He would later tell John McPhee, who wrote a book about Bradley's time at Princeton, about how he incorporated my advice into his game. Bill was one of the best ever to play college basketball, and later he gave us fits when he played for the Knicks, a team that beat us two of the three times we faced them in the NBA Finals. He was also very different, seemed to be a loner, and I respected his courage in refusing to make money off endorsements, opportunities he felt only came his way because he was white.)

I always laugh when I think about practicing that final bounce because, more often than not, it would unpredictably shoot up from my rock-strewn dirt court and smack me in the face. But I kept doing it and doing it and never stopped.

Long before Malcolm Gladwell, in his book *Outliers,* pointed out the importance of repetition, of ideally doing something for ten thousand hours, I was doing that on my court in Chelyan. So I knew full well what it meant to be a solitary boy with a ball and a fierce dream of better.

Jumping was another thing I worked on in order to achieve balance. Drawing little chalk blocks in the dirt would help me land in the spot I wanted to. And the thing that confounds a lot of people is how I can close my eyes and shoot free throws and be able to make shot after shot. I figured out how much distance there was between me and the basket, and I also figured I had one second to shoot. In a normal shot, I knew if I had a taller guy guarding me, I would have to shoot it higher, would have to change the release point. Again, these are things I learned myself; no one taught me that. So this is part of why I have always felt the sport chose me, not the other way around. As far as being able to go out there and compete, that's a gift. It's innate. Nothing more, nothing less. I used to wonder, though, if there was anything else in life I could enjoy more than basketball, something that didn't come with the torment I felt as a player sometimes. And what did I come up with? Nothing. Nothing that would have been as exhilarating and given me that same rush I got when I knew I was going to go out and play. Every night was a different story with a different theme—a new team to play—and a different puzzle to put together and solve.

What other people might have perceived as unbearable pressure and expectation, I viewed differently. It was something I embraced. For someone as anxious as I am in many ways, it is interesting how calm I would get near the end of a game. Everything would become quieter and slower and I was able to concentrate and bear down even harder. I never drew attention to myself other than through my play. These days, a lot of players are chest-bumping and hollering and whooping it up and holding their jerseys out. It's almost like an extension of the Internet, where everyone has a blog, it seems, and can sound off about anything he or she wants. And many players even have their own publicists. *You've got to be kidding me.* If you are good enough, why on earth would you need a publicist to embellish what should already be powerfully clear? If I played today, the last thing I would have is a publicist.

If I had been forced to choose a different sport to play, I would have chosen golf, partly because it is so ridiculously hard and partly because you are essentially competing against yourself. Designed by the devil, it is a game that requires exacting precision and touch. It is also a very emotional game internally (which suits me) and it appeals to me for many of the reasons basketball does: it is a game of angles, and angles fascinate me, even obsess me. I didn't start playing golf until 1961, when I got a set of Wilson clubs for participating in that year's All-Star Game as a rookie. They sat in my garage for a while before a friend named Joe Miller and my teammate Frank Selvy got me started playing, and it became a lifelong pursuit. I used to attend the Los Angeles Open when I had a chance and watch all the great players on the practice range and try to copy them. Playing an individual sport might have been less tormenting for me, but I don't know that for sure. I have broken a lot of clubs in my life. On purpose. There was a place not far from Bel-Air Country Club that repaired them, and I would often put a broken club (or two) in front of their door early in the morning, well before they opened, with no note. No note was necessary, because they knew the clubs were mine. I have even thrown some over the fence of Bel-Air. If you don't believe me, ask Pat Riley. He witnessed it.

There was a time when the thinking in basketball was that being in the air for any reason was not a good thing, that you had less control, that you could do fewer things. But Bill Russell, in terms of perfecting the art of blocking shots, and Elgin Baylor, my teammate and the first player to really play in the air (the forerunner to players like Julius Erving and Michael Jordan), proved that this was not the case. When I first got to the Lakers, I studied everything Elgin did, and I was in awe of him, one of the most dignified people I had ever met. He learned to play on the playgrounds of Washington, D.C., where the prime objective, day in and day out, was to not lose, to not have to leave the court. Long before the expression "Who's got next?" gained a kind of national currency, Elgin's answer was always the same: we do, every time. In many ways, I envied the opportunities Elgin and Oscar Robertson (growing up in Indianapolis) had to compete each day when something was at stake; my rural experience was so much different (though I also think that had I grown up in a city, I might have gotten into a lot of trouble, done things I would later have regretted).

Elgin was also the first player I had ever seen use the backboard, "the glass," as if he were shooting pool. I had never seen someone with so many moves, so many creative ideas of what to do with the ball and how to angle it. It was like getting a free education and free entertainment at the same time. In 1960, my rookie year, Elgin scored seventy-one points against the Knicks at Madison Square Garden, a dazzling performance that I witnessed mostly from the bench, as I was not starting yet. Tommy Hawkins, another teammate, always joked that he and Elgin combined for eighty-six points that day—a joke he never tires of telling and told as recently as February of 2009, when Elgin and I were enshrined together on one plaque outside the Los Angeles Memorial Coliseum.

I will never forget when Fred Schaus, West Virginia's coach, first came to visit me in Chelyan. He came in the summer of 1955, after my junior year of high school. I had just returned from Boys State, an educational program that you had to be selected for by the American Legion, and he was the first coach to try and recruit me. In those days, you didn't make a commitment to a college until you'd almost graduated from high school, and if I didn't get an athletic scholarship I would not be able to go to college. So one day, near evening, my mother and I were out on the porch and I see this car pulling up and I said to her, "Ma, is that who I think it is?" It was Fred Schaus, and as he got out of his car, I could see he was carrying something. A blue West Virginia T-shirt. I had been to Morgantown to see a game before, and I had heard of his interest in both me and Willie Akers, whom I had just met over in Jackson's Mill at Boys State.

Willie was from Mullens—his high school coach was Lew D'Antoni, whose sons Mike and Dan have coached in the NBA for many years—and was well known throughout the state as a star on the rise. I was just coming into my own at East Bank, but I soon realized that nobody was giving me much thought. In fact, one of my first huge disappointments had come that winter. Our team was mediocre, finished at thirteen and thirteen, I believe, but still I was named first-team all-conference. But when the all-state team was announced, two guys who had also been first-team all-conference had made it, and I was honorable mention. How in the world, I wondered, did something like that happen? I was crushed, though I never said a word, not one, but let me tell you, the injustice of that only added to that emotional chip on my shoulder.

Willie and I were in separate cabins at Boys State, but he has joked many times since that once he'd seen me play — to this day he loves to tell people how I blocked a shot in midair and came down with the ball — he always wanted to be on my team. Doing well at Boys State gave me a degree of self-confidence and a sense of belonging. Since I'd had very little of either before going there, even a little bit was a lot. I outperformed the guys who were there; Willie knew it, and even someone like Howard Hurt of Beckley, who went on to play at Duke, knew it.

Anyway, coming back to Fred Schaus. To actually see him in my little burg — that was something. We had some lemonade and we visited (my father tried to get involved as well, now that it appeared I was going to make something of myself, but I made it very clear I didn't want him to), and my mother told Fred that she wanted me to go to WVU and wear the blue-and-gold uniform — the same thing she would flatly state to all the other recruiters who came after Fred, making promises and offering all sorts of bells and whistles.

Fred (who had actually never seen me play) was a tall and imposing figure, standing six six and rather stern-looking. He had played at WVU himself and was one of the pioneers of the NBA. As he got ready to leave for the long drive back, he asked me to walk out to the car with him. "Hell," he said, reaching into the backseat, "I might as well give you this too."

It was a gold WVU T-shirt. By mid-April of 1956, I formally committed to play basketball for West Virginia University, beginning a relationship with that school that continues to this day.

In some ways, I also saw my call to adventure as a call to disappear, a prospect I have always found appealing. When David died, I became withdrawn. I won't say antisocial, but anti- a lot of things. I lived in that house, but I vanished. I contributed nothing verbally. I became deathly quiet. In that summer of 1951, I couldn't wait for school to start again so I could be home even less. I didn't sit around moping, but I did sit there thinking how unfair it was that I would never see him again. I can't tell you how many times in recent years I have thought how interesting it would be if I could have sat down with MacArthur and asked him what it felt like knowing he had guided many young men to their deaths. I would have asked him why he did that. I would have kept pressing him and pressing him — Did you do it for your ego, nothing more, nothing less? — and I wouldn't have stopped.

When I saw the movie *Saving Private Ryan*, it really affected me. *Band of Brothers*, same thing. My brother-in-law Jack Noel, who fought in World War II, would often wake up in the middle of the night screaming, still caught up in the horrors of what he saw. I often think of when the first atomic bomb was dropped and wonder if the pilots, once they landed safely, ever thought of how many people they had just killed; if, once they got older, they wondered, *Oh my God, what did I do?*

I say this because I often reflect back on my three years as coach of the Lakers, particularly the second and third years, and wish I could relive them and do it better this time. I was so hard on the players, particularly verbally, so hard. To this day, I feel bad about the horrible way I treated them (especially Brad Davis and Norm Nixon). I wanted them all to be better, but they could only be what they were; no matter how much you practice, no matter how hard you tried to put them in an environment where they could prosper, you couldn't make them any better.

Everybody thought I wanted them to be me, and that really irks me. I wanted them to be better so we could win and they would feel better about themselves. A certain self-esteem comes with winning; it breeds confidence. When you lose and lose, as the New Jersey Nets did throughout the 2009–2010 season, it breeds just the opposite.

When I took over as coach of the Lakers in the fall of 1976— one minute I was in an ugly lawsuit with Jack Kent Cooke, whom I didn't speak with for two years, and the next I was named head coach as part of the resolution of that suit, go figure—I immediately hired two assistants: Jack McCloskey, to focus on defense, and Stan Albeck, for offense—two men who not only showed great patience and understanding toward a rookie coach (which I will always be grateful for) but were instrumental to whatever success we enjoyed. Even though I had been a prolific scorer, I didn't have a clue as to how to coach offense. I really didn't. Defense I had a better grasp of, and becoming more defensive-minded was what I wanted for the team. The previous season, even with the acquisition of Kareem Abdul-Jabbar from the Milwaukee Bucks, the team finished forty and forty-two and missed the playoffs.

Campbell's suggestion that the hero is reluctant to move forward after hearing the call to adventure really resonated with me. He writes of the fear of the unknown, a surprising hesitation to confront the challenges that lie ahead. I was scared of everything. My shyness, my awkwardness, my feeling that I didn't fit in all contributed to this fear, even though a lot of people, particularly basketball coaches, thought I was pretty special. They didn't see this incredibly fragile part of me—deathly worried that I wouldn't succeed, wouldn't measure up, that I wouldn't be able to follow my dreams and the echoes of my mind. Here I was, having helped my team to a state championship, getting ready to leave a house that I had never wanted to be in, and yet all of a sudden I was on my way to Morgantown, hours away, and I was alone. I didn't have any of the people in my neighborhood to say hello to, and I arrived in this strange place, being around people who didn't know anything about me other than my reputation as a basketball player.

I landed in a little house at 65 Beechurst Avenue, living with two sisters in their forties, Ann and Erlinda Dinardi, who tried to get to know me and make me feel welcome, but inside of me I kept thinking, *What the hell am I doing here?* I got terribly homesick that summer of 1956 and wanted to go home, but go home to what? Other than familiarity, I guess, I had no clue. (I actually did leave Morgantown—what Campbell calls a "false start"—and Coach Schaus was so upset he phoned my friend Willie Akers, who had also committed to WVU but was still home in Mullens, and told him to bring my sorry ass back. When Willie got to my house, he found me playing with my sister Cookie on the porch.)

My real salvation that summer was a job I had as a water boy. A dam was being built on the Monongahela River and they needed someone to drive a truck and carry water back and forth. But I had never driven before—just as I don't swim now—and everyone laughed at me trying to learn how to do it. One time it rained so hard that I got the truck stuck in the mud, and they had to pull it out with a bulldozer. I say it was my salvation because these guys were everyday guys and they were fun to be around, but I am sure they were happy to have me gone because it rained hard all summer long and they were always having to rescue me from the mud.

Ann, a robust, no-nonsense woman whose home was the place where many West Virginia athletes lived over the years, and Erlinda worried about me right from the start. They worried I was too damn skinny—I weighed only 156 pounds—and they were determined to do something about it. They would send me off with six or seven sandwiches in a big paper bag and one or two milkshakes (Erlinda worked at Chico's Dairy Bar up the street), which I thought was both hilarious and ridiculous. I had so much food I used to give most of it away. There is no way I could have eaten all of it. All of this brought a certain levity and I looked forward to going out there each day. But then, back in my room by myself at night, I had no one to talk to. It's funny that this never bothered me when I was up in the woods by myself, or even at my home in Chelyan, where I didn't want to talk to anyone anyway, but it bothered me that summer, an unbelievably emotional period of my life. The strangest thing of all was that I didn't touch a basketball and, for whatever reason, I didn't even think about it.

When school began that fall, I moved into a dorm, and, thank God, I had Willie Akers with me. Willie was nearly everything I wasn't: happy, bubbly, lovable, easy, mellow. I knew he liked me, but I didn't know the depth of that at first. We were inseparable—if you saw one of us, you saw the other—and he remains a person I can share anything and everything with. When I look at Willie, I see someone with no apparent stress who manages to find fun in nearly everything he does (though you would not want to be on his bad side, trust me). Now, don't get me wrong; I can, as I've said, joke and play pranks and engage in high jinks as well as anyone.

(Willie and I were involved in a "food incident" once at the university dining facility that caused us to flee across state lines to Pennsylvania, to the home of a classmate's parents. We were laughing all the way there, but we were also scared, and we didn't return until Ann assured us that there would be no lingering repercussions. Ann took care of things on the university side, but we were not spared a real talking-to from her, the ultimate form of tough love. End of story.) But as you have probably gathered by now, I can also be testy and withdrawn and taut as a piano wire, though it is awfully hard to be that way around Willie. He pretty much doesn't allow it.

I trusted him then and I trust him now, and I feel certain that I stayed in school because of Willie. One of the saddest days in my life was being physically separated from him. If I hadn't gotten married before I graduated, I was going to bring his ass with me to Los Angeles. I never told him that, but that was my plan. He was going to be my buddy for life, my soul mate—and he is both of those things. I have known a lot of nice people in my life, but I have never known anyone nicer than him, or more loyal. The truth is, I envy Willie, I really do. He loves his life, and he rules his corner of the world, in Logan, West Virginia, where he was a successful high school basketball coach for more than twenty years. He has a bevy of sisters who spoil him and look up to him and call him the King. (His wife, Linda, spoils him as well, but she doesn't refer to him that way.)

I had made a commitment to be both an athlete and a student at West Virginia, but I often didn't go to class because I didn't want to be there. I was embarrassed that my grades were so poor (to this day I don't want my sons to see my transcript) because I knew full well that school wasn't that hard. It hadn't been hard in high school; it was only hard when I didn't study, when I avoided it altogether. I was confused and I was lost. I didn't know what I wanted. I was afraid of contact with people. I eventually had one teacher, though, who really captured my attention. He was an English teacher and he would stand on the desk from time to time to make his points. But when I first got to his class, I thought to myself, *Oh my God, we're reading Shakespeare and poetry, what in the hell am I doing here? What importance is this going to have to my life?* But that guy had such a personality, he made you so interested in what he was interested in, that at the end of each class, I almost couldn't wait till the next one. As it turned out, he also loved basketball, and we would often shoot baskets together down at the field house.

I was interested in girls but was too shy to approach them, so I would occasionally ask Willie to tell a girl of my interest. I remember he and I took a square-dancing class and it was a complete disaster; even when I was asked to make the call, I couldn't bring myself to do it. As time went on, if a girl asked me to dance, I would suggest we take a walk instead.

I couldn't play on the varsity as a freshman but our squad was so good (we went undefeated) we would often beat the varsity in practice. In the one official game we had, they beat us by a point, and I can tell you that the refs didn't help us.

The first slice of pizza I ever had was in college, at a place called Mario's, and for whatever reason I didn't relish it. Willie and I loved movies—it was the perfect place for me to disappear—and we would often see the same movie (like *Bus Stop* with Marilyn Monroe) four and five times. We lived together, played pool together, and stuffed ourselves with ice cream at Chico's, where I eventually had a dish named after me, the Jumpin' Jerry.

Once freshman year was over, I went to live at Ann's again and quickly learned that she (who became my surrogate mother, the kind of mother I surely would have chosen had I been able to make a choice) was not easy to say no to—*about anything*—and not someone to cross. Becoming one of "Ann's boys" was something I was immensely proud of, a badge of honor, a rite of passage, and I feel that way to this day (I came back from a trip to Europe in 1996 so that I wouldn't miss a surprise ninetieth birthday celebration for her). Her little house on Beechurst was the first place in my life where I really felt at home, and so it was only fitting that she be present in 2000 when part of Beechurst was renamed Jerry West Boulevard.

Ann was the first woman to graduate from WVU's School of Pharmacy, and she co-owned a drug store called Moore and Parriott for thirty-five years. She never married and was small in height, but that didn't prevent her from often reaching up and pinching my cheeks and throwing her arms around me. She would call my teachers and see how I was doing in school. If I did something she didn't approve of, she would say, "Why, Jerry, you bloody bastard." If I did something that pleased her, she would add, "I love you."

I was not used to this kind of affection. She died in 2003 and I miss her still. I will always miss her.

On the day I went to see my sister Hannah, I had stopped in Charleston to meet Willie for lunch at the Charleston Marriott. He pulled into the parking garage in his cream-colored Lincoln, the number 44 on his license plate. Many people have asked him how he was able to get hold of that, and his answers have always been vague and rather evasive. The real answer (which I only recently learned) is this: So many people asked to have that number that someone in the administration of Governor Cecil Underwood called Willie and suggested he take it in order to solve a potentially sticky problem of favoritism (unheard-of in West

Virginia politics, of course). Willie said that would be fine with him, and each governor since then has allowed him to keep it. Such is the unknown and unstated power of Willie Akers in the state of West Virginia, and the regard in which he is held. To me, his having that plate is a touching, but somewhat embarrassing, acknowledgment of how he feels about our relationship, perhaps the only one I have ever had of unconditional love.

I had last seen Willie about three months earlier, in Morgantown. We'd both been there to coach at a Bob Huggins Basketball Fantasy Camp, coming full circle as it were from all those years before at Boys State. I could never have imagined then that grown men (which included that car dealer from Wheeling who'd been so devastated when we'd lost the 1959 national championship, and his son) would one day spend a great deal of money to hang around with guys like Akers and me. I had many experiences with camps like this, running one with Earvin Johnson in Maui (Hawaii being one of the few places I can find some measure of peace, though Earvin disputes this), and I knew how much it meant to the guys who attended. They came in all shapes and sizes and were there for their own particular, and personal, reasons; what they shared was a passion for the game, a love for it that perhaps they couldn't even entirely articulate, and that is why I always threw myself into these things as if I were coaching in the NBA Finals. I love to teach; I love to be specific, to help someone improve on what they are trying to do. Whether it is an adult who wants to keep competing at a fantasy camp or a young boy or girl who comes to a regular camp, possessing the same sort of dreams that I did when I went off to Boys State, I relish having a hand in helping them. I love to see individuals better themselves, to push themselves closer to whatever it is they see for themselves in their mind's eye.

* * *

Whenever Willie and I get together, what we do is probably not all that different from what a lot of lifelong friends do—reminisce and cut up and gossip. Since we happened to be in Charleston that day, we talked about the time we had summer jobs at the DMV and put CLOSED signs in front of our windows every five minutes to take breaks that we hardly needed. It wasn't right, I know, but we were bored and didn't want to be there. We lived at my parents' house one of those summers and would drive to Charleston in Willie's car. One summer I lived some of the time with the people who owned Blossom Dairy and Restaurant, a Jewish family named Gattlieb who were very good to me and who sponsored the team I played on in the Charleston Summer League.

Throughout the years, I have never gotten used to the reverential way people treat me in West Virginia. At the same time, though, it makes me proud and it fills some, though not all, of my emptiness.

The significance of mentors in my life (something else Campbell wrote about) cannot be underestimated. From Roy Williams, my high school coach (who was also the football coach), I first learned about the importance of defense, which I have always prided myself on; in my pro career, I was named to the all-defensive first team four times. With Roy's encouragement, I somehow put five pounds on my Ichabod Crane body and suddenly felt like Superman. I mentally saw myself getting tougher because of Roy. It was always about defense and toughness for Roy, and I never forgot that. (Nor did I ever lose sight of how much Roy cared about me, as both a player and a person, and how he never stopped encouraging me.) I loved that an opposing player would think he had gotten past me, only to find that I would pick the ball from behind.

(Running away from those crazy guinea hens and from Bear had prepared me well.)

At WVU as a freshman, I found it hard to watch the varsity play and not be out there. As I mentioned, I first met Rod Hundley during my senior year of high school and thought he was a great player and a lovable guy, but I did not approve of all his antics, though I didn't tell him that at the time. Rod was an All-American and everyone said I would be the next one. But I would watch him and his showboating and think to myself that I would never do the things he did. I felt it was demeaning to the sport, and to the teams we played against—sneaking over and sitting on their bench, making a T-formation on the court as if he were a damn quarterback. I understand the importance of entertaining the fans, but he treated the game like a circus, and to this day I am not sure why Fred Schaus allowed it. Fred and George King, the assistant coach, pushed me hard once I was on the varsity, and I would often play one-on-one with George, who had played for the Syracuse Nationals in the NBA. The more I was able to beat him, the more I realized that maybe, just maybe, I could play professionally too.

Much as I loved to compete, I found that the more mediocre the team or the player who was guarding me, the worse I played. It's called playing down to the competition, and I was guilty of it. I can't tell you how many times we would get behind in a game and have to come back to win it. It caused such concern for Fred and George that they would call me in to talk about it, and Fred even threatened to take me out of the starting lineup in my sophomore year. I didn't know if he was kidding or not, but I had no interest in finding out. What I do know, and have always known, is that I respond best to a crisis, whether it is real or simply if I perceive it to be. We played in the Kentucky Invitational, in Lexington, and on consecutive December nights we beat Adolph Rupp's Kentucky Wildcats, ranked fifth in the country, and then Frank McGuire's North Carolina Tarheels, ranked first, which made us America's top-ranked team. As thrilling as those games were for us as a team, the turning point for me personally came on January 8, 1958, at the Palestra, in Philadelphia, against Villanova. The Palestra is as tough a place to play as I have ever encountered, and the fans both expect and demand excellence — not just of the home team but of the opposing team as well — and I wanted to be at my best. We started off in our customary slow way and got behind. But in the second half we came roaring back and I scored seventeen of the final twenty-three points; just in the last thirty seconds, I had two baskets and then an assist for Lloyd Sharrar's winning basket at the end. The final score was 76–75, and I had thirty-seven points in all. Far beyond the victory, though, that game was pivotal for me. I left Philadelphia with the sort of self-confidence I had been seeking on a consistent basis and that had been eluding me. I felt as if I finally belonged.

My personal dilemma aside, though, the fact is that your body simply cannot respond the same way every game, it can't, especially in the pros. You might hit twenty straight shots in practice or warm-ups but then you go out there and can't make a damn shot in the game. My body teased me all the time and tested me all the time. It doesn't matter what kind of shape you're in. I don't think fans understand that. They expect you to perform at your norm, and if you are really prideful, you want to do it against the best competition. And if you don't, that's when you feel the most disappointed, when you feel you have let everyone down. Every player sets a standard for himself, seeks his own level of play. If Kobe Bryant hits nine of twenty-seven shots, he's criticized for having a terrible night, but the reality is that there may not be another player on the team who is good enough to take twenty-seven shots, or courageous enough to take them even though he is having a bad shooting night. The next night, Kobe might make eighteen out of twenty-seven, and all of a sudden he goes from a guy who took a lot of bad shots to a hero, and I'll guarantee you that many of those shots were the same shots he missed the night before. The point is that a player like Kobe, or Michael Jordan, or Magic Johnson, has supreme confidence, and that is why they excel, why they are able to accept the responsibility of greatness, why they are the buoys of their team. Other players on the team might resent these players out of envy and jealousy, but they are also damn glad, for the most part, that they are on their team. As for me, I tended to play much better in the playoffs (my career average in the playoffs was two points higher than my regular season one), but even there I would have slumps, nights when nothing seemed to go right.

Anyway, it was guys like Roy and Fred and George who spurred me onward, and there were others too, like the WVU trainer Whitey Gwynne and the equipment manager Snoopy Roberts and, of course, Ann Dinardi, the person who helped me to have a base of support and a foundation and a belief in myself.

But none was more important, ironically, than Pete Newell. Even though Pete was the California coach who had a hand in one of my most crushing defeats, WVU's loss by one point in the 1959 national championship, he, above all, was the person who seemed to understand me and my fragile psyche best. As my coach for the 1960 Olympics, he was the one.

My third departure from home, after Boys State and West Virginia University, turned out to be my most enduring one — going to Los Angeles in 1960 to play basketball for the Lakers. And unlike my leaving for college, I didn't, as far as I can recall, feel

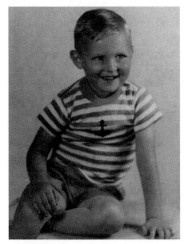

At three and a half

With sister Hannah (*right*) and my mother right behind me, holding my sister Barbara, along with other relatives

At fourteen

David in his East Bank
High School letter sweater

In Japan, after recover-
ing from hepatitis, before
returning to Korea

Sergeant David L. West

At Chelyan Junior High (I'm #12). Even then my arms were freakishly long.

Roy Williams, my East Bank coach, stressing defense

The shot that earned me the West Virginia state scoring record *(Charleston Daily Mail)*

Outside East Bank High, holding the trophy, the day after we won the state championship, March 1956

More than two thousand people came from miles around.

Willie Akers, Ann Dinardi, and me, outside 65 Beechurst in Morgantown, 1957

Willie and Fred Schaus, our WVU coach *(West Virginia University Sports Communications)*

I may look innocent here, but I would occasionally play pranks in the dining hall.

Receiving the Kentucky Invitational Classic trophy from Kentucky coach Adolph Rupp, along with Willie and Fred *(West Virginia University Sports Communications)*

Our WVU team (I'm #44) in 1959, the year we played the NCAA Final against Cal *(West Virginia University Sports Communications)*

The beginning of a lot of national media attention, which made me uncomfortable *(Morton Tadder)*

With my
parents—and
the first of nine
broken noses

Howard and
Cecile West

Battling the Russians in the semifinal game of the 1960 Olympics *(John G. Zimmerman/Sports Illustrated/Getty Images)*

Oscar Robertson and me, the co-captains, receiving our Gold Medals on the podium, one of the happiest days of my life *(© Bettmann/Corbis)*

Our entire team (I am second from the right, first row), with Pete Newell, our coach, kneeling on the right *(United States Olympic Committee)*

With Michael, David, Mark, and my first wife, Jane, in our kitchen in Brentwood

Driving on Oscar Robertson, my main rival, who played for the Cincinnati Royals *(Wen Roberts/ NBAE/Getty Images)*

With Elgin Baylor, from whom I learned so much *(George Long/ Sports Illustrated/Getty Images)*

Going up against my former teammate Dick Barnett, just as I taught myself to do years earlier *(© Bettmann/Corbis)*

Building the Forum, 1967
(Wen Roberts/Photography Ink)

Wilt was probably the loneliest person
I have ever known. *(Tony Triolo/Sports
Illustrated/Getty Images)*

With Wilt and Keith
Erickson at Wilt's house on
Mulholland Drive

Jerry West Night, March 1971—me with Jane, David, Michael, and Mark; my relationship with Jack Kent Cooke (*right,* next to his wife) was far better then.

Fishing at Crowley Lake in the mid-1960s with my Laker teammate Darrall Imhoff (*left*) and Hollis Johnson

With Kareem
Abdul-Jabbar
when he was
still with the
Milwaukee
Bucks, 1972 (*Los
Angeles Times*)

With Gail
Goodrich, my
backcourt mate
on the 1972
championship
team *(Wen
Roberts/
Photography Ink)*

After I retired, golf was practically my sole outlet.

With Stan Albeck, one of my assistant coaches, when I coached the Lakers *(Wen Roberts/ Photography Ink)*

Without Jack McCloskey (*left,* my other assistant) and Stan, I could never have done it. *(Wen Roberts/Photography Ink)*

Even though I was no longer playing, I never lost my love of shooting around.
(Wen Roberts/Photography Ink)

scared at all—at least, that's what I told myself. I had just come back from the Olympics and we had won and I was ready for the next step.

Or so I believed.

The Lakers were still in Minneapolis when I was drafted in April, but the owner, Bob Short, moved them to Los Angeles soon afterward, something I only learned about from the *Stars and Stripes* when I was in Europe, preparing for the Olympics. And that was also how I found out that Fred Schaus was going to be joining me. (Apparently, Short's first choice was Bill Sharman, who was still playing for the Celtics. In order for that to happen, Red Auerbach would have to release Sharman from his contract. He was willing to do that, but only if Short would agree to send me to Boston, which he refused to do. I didn't know any of this at the time. Had that happened, though, I often think how completely different my life might have been.)

Interesting. That was my first reaction to hearing that Fred was going to be my coach. But I quickly became frustrated when he said he wanted to bring me along slowly, that he didn't think I was ready. I was on the bench and it was terribly hard on me. I felt Fred was making excuses and that he really just wanted to give Rod Hundley—who performed many of the same antics with the Lakers that he had at West Virginia—enough opportunity to shine in the pros as he had in college. (And it also bothered me that Rod seemed more interested in having a wild and loose life-style than in being dedicated.) When I finally gained a starting position in the middle of my rookie year (and played in the All-Star Game), I told Rod it was my job now and there was no way he was getting it back.

When I went to visit Fred in Morgantown a year or so before he died, we talked about this and he said that he was worried I might have a hard time withstanding the daily physical toll of being a professional, of playing roughly eighty games a season (not including the playoffs), as opposed to the thirty a year I played in college. Nearly fifty years after the fact, Fred's confession stung me. We had had our ups and downs over the years, but I finally realized that he didn't know me, didn't know what was inside of me. He might have thought he did, but he didn't.

During the 1960s, we lost to the Boston Celtics six times in the Finals. *Six times.* If it had been six different teams we'd lost to, perhaps the pain of those losses would have been diluted. But the same team, over and over? You felt as if you were being taunted, like when you are a kid, and someone says something about your being too skinny, or too fat, or your buck teeth, or your big ears. But when you are a kid, it would usually be one on one. Here, it was ten on ten, and you had to try to take it like a man.

Those losses scarred me, scars that remain embedded in my psyche to this day. You would have to be able to see the tissue under those scars to really know and fully understand what I am talking about. The thing about scar tissue is that it keeps building, and pretty soon it's awfully sizable. I realize that I sound like a permanent victim when I say this, and I realize that I have had many more victories in my life than losses, and that many people will have little sympathy for me, given the life I have led, but I am saying all this because it is true and it haunts me still.

After the sixth and final defeat in 1969, I wanted to quit basketball in the worst way. There is a picture of me walking off the court at the Forum, shoulders slumped and alone, after Game Seven—the game that we lost by two points; the game in which the Celtics' Don Nelson hit a crazy shot near the end, and all those god-awful balloons that Jack Kent Cooke had arrogantly ordered to be put up in the rafters and released *when*, not *if*, we won, stayed right where they were and should never have been in the first place. The game that turned out to be Bill Russell's last and ended with Wilt Chamberlain mysteriously on the bench. It is a picture of defeat that, some think, rivals the one of Giants quarterback Y. A. Tittle on his knees with blood pouring out of a cut on his bald head. I scored forty-two points, had thirteen rebounds, and twelve assists in that game, and I was struggling with a hamstring so extremely strained that Frank Deford expressed the view in *Sports Illustrated* that I was essentially playing on one leg. (If our coach, Bill van Breda Kolff, had only taken me out of Game Five, when I first incurred the injury and we were fifteen points ahead, I might have been even more effective.)

I was rewarded, if you can call it that, with the MVP Award for the Finals, the only time a player from the losing team has ever received it. When I went to New York not long after to accept my booby prize, a brand-new, souped-up Dodge Charger, green, no less (it was probably intended for a Celtic), I felt like putting a stick of dynamite in it and blowing it up, right there in Manhattan. I have never admitted that before, but this seems as good a place as any to show my ingratitude. Criticize me if you want, but that's how I felt. As a team, we had let down the fans and the city of Los Angeles (just as my college team had West Virginia, ten years earlier). Somehow, I was sure, the stars were aligned against us.

The summer that followed, the summer of 1969, was one of the worst summers of my life. I was lost, and I was depressed. Wherever I went, I had a hard time making eye contact with people. I was jogging one day and somebody said something to me about how we had choked. I had a violent streak as a kid, and this so incensed me that I nearly went back and kicked his ass. I had given everything I had and still we came up short, still I felt I hadn't done enough, and the city was without a title. On two occasions I felt we had the better team—particularly in 1969—but it wasn't to be.

Probably the main reason I wanted to walk away from basketball was that I honestly didn't think I could endure any more pain. Every night I went to bed I thought about it. Every night. Every goddamn night. It was the most helpless feeling because I was sure I was going to be labeled a loser forever. After a month, I would start to get some sleep and not think about it, and then something would happen to rekindle it, and I would think about it all the next day. I didn't want to be home; I didn't want to be anywhere. Even playing golf—a game that I love because it is so solitary and because if you fail you can only blame yourself—gave me little pleasure. I never felt worse about myself, and that is when I started to get out of control, began doing whatever I could to ease the pain. I would lose myself in women, a lot of women, and I was married. I was bad—I did things I consider derelict and predatory, things I am not particularly proud of. If Campbell is right, that the hero at some point sees the dark side of his true, hidden self, the side he's always denied for most of his life, then this was that juncture for me.

I had met my first wife, Jane, in college, at the beginning of junior year. We started off exchanging notes in a large humanities class, and it continued from there. Our small Catholic wedding, in April of 1960, took place in a chapel inside Newman Hall, right on campus, and Willie was best man. Earlier that day, my parents had stopped at the home of Jane's parents, in Weston, which was on the way to Morgantown, and where they were meeting each other for the first time. And it was there that they learned what Jane and I had been keeping to ourselves, that we were expecting a child. My mother was extremely upset, as were Jane's parents, especially her father, who had never really approved of me anyway.

So here I was, nine years later, displaying no respect for my marriage and no respect for my three sons, David, Michael, and Mark. And yet I continued doing what I was doing. It was like a game, a contest, and it really became a problem and it became a sickness and it became my way of coping. I didn't seek women out. That was not me and never would be. I would go to bed some nights and say to myself, *Why in the world are you doing this? Why? Why?* And my stock response to myself would always be *Well, because you never really dated, you never knew anything about life. It's like a new adventure for you, a new form of being competitive.* But it was completely the wrong deduction. Completely. The sad thing is that I wanted people to like me. I wanted to be loved for me. That period of time has haunted me ever since.

I don't know for sure if Jane suspected anything; she insists she didn't, but I think people always know, especially women. And, as I think about it now, I realize I must have wanted her to know, must have wanted to be caught, to be found out, to be chastised. What bothered Jane most about me, ironically, was my preference for spending time with other guys, as opposed to doing things with her or with her and other couples in our neighborhood. When we first moved to Los Angeles, we began our lives in a little apartment on Century Boulevard, where every few minutes planes flew overhead and the place would shake a little and you could hardly hear yourself think. Other Laker players and their wives (whom Jane became friendly with) lived there, and we did a lot of cooking out and other social things, but Jane was far more social than me. I could go through long periods and never say a word. Jane wanted to finish school, and so we moved to another apartment, near UCLA, where she enrolled, and then in 1962 we bought our first house, in Mar Vista. We furnished it in a way that reflected the times, you could say, with orange shag carpeting throughout. And our small garage became a zoo—literally—with all sorts of reptiles as pets, including snakes (as would the garage at the home we moved to next, in Brentwood). I tried to instill my own childhood love of nature in my sons, and we would often go up into the hills of Malibu to hunt for whatever we could find, or go fishing at Crowley Lake.

There was a park up the street from the house and I would often go there to shoot baskets with the neighborhood kids. Movies such as Laurel and Hardy's *Two Tars* were shot on location in Mar Vista, and the Little Rascals rode soapbox derbies down Grand View. The actor Lloyd Bridges lived there at one time, as did Fatty Arbuckle, UCLA coach John Wooden, and Lakers' owner Jerry Buss, long before I ever met him.

Jane would come to as many home games as she could, but I would often drop her off afterward because I was so keyed up and then try to wind down at places like Tiffany's and the Fireside, but especially at La Marina Inn, where Mike Harris, the owner, and I would talk long into the night, often till dawn, about everything, everything except basketball.

Jane and I eventually went to marriage counseling. The first time we were told we were on a collision course with a brick wall; the second time that we had hit it. If I had only had the courage to say to her, *Hey, this is not going to work. You don't need this very flawed person in your life; you don't. I don't want to embarrass anyone, but the way things are going, I might embarrass you.* This was all happening around the time the world was changing between men and women; there was the pill and free love and all of that. It was the

Age of Aquarius, and Florence LaRue, one of the singers from the 5th Dimension (the group that recorded "Aquarius/Let the Sunshine In"), later became a neighbor of mine in Pacific Palisades. Small world.

Something else happened during that summer of 1969, something strange. I am almost certain that I was being followed as I drove around, aimless and sullen, in my white Ferrari. It was not unusual for kids to follow me home after a game, but my instincts told me this was something different. Not long after that, the Manson Family (Charles Manson, ironically, spent much of his childhood in West Virginia) murdered Sharon Tate (wife of Roman Polanski) and others, a gruesome story that gripped the country that summer and was later recounted in Vincent Bugliosi's *Helter Skelter*. I read the book, and imagine my reaction as I came upon the following sentence, on page 357: "Observing a white sports car ahead of them, Manson told Linda, 'At the next red light, pull up beside. I'm going to kill the driver.'" I've often wondered if that could have been me.

It was also in and around this miserable period of my life that something equally improbable happened: my silhouetted figure became the logo of the NBA, and it remains so to this day. Though I never talk about this and it has never been officially confirmed by the league, the commissioner at the time, Walter Kennedy, quietly told me one day, "Jerry, that's you," and his son later confirmed this, that his father had initiated the idea with the graphic designer Alan Siegel, and that he wanted it to be based on a likeness of me. (I have the *Sport* magazine photograph by Wen Roberts that Siegel worked from; it shows me dribbling with my left hand; ironically, that was never my strong suit, because I played forward in college and didn't have to handle the ball very much.) And so, years later, I acquired one more nickname: the Logo.

*   *   *

Even when the new season began, that autumn, I still felt as if people were laughing at me, and I don't think any of us wants to be laughed at. Hell, it was a real struggle just to go to training camp, even though I was there with people who were feeling the same emotions. But I would get easily frustrated with them because I felt they had forgotten. It was almost as if I were looking for someone to say something negative so it would make me even madder, and more determined.

But if you are really determined to begin with, as I am, you can't make yourself more determined. You can't. There's no way. You know, everyone says, "Well, we gave a hundred and twenty-five percent." That's bullshit. You can give 100 percent, but you can't give 125 percent. I hear people use the phrase "Well, it was in the moment." What the hell does that mean? You're "in the moment" every time you walk outside, not just on a basketball court. If somebody can explain what that phrase means, I'll kiss their fanny. Because it applies to everything we do every day of our lives. Whether it's pleasurable, whether it's stressful, whether it's fun. It's the way life is. You can't get around that.

But life is also very cold. And in basketball you're not going to have any ties (as there used to be in football). There's a finality to it, and that finality sometimes is a problem for some people, and it certainly was for me. Can you imagine what it's like to feel you have a game won, and then you don't? One shot, one play, one call? In 1962, had Frank Selvy made a fifteen-foot shot at the end of Game Seven, we would have won the series against Boston and it might have changed the whole nature of our rivalry with the Celtics. What people forget is that Frank made two shots before that, and those baskets put us in a position to win. With sports, you never know. What I do know is that it hurts, it *really* hurts, and that's when you know who your friends are. And in 1969 particularly, that's when you also know the ones who are saying behind your back, "Those guys choked."

When Campbell writes about the supreme ordeal the hero faces, the efforts he makes to draw from the parts of himself that terrified and shamed him earlier in his life, my relationship with my father is all about that: even though he terrified me, I am ashamed of the fact that I can neither forgive nor forget the horrible feelings I have toward him. At that point in my life, either I was going to die or he was. If I had actually pulled the trigger of the gun under my bed and killed him, I feel sure it would have been seen as a calculated act, as something that had been building and building for quite some time. I don't think the truth of my circumstances would have protected me, would have led to anyone's viewing it as self-defense. What I am revealing here—that I would have gone through with it—very few people know. Had I done it, my life would have been over. I would never have gone to West Virginia University. I would never have played for my country in the Olympics. I would never have played for the Los Angeles Lakers. It all would have been such a waste. But I can honestly say I would have done it because I was that terrified. I'd go into my room after being beaten—not hit, but *beaten*—and I remember just sitting there, filled with every disgusting thought, hating the mere sight of him. And then as I got older and started to make the West family proud—because of my physical accomplishments, not my mental ones—all of a sudden, this person reappears as the father of the golden child. I didn't want him around, didn't want to interact with him in any way, shape, or form. I was proud of myself for taking a stand, and I know it is the thing that has made me defiant to this day, but I also feel it has affected the kind of father I became. I certainly disciplined my first three sons—Jane wouldn't do it, felt it was my job—but they were rarely spanked, and never beaten. I certainly wish I were more demonstrative with affection toward all five of my sons (and toward people I like), and it makes me sad that I am not. There's a barrier there that I seem unable to remove.

I compensate for all this by being generous. I want to make sure the people who work for me know that they are taken care of, that I appreciate all they do, that I enjoy working with them. Christmas and birthday gifts, flowers, thank-you notes, a phone call, presents from my travels, unexpected money that might help someone with a bill—giving all of these things is easier for me than showing affection is, including and especially to members of my own family.

But if a member of my family does something that displeases me, I am not quiet about it. One of my sons visited West Virginia around the time a big Walmart opened in our area and he made an elitist comment about the people who worked there. About how everyone's IQ put together wouldn't be as high as his. I said, "Who do you think you are? You gotta be kidding me. You don't know anything about this state. You ought to be embarrassed. You ought to apologize to everyone in here. Do you know that this might be the only job some of these people can get? That there are people in here who are probably a hell of a lot smarter than you that never got the opportunity to go to school?"

He apologized, but it took me days to cool down.

If you are reading this and thinking I've completely lost sight of the series of mountains I reached the tops of in my life, trust me, I haven't. The 1956 state championship. The Olympic Gold Medal in 1960. And, finally, the 1972 NBA Championship. But winning that championship was marred for me by the sad, conspicuous absence of Elgin Baylor—by the fact that someone I loved as a player, a teammate, and a friend retired nine games into the season. It seemed so horribly unfair for him not to be playing when we finally won. I mean, Jesus Christ Almighty, the guy that shared all the blood, sweat, and tears wasn't there to realize what it felt like. And yet I have never told Elgin I felt that way, which is another of my many flaws.

The year I made the All-Pro first team, in my second season with the Lakers (I was an All-Star in each of my fourteen seasons, but the All-Pro team, which I made ten times, was composed of just five players), was very significant too, because it told me that I belonged in professional basketball. I was unbelievably proud of myself. Even though I had so much to learn and felt so far behind certain players (Oscar Robertson being the main one), I was able to take another step in my career. As my career went on, there were a couple of years when I felt I was the best player in the league. But, generally, smaller players didn't get as much credit as bigger ones, with the exception of Oscar, the one year he won the MVP Award. In the 1969–70 season—the season following the one when I almost walked away from the game—I felt I should have gotten it for sure: we started two rookies, and Wilt got hurt and then Elgin, but I had an incredible year, leading the league with an average of 31.2 points per game, and I stayed healthy (until the playoffs). I couldn't have played any better—for me to say something like that is almost unheard-of—in every facet of the game. And not winning the MVP Award was probably the single most disappointing thing to me individually. The award went to Willis Reed, and much as I respect Willis, I didn't think he was even the most valuable player on the Knicks that season; Walt Frazier was.

4

Drawing the Curtain

Leaving the floor of the Forum, 1969,
and wondering, "Where do I go?"

When I decided to retire from playing basketball, in the autumn of 1974, I had an initial feeling of pure elation, of being unburdened. President Richard Nixon had just been forced out of office, but I was leaving of my own free will. I played well in an exhibition game against Portland and then told our trainer, Frank "Piggy" O'Neill, that I wouldn't be needing my uniform anymore. Piggy completely misunderstood me—or chose not to hear me—and proceeded to pack it for the next game. So I told him again, more firmly: "Frank, I'm through. I'm retiring." Frank, being the stubborn Irishman that he was, refused to believe me, and once again put number 44 in the bag.

I spoke with Bill Sharman (my coach for the previous three seasons) and Pete Newell (our new general manager) about it the next day, and they were shocked, did everything they could to talk me out of it, urged me to please think it over. They felt I could easily play for another couple of years. "I can't do it anymore," I said. "I just can't make myself play anymore. There's nothing left inside me." When you lose a passion to do something, you shouldn't do it. At least that's how I looked at it. I was thirty-six years old and I simply felt that I could not play up to the exacting standards I had long ago set for myself—a standard of perfection that everyone thought was crazy and unreasonable and that constantly tormented me. I did not want to cheat anybody—the fans, the Lakers, the owner, or myself. The last thing I was going to do was just hang on and collect a paycheck. But out of respect for both Bill and Pete, I agreed to think about it. But two days later, my position hadn't changed.

For as long as I had played, I had looked forward to going out and competing, and that spilled over into everything I did: golf, cards, fishing, hunting, you name it. (Even the writing of this book in a weird way became a form of competition, something I wasn't conscious of until Jonathan pointed it out.)

But I had reached a point where going out on the court was becoming harder and harder to do. Your body begins to fail and what energy you could muster before was becoming increasingly difficult to summon. If you played on a Tuesday night in San Francisco and flew overnight and played in New York the next evening, you might only get a few hours of sleep. We didn't travel on private planes back then. I remember one time getting to the Hotel Manhattan in New York in the early hours of the morning and hearing dogs barking constantly (much the way my three spoiled dogs do now). So I called down to the front desk and asked what the hell was going on. "Mr. West," the guy said, "I am terribly sorry. But the dogs are guests in the hotel just as you are. They have been competing in the Westminster Dog Show at the Garden."

If I hadn't been so exhausted, I would have found it funny. The finals of the competition had been a few hours earlier, I learned, and some lucky dog or dogs were celebrating. We were going to play the Knicks that night. I got off the phone and then did what I did in every city I traveled to: I got out my duct tape and taped the areas between the venetian blinds (there were no plush thick curtains back then). If I couldn't control the noise, I could at least keep out the light.

Much as I might have complained about the amount of travel, about having to be at an airport at five thirty in the morning, about arriving in Chicago by train fully dressed in my uniform and then stepping in a puddle of slush as I got out of a cab and having to play twenty minutes later in socks and sneakers that were soaked, I was going to miss the camaraderie of my teammates. Players were so much closer then. I will never forget my rookie year and rooming with Ray Felix—one of the best and smartest things Fred Schaus ever did was make roommate assignments by race, ensuring that a black player roomed with a white, that we would have no choice but to get to know each other. It was my rookie year and we were in a motel in Bangor, Maine, barnstorming with the Celtics. I was having even more trouble sleeping than usual because no sooner had I got back to West Virginia from Rome than Jane (who had grown weary of living at my parents' house and calling my mother "Mrs. West," which she insisted on) and I headed to Los Angeles. We had two practices in one day, then hit the road for all these exhibition games (in those days, we played those games as if our lives depended on it; today's preseason games are so lacking in anything it is wrong to even charge the fans to come).

Anyway, it was a hot September night—too hot for my taste—and I was perspiring, so I got up to open the window around two in the morning. Well, the next thing I knew, "Baby Ray" (who stood seven feet tall and was seven years older) was towering over me and shouting, "Goddamn it, rookie, I'm going to catch pneumonia. If you ever do that again, you'll be sorry."

Thinking of Ray always brings to mind two other things. We were rooming in St. Louis later that year and I suggested a place we might go for dinner. "Jerry," he said slowly, "I can't eat there, man." At first, naïve as I was, I didn't know what he was talking about. (In fact, I didn't even know that a year before, Elgin Baylor had refused to play in a game in Charleston, West Virginia, because the black players were told that they couldn't stay at the hotel the team was supposed to stay at.) But once Ray informed me about how segregated St. Louis was (a city I had never been to), I said,

"Hell, I'll go out and get some food for us and bring it back." Then, the following year, when we lost to the Celtics in Game Seven of the 1962 Finals, we trudged back to the visitors' locker room at Boston Garden, which had no lockers, just hooks, and that you had to walk down some narrow stairs to get to, like descending into the catacombs of hell. The room was dank and gloomy and unbearably hot, and set at such an angle that the tallest guys, like Ray and Rudy LaRusso, had to dress in the front part of the room. We were all miserable and Frank Selvy felt awful about missing that shot and Fred Schaus didn't know what to say and we were far from home. Suddenly, out of nowhere, Baby Ray pipes up, "That's okay, boys, we'll get 'em on Tuesday!"

It's one thing for a player to not know what the score is in a game, or not know how many timeouts his team has, as Chris Webber of Michigan demonstrated in the 1993 NCAA Final. But to not know that a season is *over?* You gotta be kidding me. At the same time, it reminded me of how much Ray loved to play and how he was able to inject some much-needed levity into that locker room. Knowing me, had he not said that, I'd still be sitting there, staring into space.

Dick Barnett was a player who was always kidding me, who always made me laugh. He was both a teammate and, later, a formidable rival when he played for the Knicks during their championship years. His jump shot was so unique — he had a way of falling back and kicking his legs up — that his nickname became "Fall Back Baby." When the Lakers traded him away in 1965, I was incredibly disturbed that we would part company with a player of his ability. I loved rooming with Dick and will never forget the time he came back to the room with some shirts he had bought from a guy on the street in New York. He was so excited about the great deal he got and couldn't wait to show me. The only problem was that the shirts he'd bought had no sleeves. They were in a cardboard box, and Dick didn't think to pull them out before he bought them. We both cracked up; it was a little private joke we had, and even years later, whenever we saw each other, one of us would begin to recall the incident. After he retired, Dick became a much more serious, and reclusive, individual. He earned a Ph.D. in education from Fordham and would insist people call him Dr. Barnett. To this day, I am not sure I ever told Dick how much I respected him as a player and cared about him as a person.

I look back and remember the 1964 All-Star Game in Boston, the first one ever televised. It had been snowing heavily all day, and it wasn't certain if everybody who was scheduled to play would be able to make it by game time. There was another problem too: The players, led by Tom Heinsohn of the Celtics, head of the NBA Players Association, had decided they would boycott the game unless all the teams' owners came up with an acceptable pension plan. (The players also wanted their own trainers to travel with the teams, and they wanted the league to agree that no team should have to play a Sunday afternoon game if they'd played the night before.) I have never been more nervous or scared in my life. This was my livelihood, and Bob Short, our absentee owner (he'd stayed in Minneapolis when the team moved to Los Angeles), somehow got around a security guard and into the trainer's room and was shouting through the wall that if Elgin and I didn't play, he would personally make sure we never played again. It was my fourth season and I was coming into my own, and I didn't know what to do. (The first vote we took was 11 to 9 in favor of playing. The second vote, though, was 11 to 9 *against* playing.) But Elgin, who was stronger than I in this regard, reassured me that Short needed us far more than we needed him, that it was important that we make a stand, not only for ourselves, but for the players who would come after us. We got assurances from Walter Kennedy, the commissioner, that the owners would come up with an acceptable pension plan by summer, and we knew that a future television contract was at stake, so five minutes before the scheduled tipoff, we decided to play, and the game began fifteen minutes late.

The stand we took that day was the right one, and I will always admire Tom Heinsohn for believing that his position as head of the Players Association was more important than the close relationship he enjoyed with Walter Brown, the owner of the Celtics, who remained angry with him for some time afterward. Our refusal to back down made our organization as powerful as baseball's, and within ten years, even more so. It led to the end of the reserve clause, a fight spearheaded by Oscar Robertson; now, a player no longer had to play for one team his entire career, and the way was paved for free agency.

Oscar Robertson. The Big O. Our names will be as entwined and enmeshed in the history of professional basketball as my name and Elgin's, but it goes even further. We were not only co-captains in the 1960 Olympics but the top two picks of the 1960 draft; Oscar was taken with the first, as a territorial choice of the Cincinnati Royals, and I was taken with the second. The beauty of Oscar was that he was such an advanced player—so much more advanced than I was that it was a joke. He was bigger than I was (he was six five; I was always listed at either six feet two and a half inches or six three, though I am closer to six four and a quarter), and he was stronger than I was and he could do everything. We both played forward in college (though he was needed to handle the ball more) but switched to guard in the pros. He averaged a triple-double in his second season—double digits in points, rebounds, and assists—the only player to ever do that. He had polished his game on the playgrounds of Indianapolis, in a state that was—and is— a hotbed of basketball. We both had chips on our shoulders; his had to do with race, beginning with the various struggles his Crispus Attucks High School team had in being recognized, whereas mine, as I've said, was fueled by anger toward a father who found fault with me at every turn, as well as a personal mission to fulfill: a desire for perfection and a way of replacing my dead brother. When our team played in the Olympics, I was determined we were not going to lose to the Russians. There was no way, no way I would not display my own personal rage toward Communism in a productive way. Of the six games we played, the one I cared about the most was that much-publicized, tension-filled semifinal game against the Soviet Union, and we won by a score of 81–57. I learned recently that there was a rumor that the CIA tried to recruit me as a spy before the Games began. They did not. I am extremely patriotic—which does not change my hatred of war—but espionage is something I only enjoy reading about. Ever curious, I checked and found I don't even have an FBI file.

Tex Winter said recently that there was a small number of players who fit in the category of alpha males, players who had that little something extra in terms of drive when they went out on the floor to compete: Oscar, Michael Jordan, Magic Johnson, Larry Bird, Kobe Bryant, and me. I don't particularly care for the term *alpha male,* but I have always believed in the notion of gold dust, of there being something innate in a person that can't easily be defined, something that propels you onward and keeps you fighting, no matter what, until the bitter end. I don't think that I and the other players Winter mentioned are the only ones who have it, but we do possess it, that's for sure.

If Elgin was the player I studied when I came into the league, Oscar was the player, honestly, that I tried to emulate. He felt that the press always favored me, the implication being too much so; in his book *The Big O,* he said, "America looked at Jerry fondly." But he also wrote that I was the best clutch shooter he had ever seen, and quoted Bob Ryan of the *Boston Globe* as saying Oscar had developed more different skills than any player he had ever seen whereas I perhaps had more desire.

It must be left to others to determine all of this, but I do know that Oscar was never a rookie, not even close. I also think that halfway through our careers I caught up with him and, in the minds of some, perhaps surpassed him. We both won one title apiece, a year apart. His came in 1971, with Kareem Abdul-Jabbar, when they played for the Milwaukee Bucks, and mine a year later. Ironically, it was the Bucks who stopped our thirty-three-game win streak in January of 1972—a record for consecutive wins in professional sports that still stands.

Because of his push for free agency, Oscar was vilified by the league and team owners and has never been able to find the sort of front-office job that I did, and I know he has been bitter about it. Just as Curt Flood found out in baseball, actions have consequences, and there is no way to determine how it affected their future prospects. Each of them did what he thought was right, what he thought was in the best interests of present and future players. I never had a chance to find out my real worth to other teams because of my contractual arrangement with the Lakers. But I always wanted to, and that had nothing to do with not feeling loyal.

I have always found it interesting that Bill Russell has never liked the term *rivals* and prefers *competitors* instead. He said that partly because, for the longest time, he and Wilt Chamberlain were good friends off the court and would often eat together before games, which is not something that many people realize. It is not something I was comfortable doing myself. I simply didn't believe in that kind of fraternizing with players on other teams. If it happened after games (when we occasionally played cards with the Celtics), fine, but not before. I needed to be alone and thinking about my opponents, working up the suitable amount of intense focus necessary for me to go out on the floor and destroy them. Early in my career, Elgin Baylor did take me to a few meals with Bill Russell before a game. It made me uneasy, frankly, but I was also flattered that Elgin would do that. Bill would later say that if Elgin brought me, it was fine with him. And when I look back on it now, I realize how much that acceptance by black players meant to me, especially during those turbulent, segregated times, how I always felt more comfortable around them than I did my white teammates. In the company of those two individuals, two guys who, each in his own way, had a commanding presence, I was like the child who was seen but not heard, soaking up whatever was being discussed (and it was rarely about basketball) but too painfully shy and reserved to contribute very much.

Friendships can run their course for a variety of reasons, some justified and complicated, some not. The disruption of the friendship between Bill Russell and Wilt Chamberlain is something that Bill now accepts full blame for, but it took him thirty years, until Wilt died, to own up to it. Bill resented the fact that Wilt wasn't on the floor at the end of the final game Russell played, Game Seven of the 1969 Finals against us at the Forum. No one knew Bill was going to retire, not even Red Auerbach, the Celtics' general manager. Bill's rivalry with Wilt was unparalleled in the history of basketball, and Bill's resentment had to do with the fact that his greatest competitor was not pushing him till the end. (Wilt wanted to go back into the game—he had gone out with about five minutes to go, complaining of injury—but Bill van Breda Kolff, who had with Wilt perhaps the worst and most bizarre relationship I've ever seen between a coach and a player, would not hear of it. It turned out to be his last game as Lakers' coach too.) In a way, I can understand Bill's position, irrational as it might be, emotional as it was. I can understand it because I too can hold on to things, long after I should probably let them go.

I had been surrounded for fourteen years by guys like Oscar and Elgin, by Wilt and Bill, by Jerry Lucas and Walt Bellamy (also Olympic teammates), by Bob Pettit and Jerry Sloan, by John Havlicek and Walt Frazier, by Bob Cousy and the Jones boys, K. C. and Sam, by Dave DeBusschere and Earl Monroe. Within a short period all of us had left the court, had vanished. The reason I find a particular NBA commercial so poignant—the one that airs during the playoffs and shows players from a certain era on the court, then disappearing into smoke almost, only to be replaced by the next era of players—is that it underscores the reality of what we do. We have a limited, brutally narrow time to do what we do at the highest level, and one of the cruelest ironies about what we do—unlike many other professions—is that the smarter we get about what we do is in direct contrast to the erosion of our ability to do it. In my opinion, I peaked as a player about halfway through my fourteen-year career (so why I think my best season may have been 1969–70 is somewhat hard to explain). When we won the championship in 1972, I was asked to play a different role for that team, becoming more of a playmaker (leading the league in assists with nearly ten a game), happy to do whatever it was the team needed of me. Many people think that Gail Goodrich and I were one of the best backcourts in NBA history—each of us averaged nearly twenty-six points per game—but I knew that I was no longer the player I once was, even though I was the MVP of that year's All-Star Game. Time catches up to you; it catches up to all of us. Bill Sharman and Pete Newell were right: I could probably have played a couple more seasons before I retired, but I had gotten to the point where I no longer wanted to do it.

The elation I initially felt upon retiring quickly faded. I was lost. I no longer had my cherished routines, nor did I have an official connection to the Lakers. The already-mentioned lawsuit between Jack Kent Cooke and myself was filed in the spring of 1975. His position was that my contract was signed with the distinct understanding that I would continue playing; mine was that I would be available to the club to do whatever they wanted me to. When two people divorce, it is never just one thing that causes them to break apart. There was a lot of unhappiness and hard feelings between us and that no doubt fueled much of the misunderstanding and distrust that ensued. He had lied about me and to me before, and he would lie about me again. For the longest time, I had always heard I was his favorite Laker, the fair-haired boy, you might say. But that took a dramatic turn in the fall of 1973. I was still upset by his decision to have those balloons suspended from the ceiling of the Forum before Game Seven of the 1969 Finals against the Celtics, so certain he was that we would win the series. I felt it was disrespectful to the Celtics. It only served to anger guys like Bill Russell and John Havlicek, who got hold of Cooke's memo about the victory celebration he was sure would follow and used it as extra motivation, as if that team ever needed such a thing in the first place. If Cooke was so certain of victory, then why did we go out and play, why does anyone go out and compete? It is the uncertainty of it all that makes it interesting.

But the situation in the fall of 1973 had to do with my understanding from Cooke that Wilt Chamberlain and I were earning the same amount of money—$250,000—only to discover that Wilt, in a side agreement with Cooke, was making much more because much of what he was getting was tax-free. I was hurt and I was angry, mainly because I felt that Cooke had deceived me. So I decided to hold out that autumn, a decision that I am still not sure was correct, but it doesn't matter now.

Loyalty to an organization is one thing. Lying and deceit are something else, though, and they are things which really offend me. If I would have had anything else to do with my life, I wouldn't have gone back and played. Once I returned, I suffered a severe groin tear that limited me to thirty-one games that season. I couldn't sleep for three months. I was near the end of my career, I knew that. It is the hardest thing an athlete has to face, particularly one who tried, as I did, to give his all every time he stepped onto the court. So what did I begin to hear? I heard that Cooke—someone I had bled for—thought I had perhaps overstated the seriousness of the injury because of the tension that my holdout had created. Honestly, this was more than I could bear. No one had ever questioned my heart before. No one. I had broken my nose nine times. I had played in so many games when I should not have been playing, but I would get shot up like a horse and go out there and do what I loved doing my whole life—what I did best—competing. In Game Seven of the 1970 Finals against the Knicks, the game in which Willis Reed famously limped onto the court at Madison Square Garden and gave his team an emotional lift, my hands were badly injured, but I knew I had to play. Dr. Robert Kerlan did what he had to do—injected my left and right thumbs, both before the game and at half-time—and with a lot less fanfare than Willis, I went out there.

(Dr. Kerlan told me I was the "craziest competitor" he had ever come across.) I didn't have one of my better games, to be sure, but I didn't need Wilt complaining that Walt Frazier had kicked my ass. These days, players have a little tweak of this or that and they may sit out for five games. Give me a break.

Not long after I retired, I moved out of the house that Jane and I had shared on Bristol Circle South in Brentwood. The distance that I felt in 1969 had continued to widen, and I had, for a time, been seeing someone who was also married. I got married far too young and had children far too young and I never felt I was a particularly good father to David, Michael, and Mark. I was gone so much and, even when I was there, I did things with them, but in my opinion, I wasn't emotionally present in the way a husband and father should ideally be.

Needing to do something, I began playing more and more golf. Every afternoon at one I would tee off at Bel-Air Country Club with Bob Falkenberg (who had won Wimbledon in 1948), Ken Jones (a young man from Mississippi who was an assistant pro), Bill Bastien, Art Anderson, Craig Crockwell, Steve Sparks, and my friend of many years Joe Miller, a real estate guy who found me my first apartment and who helped me invest in apartment buildings in Los Angeles.

I have always wished I had begun playing golf earlier in my life. At that time in particular, though, it filled an enormous void. Even more than playing against others—always with a friendly wager involved—I love (especially today) going to the practice range and hitting ball after ball by myself, knowing instantly from the sound each one makes if it is heading where I want it to. I love challenging myself with harder and harder shots, doing things over and over again—the key to getting better. I always did this with basketball and now I was focused on golf.

Golf would often be followed by dinner at Falky's home, where I would then attempt to play paleta (a variation of Basque pelota and similar to jai alai) well into the evening and spend time with Bob's family.

I was adrift and had never lived alone before, so I asked Ken Jones to move in with me and, in exchange for free rent, help me do the sort of things that Jane had always done—shop and cook and run errands—or that had been done for me by the Lakers. You get spoiled being a professional athlete, even back at the time when I played.

We went out to eat a lot—even though Ken was only fifteen years younger than I am, he became a kind of surrogate son to me—and I always insisted on paying, no matter how many people joined us. (In fact, it is something I still do, though from time to time people foil my attempts and it irritates me. On a couple of occasions, Michael Jordan has had the bill "taken care of" before we even got to the restaurant, mainly because he likes to mess with me and see me get riled up, I think.) Aside from the fact I eat very quickly, I am also particular about what I eat (as I am about what I wear). One time I went to a little Italian restaurant in Los Angeles and I ordered a caprese salad with heirloom tomatoes. When the salad came out, I could see right away the tomatoes were not heirlooms and told the waiter that. He assured me that they were and I insisted they weren't. So he went back into the kitchen and checked with the chef and came back to report that I was right.

For some reason, I was curious why one of the two women at the table next to mine was having a beer with her pasta instead of a nice glass of wine, and I asked her about it. "Well, Mr. West," she said in a kind of redneck accent, "I don't know any better, I was raised in a trailer park." It turned out she wasn't, that she was actually a financial analyst and was putting me on, and so I bought their dinner. I don't entirely know why it is so important to me to pick up the tab, but I know it has something to do with the fact that I love to be generous. But it also might have to do with my need for control. I certainly don't like to be beholden to others.

Gary Colson was the head basketball coach at Pepperdine University and just before Thanksgiving of 1974, he asked me to come up and give a talk at the team banquet. Shortly after I arrived, I happened to notice one of the school's cheerleaders and asked Gary to introduce me to her. Her name was Karen Bua, and she had long dark hair and was, quite frankly, one of the most naturally beautiful women I had ever seen. I don't say things like that lightly. I have never been good about initiating conversation, particularly with women, and unless a woman came right up to me, and many did while I was playing, I would never say anything.

That evening, after the banquet, I told Gary to ask Karen if she wanted to join me for a drink. She said she would go only if Gary came along, that she figured I was interested in her for just one thing. So we all went, along with some other people, to Tiffany's in Marina del Rey (where Gary lived on a houseboat), but I did manage to speak with Karen alone for much of that time. Karen grew up in Los Angeles and loved sports and she knew I had played for the Lakers. When she recalls our meeting, what she remembers most of all is that I struck her as the saddest man she had ever met. I poured my heart out to her about everything, and, probably because she felt sorry for me, she eventually agreed to go out with me. I was still living with Jane at the time but was desperate to move out. I asked Karen if she could help me find an apartment, but she was noncommittal, thinking to herself, *I'm a senior in college, living in a dorm, what do I know about helping a grown man find an apartment?*

Eventually Karen did help me, and that turned out to be the apartment that Ken Jones and I moved into, a condominium on Almayo, off Beverly Glen, in Century City. For someone as solitary as I am and can be, it was interesting to realize that I did need people around me, especially during that weird, empty time of my life without basketball.

Bel-Air Country Club became a haven for me, a home away from home. I had only been a member for a few years at that point, but it gave me, most of all, a place where I could just be Jerry, not "Jerry West," surrounded by people who had accomplished much in their professional lives, people like Jack Nicholson and Sean Connery, Fred MacMurray and Dean Martin, Robert Wagner, Joe Hamilton, and Dave Moore, the broadcaster Vin Scully, business titans like Barron Hilton (who would become a good friend and someone whom I go on fishing trips to Alaska with, along with Chuck Yeager, the first test pilot to break the sound barrier and a fellow West Virginian). Barron—who, aside from running the family hotel business, was the original owner of the San Diego Chargers of the American Football League—and I are so competitive that if he catches a fifty-five-pound salmon, I will stay out there all day in order to catch a larger one, just like I did as a boy back home. Barron, sadly, stopped coming to Bel-Air not long ago because they banned cigar smoking in the Card Room, where I play gin a number of afternoons a week with my friends Walter Lack, Asher Dann, Brian Wynn, and others. Barron's feelings on the matter were clear and good-natured, as he is, and in no way bitter: if they don't want my cigar, they can do without me. Barron is also someone you can't really do things for. When you go to Alaska with him, you fly up on his private plane and you are always his guest. I always bring along fine steaks and, of course, heirloom tomatoes.

One thing I have never told anybody before is that when I am invited somewhere and surrounded by people who have more money than God, even people who have become friends, I always say to myself, *What are you doing here, Jerry? You don't belong here.* Even after all these years of success and accomplishment, I still have some deeply rooted insecurities as to where I fit in, of feeling and being the odd man out.

When an athlete's career is over, perhaps the hardest thing to get used to is the dimming of the lights, the deathly silence in the arena. More than anything, I played for the fans, not just in Los Angeles, but wherever they might be. The colors of my college team, old gold and blue, were not that different from the Lakers' colors, gold and purple, though Jack Kent Cooke insisted on calling the purple "Forum blue." Wearing the Lakers' uniform (which started out blue and white but was changed by Cooke when he bought the team, in 1965) had meant something to me (though not quite as much as my Olympic uniform), and now I wouldn't be wearing it again, or the Converse (later, Adidas) sneakers that were more like bedroom slippers for all the support they gave you. My career was over. My numbers—my "stats"—and my list of accomplishments would be permanently enshrined in history (they are in the back for those who are interested). I wouldn't be adding to them—a death of a different kind, like turning into a museum piece or a statue (which I would eventually do, *twice*), frozen in place and time. They were impressive, I knew that, but I wasn't impressed by them. I wouldn't be making a comeback, as Earvin Johnson and Michael Jordan did, not once but two times. I was relieved to have won one championship, but had hoped for more, much more. That's the raw, unvarnished truth. That feeling of having been a prince far more than a king continues to gnaw at me. I dislike the color green. I rarely go to Boston. Is this, *any* of this, in any way rational? No, of course it isn't, but then again, neither am I.

My relationship with Karen blossomed at an important time. When I wasn't playing golf or cards, I was reading. I have always been a huge reader, and now I had a lot of time on my hands to do more of it. (At that time I almost always read mystery novels or thrillers, but now I read much more nonfiction, mainly history and about war.) Jane and I were separated, and she was furious when she learned I was seeing someone else. She was under the impression that we were going to continue to work on things, but I knew that wasn't going to happen. Karen was a rock. She might have been in her early twenties and I might have been "a grown man," but I needed her in ways, I see now, that I couldn't fully articulate. And, as I would learn, she needed me, but not for the stereotypical reason some might think: that I was a big star and she was drawn to me mainly because of that. She offered a stability that I wanted and desperately needed; she was someone I instinctively knew I could completely trust; and she had a big, warm, occasionally loud Italian family who embraced me at a time that I needed embracing. (Her mother, Trudy, will often confide things in me that she would be unlikely to discuss with Karen. The peculiarity of family life, I suppose you could say.)

I will never forget our first trip to Hawaii together. It was in January of 1975, not long after we met. I had flown out separately, and Karen was delayed in Los Angeles by fog and didn't make it there until the next day. I don't think of myself as a very romantic guy, but being in a place like Hawaii certainly helps. On one occasion, we were walking on the beach when the skies opened up. Everyone has certain moments in his life he remembers — always — and this was one of mine. The song "Laughter in the Rain" was popular then, and it became the one that has had the most meaning to us ever since. To this day, whenever I phone Karen on her cell, that song is the special ring that lets her know it is me.

My getting to know Karen aside, coming back to Los Angeles was coming back to the harsh reality of my life. I was depressed and I was sad and I was angry. In addition to the lawsuit against Jack Kent Cooke and the Lakers I was getting ready to file, I was in the beginning stages of what would turn out to be a messy and ugly divorce. Seeing the pain it caused my children was very difficult. The night that I told them that their mother and I were permanently splitting up was one of the most painful times of my life. I came back to the place where Ken and I were living and sat down and cried. Boys need a father, and that is why I found a place that was close by. I was not going to abandon my kids. Not long after that, I moved into a little house on Bowling Green, off Bundy — a place that belonged to Pat Riley, who had gone to play for the Phoenix Suns and rented it to me.

And it was to Pat's place one day that Jane drove over in a rage and dumped all of my personal belongings — my clothes, my trophies, my shotguns, *everything* — onto the front lawn. You see this kind of thing in the movies all the time, but I never imagined it would happen to me. The thing that bothered me most, though, was that she brought the boys with her (and later phoned Karen to tell her what she had done). To this day, I resent that she did that, because I felt it was wrong, that they didn't need to witness that. Anyway, I dragged everything inside, but when I moved out, I left nearly all the trophies and mementos there and forgot about them — except my Gold Medal from the Olympics and my uniform. (Even though I was known for wearing number 44, it was the USA and the number 3 below it that I cared about most.) After our family fire in 1962, wherever I went, those items went with me.

I worried constantly about my sons and how sad they were. They had accepted, or so they say now, that I was away a lot when I played, and their pride in me outweighed whatever feelings they had of wanting me to be there more. When I was around, we played basketball in front of the house, went fishing, and continued to bring home all kinds of wildlife. Other kids would come over too, kids who turned out to be professional players themselves, kids such as Kiki Vandeweghe, whose father, Ernie, was my sons' pediatrician (and who played for the Knicks in the early days of the NBA), and Steve Kerr, who was friendly with my son Mark. I would also invite people to stay for open-ended periods. Barry Parkhill, an All-American from the University of Virginia, whom I first met at Camp Wahoo (one of a number of summer camps I have been connected with over the years), was coming to play in the Los Angeles Summer League after his rookie season with the Virginia Squires of the ABA. I told him to stay with us and gave him all sorts of clothes and sneakers to keep and one of my cars — my beloved gold Ferrari, a Daytona Spyder — to drive. I love cars and I am crazy about clothes. Even now, I may wear a suit once or twice, then give it to someone else. It all goes back to how little I had growing up and my desire to share with others.

But this was different. This was a divorce and it dragged out and I blamed myself for it. I hate the term *grew apart* (nearly as much as the word *closure*), but we had. One difference between us was that an important part of me missed West Virginia, and Jane never did. I also had never reconciled myself to the distinct feeling I had that her parents initially thought that Jane was marrying beneath her, and it then irked me that, like my father, they only seemed to embrace me when they saw I actually might become something. I hated that, and hate that about people in general. I can see through that a mile away. All that aside, it's not easy to be married to a professional athlete, and I *know* it is not easy to be married to me. But I certainly didn't think it needed to become as ugly as it became. As I've said, Jane was very social. She liked being Mrs. Jerry West. She even wrote a book, published in 1970, called *A Wife's Guide to Pro Basketball.*

I did not want Jane to be approached about this book, but Jonathan and Karen persuaded me that it would be wrong not to; we'd been married for quite a long time and we had three sons, and there are two sides to every story, especially when it comes to divorce. One of the reasons I didn't want Jonathan to speak with her had to do with something that happened the night before my son Mark was married, back in the mid-nineties. We were all sitting at a table for the rehearsal dinner, and Jane, who had had a few drinks, informed everyone that I had left her "high and dry" financially (which was completely untrue) and that Mark's future father-in-law was much more of a father to Mark than I had ever been.

Jane's comment made me so furious I considered not going to the wedding and was determined never to speak to her again, and I pretty much haven't. When our son Michael remarried in December of 2007, Jane came to the wedding with her new husband, Jim Montgomery, and I spent time speaking with him. I had known Jim for years, though not well, as he was connected with Great Western Bank, which held naming rights to the Forum for a long time.

I know of many people who go through a divorce and eventually find a way to forge a friendship of sorts, especially if they have children, and which they do primarily for the children. In my case, I simply lacked the capacity and desire to do so, and that would be true even if Jane had not made that comment, which I have never forgiven her for or forgotten. I accept the entire blame for our marriage not working out. I know that makes me seem, or sound, like some sort of martyr, that some might say it is easier to say something like that than face the real reasons, or that I am smart enough to know it takes two people to cause the end of a marriage, but I honestly did not know what it took to make our relationship work, and maybe I didn't want to know. I certainly had no model to work from, that's for sure.

When Karen and I got married on May 28, 1978 (my fortieth birthday), at the Beverly Hills Hotel, she planned everything, and it was elegant. That's Karen. She asked me to do something I had never done before, and have never done since: wear a tuxedo.

But the few days leading up to our marriage, including the day itself, were filled with tension. My lawyer wanted Karen to sign a prenuptial agreement—my divorce from Jane had been expensive—and though she eventually signed it, she was not happy, and even felt ambushed. We barely spoke. On the day of the wedding, as our attorneys spent the morning working out the details, I tried to soothe things by saying, "I hope this is the worst thing that ever happens to us."

Later that day, when Karen walked down the aisle, nobody would ever have guessed what had been going on.

It's probably good we waited as long as we did to marry. The length of time it took me to get divorced from Jane aside, it gave Karen a chance to see how intense and moody and difficult I could be. It wasn't until the end of my second season of coaching that we got married, and that second season was horrible for many reasons. She had experienced the bitter lawsuit I had with Cooke and she experienced the wrath, however indirectly, of being "the other woman," so to speak, even though she was not. She also experienced the indignity and hurtfulness of being ignored by people who would come up to me and act as if she weren't even there. I didn't like it; even if I said, "This is Karen," no one paid her much attention. Prior to meeting me, she was used to being one of the first women you would notice when you walked into a room.

Throughout much of my professional career, women would approach me and make their interests known, quite blatantly, and give me their phone numbers. If you think that I am suave in situations like this, think again. I am still in many ways the same awkward, shy person I have always been. During the period I was single, I saw women, don't get me wrong. But getting married and settling down with Karen was what I wanted to do. I'm not cut out to be single. That's not who I am. I wanted a second chance, a chance to do it better and do it right. I wanted to have a domestic life and a routine again, and I wanted to have more children — five more — and I sensed that Karen would be a terrific mother, and she is. In fact, in my low moments, I am convinced that our home and our boys, Ryan and Jonnie, are what she values most, more than she values me. But at other times, I am not sure I really believe that. And yet, on some deep, troubling level, it is hard for me to accept being loved, to feel I am worthy of it.

Of all the things that plague me and keep me up at night, be it the losses to the Celtics or my own lingering insecurities and internal struggles, my own conflicted attitude toward quietly liking recognition for my accomplishments and yet being very uncomfortable about being singled out, I continue to be harder on myself than on anyone else around me, continue to punish myself in the same way that my father punished me.

In all the years I played, I dreamed about playing the perfect game. I am not alone in having this kind of fantasy. In Bill Russell's view of what a perfect game would look like, he would be able "to use all the different skills I had and the other team didn't really exist. The game would be played in a box. The place would grow silent. When a shot was taken, I could see all the grains on the ball, see the rotation. I could hear footsteps. The loudest noise was the ball bouncing. But in reality, it all came down to mathematics and equations: I would always come up missing some element of my game that was important. So I would have to go and do something else that would help the team and emphasize that for the night. Even with the really great players—and Jerry is one of the very few in that category, from 1949 to the present—if you play a hundred games, twenty of them you will come up empty-handed in some way. You got to struggle through without anyone knowing you are struggling. That's one thing I noticed about Jerry. In the Finals, I never caught him having a bad game."

I wish I could be as eloquent as Bill and I wish that he were more accurate. I had a lot of bad games in the Finals. But in 1965, I averaged over forty-six points a game in the Western Division finals against the Baltimore Bullets, a record for a playoff series that still stands. Elgin seriously injured his knee and it was incumbent on me to carry the load. I had broken my nose during the season—this was nothing new—but still managed to play in seventy-four regular-season games. I didn't read much, if anything, that was written about me, but someone showed me an article in the *Los Angeles Times*. In it, the writer, Dan Hafner, said,

"They used to say that pound-for-pound and inch-for-inch he was the best in the game. Right now the experts are beginning to believe he is the best period." I laughed out loud when I read that. We hadn't won a championship yet, and that was what mattered. I was playing a team sport and I never forgot that. That whole series, the Bullets had someone hanging on me and I had to take many more shots than I normally would have or would have wanted to. But I had no choice. Elgin was out. That was our biggest problem, and it had been since I had joined the Lakers five years earlier: the team was far too dependent on us to score, and we didn't have a center who could deal with Russell and help us defeat the Celtics.

This would be the third time in four years we faced the Celtics in the Finals, and I knew that Fred Schaus was obsessed with beating Red Auerbach. Red knew how to get under Fred's skin — Red knew how to get under *every* coach's skin, as well as many players' — and I always thought we were at a disadvantage because of it. Fred was convinced that Red always got the upper hand with the officials. That he had a way of baiting and intimidating them but without taking it so far that he got his ass thrown out.

Red was one of the pioneers of the league and so was Fred. Fred had a burning desire to win, but we came up short. It always irked Fred that a point here or two points there and it would have been the Lakers holding the trophy, not the Celtics (though not that year; we lost, 4 to 1). Don't get me wrong; losing made all of us just as livid. But the fact that Red was able to get Fred unhinged was not good. Red knew how to work the sportswriters too. The All-Star Game in 1963 was played in Los Angeles, but you would have thought it was played in Boston for all the media attention Red commanded. Red understood how psychology could play such a crucial part. How creating just the slightest bit of doubt in the other team could result in something positive for the Celtics.

I secretly liked and admired Red's brazen ways, and he is one of the coaches I would have loved to compete for. The league was extremely rough when I played, and most of the fans, other than the fans out West, especially liked it that way. In fact, Red always said Lakers fans were too polite, that they weren't real fans at all. In cities like Boston, Chicago, St. Louis, and Philadelphia, but particularly Boston, fans were used to hockey, and they were full-throated, and, according to John Taylor's *The Rivalry*, they threw stuff—oranges, batteries, tomatoes, paper, potatoes, you name it. (For whatever reason, I only remember the paper.) They loved to see fighting, they wanted to see fighting. Punches were thrown all the time. Hand-checking was fierce. Guys like Clyde Lovellette and Jim Loscutoff were figures to be feared. In one altercation, Lovellette elbowed Wilt Chamberlain in the mouth and messed up Wilt's teeth so bad that he never fully recovered. It took a long time to get Wilt riled up to even retaliate against anybody, but he did exact his measure of revenge on Lovellette. Wilt was very self-conscious about his size and his strength (he was probably the only player in the entire league who lifted weights, but he did it because his first love had been track and field), and he was reluctant to be viewed as a villain. He wanted to be loved more than anything else, and yet he was convinced that "nobody loves Goliath."

Red, however, couldn't have cared less. Red was the figure everyone loved to hate, and he didn't mind it one bit. He didn't mind being the villain. He would be anything you wanted him to be as long as it helped the Celtics win. On most teams, players' salaries depended in large part on their individual statistics. But not on the Celtics. If you tried to get more money out of Red by boasting about your numbers, he would throw your ass out. He had his own way of determining how much you were worth to the team, how much you had contributed. (One of my biggest beefs with Fred had to do with a promise I felt he had made after the 1965 season—to go to bat for me with management for more money. But he never did. Given that Fred had recruited me to play for him in college, I expected more from him, and so my disappointment in him was greater—and much more so for the reasons he said he had for bringing me along slowly during my rookie year.)

Of all the places I played, Madison Square Garden was my favorite, and Boston Garden my least. I had secretly hoped the Knicks would draft me (and Ned Irish did try to swing a deal with Bob Short) because I had loved playing there in college. But I also secretly worried that I would somehow get lost in the city, a small-town boy far from home. (In fact, the only times I left my room when we played the Knicks were to go to Broadway shows—*Man of La Mancha* is my all-time favorite—and, once or twice, to Small's Paradise, the famous Harlem nightclub that Wilt briefly owned and where Ray Charles often performed.)

Still, the life that I led playing for the Lakers and for the city of Los Angeles, starting at the Sports Arena and ending at the Forum, was more in so many ways, far more, than I could have ever imagined when I flew west fourteen years earlier.

But I still wish, and will always wish, my playing career would have caused me less anguish and brought me a greater level of satisfaction.

5

What a Time It Was

Kareem Abdul-Jabbar, James Worthy,
Magic Johnson, 1980s

In early September of 2008, I flew to Springfield, Massachusetts, for the induction of Pat Riley into the Hall of Fame as a coach. Earvin Johnson and I were going to be his presenters, which meant we would walk Pat to the podium and stand there as Pat gave his remarks. (When I was inducted, in 1980, they didn't have such a thing as a "presenter.") I have always had ambivalent feelings about the Hall, have always felt the selection process was far too political and, to tell you the truth, not selective enough.

It is nearly impossible to go anywhere without people coming up to you for autographs. I don't mind signing autographs, never have. What I mind is when the same people—adults much more so than kids—come up to you again and again. (Fran Judkins, who works for the Hall, said that she thinks of me as someone who "sees the big picture without wanting to be part of the big picture." She is probably right about that. She also worries that I don't enjoy myself enough when I come, and she is determined to change that, even though I tell her not to worry about it.) Bill Russell took constant criticism for never signing autographs during all his years with the Celtics and I always respected his right to say no, even if I didn't entirely agree with it. But then again, Bill's relationship with the fans in Boston was always fraught. They loved how he played, but they didn't particularly like how outspoken he was about race relations in Boston and around the country. The Celtics were the first team to start five black players, and yet the Garden was filled with people from South Boston, people whose last names were O'Shaughnessy and Rourke and McGrady, Irish Catholic to the core. When Bob Cousy retired, the city went into mourning. Nonetheless, Boston was a town that idolized the Bruins, so the Celtics, despite all their championships, always played second fiddle.

I, on the other hand, always seemed to be a fan favorite. Part of the reason, I guess, was the way I played—giving my all each and every night—and part of it was no doubt because I was white. I have heard that I was the most popular visiting player ever to compete in both Madison Square Garden and Boston Garden (Johnny Most, the Celtics' announcer, called me "Gentleman Jerry," though perhaps he was subtly mocking me), but that didn't stop people from heckling us. Kids would meet our plane in New York and yell that Walt Frazier was going to shut me down and that Willis Reed was going to make sure that Wilt would suffer all game long and regret not staying home. New York fans have always been passionate that way and I love it. They have a deep understanding of the game and appreciate those who play it. In recognition of my college career, I was made a member of Madison Square Garden's Hall of Fame, but I never did what my son Jonnie, who played for my alma mater, did during the Big East tournament in 2010: on the very first shot he ever took at the Garden, against Cincinnati, he hit a three-pointer at the buzzer to end the first half, and he ran off the court quietly and humbly, his father's son, with no visible display to the world of how excited and proud he surely was. What Jonnie did was more thrilling to Karen than anything I ever did during all my years with the Lakers, and, frankly, it should be. She will talk about that for the rest of her life. Jonnie is her son, and she worships the ground he and Ryan walk on, and you don't ever want to get between Karen and her boys. I know, because I have tried at times, and it doesn't work. Trust me. She is Sicilian and feisty and she has stood her ground with me all these years.

*　　*　　*

My relationship with Pat goes back many years and has been tense and complicated at times, but I couldn't have been more pleased for him that he was being inducted. And in typical Pat fashion, he was going all out, no expenses spared.

There is footage of the two of us running off the court after we beat the Knicks for the 1972 title, and he has me in a headlock and looks a lot more excited than I do. His hard-knocks upbringing in upstate New York and difficult relationship with his father were similar to mine in West Virginia. Pat was, and is, a fierce competitor and very tough (he was drafted to play football by the Dallas Cowboys), and he's never in anything but top physical shape. But he was always going to be a part-time player, never a consistent starter, in the NBA; in his best season with the Lakers, he averaged eleven points a game. His main job on the Lakers, as outlined by Fred Schaus, was to beat the hell out of me in practice (but not "kill me," as he often tried to do) and play the role of whoever was going to be guarding me in the next game. When he got into games, he played his heart out—he didn't get in as often, or play as long, as he would have liked, but this only drove him all the more. When he returned to Los Angeles after one year with the Phoenix Suns, I had just been named coach of the Lakers. He wanted a chance to make the team, but we didn't give him one. Even though it wasn't my decision alone, I recently learned that he blamed me for it. We may have been best friends, and I may have rented his house from him, but the NBA is a business and it was a business decision—something he came to appreciate fully once he became a head coach and, later, a general manager.

Pat joined the legendary Chick Hearn in the broadcasting booth and then became assistant coach to Paul Westhead. Westhead had taken over for Jack McKinney after Jack had an awful bicycle accident, and he was one of the oddest individuals I had ever met. Even though the Lakers won the championship in 1980, Earvin Johnson's rookie year, I thought Paul was not the right coach for the Lakers. He was unbelievably bright, a Shakespearean scholar, and yet he struggled to find the right way to communicate and get along with his players, Earvin in particular, who exploded in the locker room after a game in Utah and expressed his displeasure with Paul, demanding to be traded. The Showtime era had already begun, yet Paul suddenly wanted to install a different offense, to slow down a team that was talented enough to adapt to anything but was really born to run.

Everything else aside, though, I learned an expression from Paul (which originally comes from Thomas Merton, who wrote about social justice and pacifism) that I have always loved, always felt applied to me in terms of how I tried to conduct myself both on and off the court: *The almond tree bears its fruit in silence.* That no matter what people may say about you, no matter how untruthful or hurtful or unfair it might be, it is crucial to retain a sense of dignity, a sense of who you are. But as an executive—given my background, the great deal of anger I have inside me, and my fragile ego—that had not always been easy to do, and I had not always been able to maintain it as more and more people are able, through the Internet mainly, to say whatever the hell they feel like it about you—even in West Virginia. When I mentioned earlier that parts of Beechurst Avenue in Morgantown were renamed Jerry West Boulevard in 2000, what I didn't say was that someone wrote a letter to the editor questioning why, saying I had given nothing back to West Virginia University. I was enraged by this and felt compelled to say something. To say that I had quietly been giving money and funding scholarships there but didn't want to make a big deal out of it. I have, as I hope I made clear earlier, always felt that the essence of giving is to do it without ever wanting or needing recognition for it. The letters I have received from those students who have been able to attend college there because of this mean more to me than virtually anything else I can think of.

Before Paul was let go by Lakers' owner Jerry Buss—the term I much prefer to *fired*—Jerry had me and Bill Sharman come to Pickfair (the home he lived in, which used to belong to Mary Pickford and Douglas Fairbanks). He said that he wanted me to take over as coach. I had been consulting for the Lakers at that time and working closely with Bill, who became general manager when I began coaching in 1976. I told Jerry, "No way," no way that I wanted to resume doing something that had made me so miserable and that I didn't think I was very good at anyway. I told him that he should make Pat the coach, and Jerry simply couldn't see it. Couldn't see making a broadcaster the coach, even though Pat was already an assistant. Jerry agreed to a compromise (he apparently felt certain I was on board, even though I hadn't actually said I was): Pat would be the coach and I would be the offensive coach, and he scheduled a press conference at the Forum later that day, shortly before Thanksgiving of 1981.

No sooner did Jerry Buss make the announcement that Pat and I would essentially be co-coaches than I got up there and said that wouldn't be the case. Pat was going to be the head coach and he would be a terrific one and I would assist him on the bench for a while, perhaps a month, and then I would be gone. "I'm going to be working with and for Pat Riley," I said. "He is the head coach. I hope my position will be short-lived." To this day, I am still surprised I did this. But then again, I often do things that surprise me, not to mention others.

My time on the bench was brief, and I know it was a relief to Pat when he felt he was his own man. By the spring of the following year, the Lakers had won their second championship of the 1980s, and I replaced Bill Sharman as the general manager. Bill's vocal cords, strained many years before as a coach, made it impossible for him to go on. I love Bill (who was elevated to team president), and I learned a lot by working with him, but I hated getting the job this way, a job I had no reason to think I could even do. We only overlapped one year in our playing careers, and let me tell you, when I was a raw rookie, he was no picnic to play against. I always like to kid Bill that he threw a punch at me, and he gets all red-faced and says it isn't so but he always adds that he never backed down—from anyone. He was in the first wave of pioneers to play the game (which he chose over baseball; he was a member of the Brooklyn Dodgers); not only were he and Bob Cousy a formidable backcourt combination, but Bill was one of the greatest free-throw shooters in the history of the league. He also is only one of three people to go into the Hall as both a player and a coach, and one of only two coaches to win championships in both the NBA and the ABA. Of all the coaches I played for, Bill, who coached the 1972 championship team, was my favorite.

Putting together a team is really no different than working the puzzles I so loved in my youth. I liked the idea of having more control over each component than I'd had as a player. During that Hall of Fame weekend in Springfield, many of the players who had been on the Showtime teams under Pat came together for a private roundtable to look back on those years, those games that Jack Nicholson insists were the best entertainment to be had anywhere in the world.

It turned out to be a very emotional, embarrassing hour for me. Sitting around and talking with other players about basketball and about all the things that make up a team, a band of brothers, can make me well up in about two minutes. That Friday in Springfield was just such a day.

Bob McAdoo, who now works under Pat for the Miami Heat, was there, and it brought back a sharp memory for me of how nearly everyone thought bringing him in midway through the 1981–82 season would be a disaster, partly because he had gotten a reputation for being difficult and there was a concern that he was washed up. He had a bone-spur injury and we needed to find out if he could still play, find out if he was still, more or less, the same guy who had led the league in scoring three years in a row and been the MVP for one of them. Dave Wohl, one of our scouts and a close friend of Bob's when they were teammates on the Buffalo Braves, flew to New Jersey to watch him work out. I didn't necessarily see him as a starter, but Bob certainly did, and that created problems for him at first when he signed with us for a minimum-wage contract. We were bringing Bob in because Mitch Kupchak had suffered a serious knee injury. I talked to Bob at some length about what we needed from him — his scoring as a way to open up the floor and take pressure off Kareem, and his defense (which was not something that had ever been asked of him before). I told him he would need to adjust to not being the number one, or even the number two, option. But if he could do what I had outlined, he had a chance to win a championship. (Bob would later say how difficult it was for him to make the transition to coming off the bench, but he couldn't have been more surprised by how readily he was accepted by his new teammates. With the exception of Kareem, that is, with whom he never had any real relationship to speak of.) I had first seen Bob play when he was a senior in high school, at a summer camp in North Carolina, and I told him at the time, "Son, you've got the ugliest shot I've ever seen. But don't change it, because it goes in."

Bob did everything Pat asked of him—including play tough defense—and there was no way we won the 1982 championship against the Philadelphia 76ers without his contribution. In that series, he averaged more than sixteen points and was the runner-up to Magic for MVP. And we didn't win the one in 1985 either; we defeated the Celtics, and for "Doo" it was almost a personal vendetta. He was shocked when the Knicks sent him there—Boston's reputation, in Bob's view, was that of "a graveyard where black players went to die"—and he almost didn't report. And once he got there, he wasn't there long, because he was brought in essentially without Red Auerbach's approval. John Y. Brown was one of the Celtics' owners and had been connected with the Buffalo Braves when Bob played there. Anyway, it didn't work out in Boston and Bob felt he'd been both mistreated and misused during his time there and so he had some extra juice flowing. But for three and a half very productive years, it worked out for both of us. At the roundtable, he looked right at me and said how grateful he was for the opportunity to be part of something that had eluded him for ten years—a championship team. Doo was a terrific puzzle piece and fit like a glove. I am glad he listened to me when I told him not to change his crazy, unorthodox shot all those years before. He was one of the greatest pure shooters ever, and someone who, as a fellow North Carolina Tarheel, was close to Mitch and a good mentor to James Worthy, who idolized him growing up.

Because of a deal the Lakers had made two years earlier—sending Don Ford to the Cleveland Cavaliers for their first pick in 1982—and the luck of the coin flip, we wound up with the top pick because the Cavaliers finished last in 1982 and there was no lottery then. We had just won the championship and now we could add to our team whoever we decided was the best available player. This was unheard of. We were the first team in the NBA ever to be in that position. Of the three players we felt were the best in the draft — Terry Cummings of DePaul, Dominique Wilkins of Georgia, and James Worthy — we chose Worthy because we felt he would be a perfect fit for the kind of fast-break offense we ran, a player who could eventually replace Jamaal Wilkes and hit the ground running. Fast. That he came out of Dean Smith's system at UNC was a big plus in my opinion. It meant he would be a team player. Like McAdoo, he would be trying to find his place among a group of guys who were already exceptional.

On that Friday in Springfield I looked over at James — who would, in time, acquire the nicknames "Clever" and "Big Game James" — and remembered picking him up myself when he flew to Los Angeles in 1982 for a predraft physical (he had broken his ankle during his freshman year and we wanted to make sure he was okay), something he talks about to this day. Mary Lou Liebich, my assistant (though in truth, I really worked for her, not the other way around), told James I would be meeting him at the gate, but he kept asking her over and over whom he should look for. And over and over, she said, "Jerry West is coming to get you himself." What James came to realize is how much I like doing stuff like that. Hell, I have picked up more people at the airport than most cabdrivers. Maybe it's the Southerner in me, but I am too restless to stay in the office for very long in any case. In fact, any time I felt overwhelmed in the office and pulled in fifty different directions, felt the need to get away from the constant barrage of phone calls that came with the job, I went off on scouting trips, doing the thing I loved most: discovering and sizing up talent. Another thing I loved doing was getting my hands on the schedule for the coming year as soon as it came out, and, right before the season started, after training camp and the meaningless preseason games, I would take a pencil and circle the games I thought we would win and the ones I thought we would lose, and I would put the piece of paper in an envelope and date it. I was never entirely correct, but I would come close, within two or three games, a checks-and-balances system on myself. Ultimately, the responsibility—of building a team and acquiring players and having someone who can coach those players—fell on my shoulders. It was an enormous burden, a burden I happily carried, but one that also took quite a toll.

James Worthy had a terrific rookie year—he shot nearly 58 percent from the field—but broke his leg just before the regular season ended and missed the 1983 playoffs, a real blow to us, as we were swept by Philadelphia in the Finals. I have never seen a player maneuver and find his way out of tight spaces better than James. He was explosive, an impossible matchup, and he could burst to the basket with either hand. He was long at six feet nine inches and had a great low-post game, and his jump shot was so quick it was a joke. Anywhere from twelve to eighteen feet out was nearly automatic. James was a winner and he didn't interfere with anyone's game. Because Earvin and Kareem were the focal point of those teams, you didn't have to throw him the ball; he didn't want or need the ball, he just played. But as Kareem's role diminished, James's became more prominent. In the beginning, though, I didn't think he played hard enough, felt he was coasting. I knew he was homesick—he was a country boy, a long way from home, and I could empathize with him as he struggled to find his way in Los Angeles (though he didn't help matters when he gave an interview to *Sports Illustrated* in which he suggested people in Los Angeles were plastic). At the same time I felt he was a bit soft and might have been taking his guaranteed contract for granted. He made a terrible pass in the 1984 Finals against Boston that had led to a Celtics victory.

One of the toughest things about being a general manager is that you are judge, jury, and executioner all in one. Some of the most agonizing days of my life were going through training camp and saying to myself, *How in the hell are we going to tell this kid, through his agent, what his deficiencies are, what he has to keep working on, and that he is so close, but not close enough.* But that is exactly what I had to do. That was my job. At one time the roster was ten players, then twelve, and now fifteen. It creates an environment that usually doesn't allow those two or three players at the bottom to do anything other than go to practice and compete in practice. Now, if they were legitimate NBA players, it'd be completely different. You have those extra players because everyone else does. But it's costly, and now the league is losing millions and millions of dollars a year and ticket prices are far beyond the reach of the majority of people.

Every once in a while one of those kids turns out. Through an injury to a teammate, usually, he gets a chance to perform and he performs well and he achieves his ambition. One of the saddest things, I mean really sad, is to see these guys in the summer leagues, at thirty or even thirty-five, chasing a rainbow and competing their fannies off. I would go to these games and a player would tell me, "I want you to watch me tonight, I know I can make it," and I had seen the same player two years earlier and he is still the same player except he is two years older. And that is why having the chance to play in Europe and do what they love to do and get paid for it is so great. The story of J. R. Holden, who moved to Russia and even became a citizen there, is the first one who comes to mind, but there are many more.

Now, a player like James Worthy was not in that category (though there have been many top picks who turn out to be either just average or constantly plagued by injuries or disappointments — Kwame

Brown, Sam Bowie, Michael Olowokandi, and Greg Oden are a few examples). But when I called James in to talk with him about some of my concerns, it was the right thing to do. Even though I didn't want to get rid of James, sometimes you have to do whatever it takes to get a player's attention. Two years after that (with the 1985 championship in hand), on the night of the 1986 draft, Jerry Buss and Donald Carter, owner of the Dallas Mavericks, were talking about a deal that would move Worthy to Dallas for Roy Tarpley and Mark Aguirre, a close friend of Earvin Johnson's. Earvin, Aguirre, and Isiah Thomas, who played for the Pistons, not only were tight but they all had the same agent, and Earvin wanted his friend to have a chance to win a championship. Earvin, as the vocal leader of the team, came to me with suggestions all the time and I listened, but he never came to me on this one. My real disappointment, though, was with Jerry, for not talking to me about this and for dealing with Carter directly.

Owners of course can do anything they want, but our communication had always been first-rate. What was great about working for Jerry was his loyalty. He kept the same people for years, and there is something to be said for that. It takes a while to get the right people working in an organization—people who know their job descriptions and try not to overstep. Some people are so ambitious that they go beyond that job description, and pretty soon you see something in the newspaper about a trade or a conflict internally; if it turns out to be true, you certainly don't want to see it in the damn paper.

With Jerry (as opposed to Jack Kent Cooke), I could sit around the office until seven or eight at night, which I frequently did, talking about the team and, more often, just talking about life, talking about boxing, laughing and having fun. We had both come from impoverished backgrounds—his was in Wyoming—and we had both succeeded in very different ways; he (along with his business partner, Frank Mariani) had made a fortune in real estate. He had had a very difficult relationship with his stepfather, and I was able to open up to him about mine with my father. We were close to each other in age (he was five years older) and I could relate to him in the sort of normal, easygoing way that I could never do with Cooke, who always acted kind of above you and treated you as if you were subservient. He was the Lord of the Manor (and dressed the part in his tweedy, three-piece suits) and the rest of us were basically peons. You felt like you should bow before him or something. (It's one of the reasons I have always been curious about the royal family in England: What the hell have they ever done to make people feel like servants?) I didn't feel that way about Cooke at first, but it soon became apparent that he viewed me as a hired hand. He thought nothing of using the PA system to say, "Would Jerry West please report to my office," as if I were a schoolboy who had misbehaved in class. I will never forget the story John Wooden told me of how Cooke threw him out of his house when John said he had no interest in coaching the Lakers. When Fred Schaus was general manager, he asked John to come and see Mr. Cooke, and John had said there was no point, that he was very happy at UCLA. But Fred persisted, asking John if he would come as a personal favor to him, and so John reluctantly agreed. They were ushered into Mr. Cooke's study and he made his pitch, and John politely said it was a waste of everyone's time. Undeterred, Mr. Cooke proceeded to write a figure down on a piece of paper and then push it in John's direction. John took a long look at it before saying, "No coach is worth that kind of money." Cooke reddened for a second—he was not used to being rebuffed by anyone—and then brusquely said, "Fine, now get the hell out."

*   *   *

Knowing that Jerry and I had the sort of relationship where we could talk about anything, that whenever I felt unsure about something he would often give me reassurance, that I never felt I had to edit myself, I phoned him and, straight out, asked what the hell was going on? He told me that the trade of Worthy was essentially a done deal, and I told him that the deal could be *undone* and I would call Carter and tell him so, with his permission. I was very upset and was prepared to walk away if the deal went through. Just because we were not as successful as we had hoped to be during the 1985–86 season, I told Jerry, that was no reason to make such an emotional decision, that the trade he had in mind was not at all the direction we needed to go. Jerry backed off. (In fact, he later said in a newspaper interview, "Jerry and I have kind of developed a lot of rules. I can speak my mind and tell him exactly who to play, how to draft, what coach we should have, what style basketball we should have. And after I finish my speech on all of these things, he then tells me how we're really going to do it. So I'm placated because I get to rant and rave, and he's very happy because we do it the professional way—which is his way.")

I spoke to Carter and told him he knew perfectly well that a lack of communication within an organization could create internal problems and that he really shouldn't have been doing what he was doing—dealing with another owner instead of letting Rick Sund, his general manager, deal with me. (If the trade had been made, though, and the general feeling was that it was a bad one, I knew that it was my job to deflect public criticism away from Jerry Buss as much as possible; I was the one who would have to absorb that blow from either the public or the media. I had always had a good relationship with the press, but it would burn me up if they wrote or said something inaccurate just to sell papers or increase ratings. If they wanted to blame me for a player not living up to expectations, fine, I accepted that; I'd say that it simply hadn't worked out as we'd hoped, and I'd leave it at that. The real issue, though, was whether that player really had the ability or the courage to do what we needed him to do. How a team as a whole does over the course of a season depends to some degree on luck and staying free of injury. But if an individual player is healthy, his performance has less to do with luck than with ability. Wanting the responsibility of making these decisions—what I call pulling the rip cord—was similar, I see now, to my wanting the ball at the end of the game, wanting the pressure and expectations that come with trying to make the last shot. If you pull the rip cord and it works out, you're really smart. If it doesn't, you're a dumb-ass. And that's where the second-guessing and the backstabbing come in. It's all part of the culture of basketball, which is filled with more criticism, more innuendo, and more fabricated stories than anything imaginable. No one's going to get a free pass. If you're a confident person and can do these things, then it doesn't seem like pressure and you feel empowered. The only difference is that I was calmer on the court as a player than I was off it as an executive, where, every day, you deal with the stress of making a decision that can affect an entire organization, determine the fate of a franchise.)

By not making that deal with Dallas and keeping James Worthy (even Earvin eventually agreed that trading James would have been a huge mistake) and by acquiring Mychal Thompson the following winter (a player who we felt could counter Kevin McHale of the Celtics), we won the championship the next two years—something that would never have happened without them, especially James, the MVP of the 1988 Finals.

*   *   *

Two months after that weekend in Springfield when Pat Riley was inducted into the Hall of Fame, James was sitting with Jonathan in the Hotel Angeleno, right off the San Diego Freeway. (I was not present because I in no way wanted to inhibit anyone from saying whatever the hell they wanted about my crazy ass—nor was I going to attempt to "edit" *anything* that came out of these discussions either, unless I knew it to be factually inaccurate.)

Alien was the first word James said he would use to describe me, because I was nothing like anyone he'd ever encountered. What James was talking about was this: "If you were to take Jerry away from his whole sports career, he would still be a very unique individual in the way he thinks, the way his many facial expressions—a slight smile, a grimace, a frown, a certain stare—communicate with you, the way he can be distant at times and close at other times, the way he internalizes his thoughts so much it looks like pain.

"He is passionate. I have never seen anybody so passionate and who cares so much and loves so much and loves so many people, but for some reason he did not always show that. Not right away. You had to be around him for some time for it to come out. It takes a while to get inside that shell: he can be all business, or he can be your father, or he can be your brother, or he can be the disciplinarian. He was always honest…to the point where he didn't want to be honest because he is so brutally honest, if that makes any sense. So you could see him holding his tongue and internalizing and creating not so much negative distance, but a sense of 'I am going to cool off so I can communicate and get my point across.'

"I will never forget coming to LAX and there is Jerry in his Nine-forty-four Porsche two-door and he is dressed cool and he looks like Mannix from the TV show, or like some sort of rock star. You could tell he had the power, that sense of confidence. He took me around Loyola Marymount, around the practice facilities, took me for my physical, took me to see Pat Riley and took me to a party at Dr. Buss's estate.

"I was shocked to be drafted number one. To be drafted over Dominique Wilkins, a top scorer, and Terry Cummings, who was a better rebounder and defender than I was. But Jerry just had this special talent for knowing who and what would fit in.

"When Jerry called you to his office it was for something vital. He didn't call you up for foo-foo conversation and tell you how good you were. He would call you up to tell you were stinking up the place — either on the court or how you were dealing with your life. I wasn't used to playing eighty-two games, the whole routine, and Jerry was in tune to that kind of stuff. Some days I would come in and I would be tired. And he called me up and I will never forget this, because this was the beginning of my turnaround as far as my work ethic — coming to work and realizing what job I had chosen. Jerry calls me in and he reminds me that even though I have a five-year contract, the Lakers could trade me *at any time*. He told me that I needed to play as if I were committed, and not like someone who was just comfortable, who gets a big contract and thinks, 'I got five years and I am cool with that.'

"I was conscious of it and Jerry was calling me out on it. I wasn't going through the motions, but I was frustrated because I had come from a program where I had flourished and he saw that I was having difficulties playing Julius Erving one night and Larry Bird the next. Pat was pushing me because he wanted me to be part of the program. My conditioning was a little off, I wasn't doing everything I needed to do mentally, and Jerry waited for just the right moment to give me the straight truth. He really knew how to monitor people constructively. Had he chosen to be a psychiatrist, he would have been a damn good one, because that is pretty much what he is.

"Some people would play here for years and never understand Jerry. It took me a couple of years to understand him, to understand how much he loves and cares about the players—whether it was the twelfth player or the superstars. When I learned that he never would go back to Boston Garden, just wouldn't go near the place, man, to be able to win the first one against the Celtics in 1985 and realize we were not only representing ourselves but guys like Jerry West, that was a big moment for us to be able to give that to him.

"Jerry could see certain things, in the same way he could see the court from all angles when he played. He could see something in A. C. Green. He could see that Kurt Rambis was the key to our fast break, not Magic. Kurt got the ball out of bounds in like a half second (on a made basket by the other team), his whole technique of *one foot out and boom*. It was amazing how Jerry could see the exact parts the engine needed in order to run.

"Occasionally he would come down to the floor and watch practice and just sit there. Most of the time he would stand up in the tunnel—the same place where he would watch the games. But on the days he came down, those were the days of nonverbal communication. He didn't have to say anything; we knew he wasn't happy about the way we were playing. Maybe he would pull you aside, but he would mostly sit there, looking concerned. But if he did pull you aside, he was doing it because you were struggling and he was trying to help you *before* you blew up.

"He could watch you in the layup line and know if you were ready or not. He would watch the bench during the game and could see if you were paying attention or pissed off if you weren't getting in. He was always on the ball. Whether it was something you were doing on the court, or in the community, he had a pulse about *everything* that was going on.

"When there was talk of trading me in 1986, Jerry was the first one to step up and say he was quitting. That is a strong statement, and I didn't know how to handle that, to be honest. I mean, I know that getting traded is part of the game, but for a GM to step up and say no, that is pretty powerful. I guess that is when I knew, really knew, how much Jerry cared about me. He cared about all his players and we are all special to him. But I believe he really had a special place for me.

"Jerry knew the end of my career was near for me even before I did. He could tell that I lost that appetite to get up in the morning. When you don't want to go to work, everything hurts. When you want to go to work but you have an aching knee, you get through it, or you should. I had played with a group of guys and we were so close-knit and now they were gone and I couldn't relate to the Nick Van Exels and the Anthony Peelers. My mother passed away. Even before I took some time off, Jerry had already noticed. He pulled me into his office and he said, 'I look at you, I look at your mannerisms, I look at your face, I look at you coming into the locker room and you are not happy. You don't want to do this any-more. You have a little nagging knee injury, but that is not the reason: you don't want to be here anymore. I don't know what to do with you. I don't want to trade you because you just don't want to do it anymore.'

"Jerry was right. I was having trouble with my knee but I could have gotten through that. I wasn't a starter anymore — they had brought Cedric Ceballos in — but it was more than that. Jerry told me to think about it. So I went off to my mother's funeral and was gone for about a month. Since I still had time left on my contract, Jerry worked it out so I could do things that would benefit myself and the team and avoid any legal problems. Jerry did tell me that a team in Greece had called him and that he thought it might be good for me at the end of my career. Typical Jerry—always looking out for you. I decided against it—Dominique Wilkins went instead—and I retired a Laker in 1994. And in 1995, they retired my number."

Jamaal Wilkes was in Springfield that day too. As Keith Wilkes, he had been a big star at UCLA, then played for me when I coached, and was part of three championship teams (plus one with the Warriors). He had the nickname "Silk" for a reason. So gifted, so smooth. He had great hands, a soft touch, and could run like a gazelle. Earvin said at the roundtable that it didn't matter how he passed the ball to Jamaal—even rolled it to him on the floor—Jamaal got it and made the play work. Chick Hearn always said that a twenty-foot shot from Silk—like McAdoo, Jamaal had an odd-looking shot, launched from who-knows-where behind his right ear—might as well have been a layup. Jamaal had grown up in California and followed the Lakers, so when he came to us from the Warriors, it was essentially a dream come true for him. Because he had idolized me as a player, he wanted to do whatever it took to make me happy when I coached him.

The frank discussions I would have with Jamaal, as I would with most players and which he apparently appreciated, concerned their striking a balance between their life on the court with their life off it. If Jamaal spent too much time socializing at night, he wasn't going to have enough energy to play the way he was capable of. I helped him understand that he was not in college anymore—that he was a professional and there were all sorts of distractions in the city of Los Angeles—and helped him learn how to avoid and recognize trouble, or the potential for trouble, before things would happen that might be beyond his control.

I also recall talking to him about his defense, and he does too.

For whatever reason, he stood up straight too much of the time, which meant he was standing around, as opposed to being in a flexed position, your knees bent closer to the ground, which enables you to do so much more. It's not as if he hadn't learned the proper way to play defense from John Wooden, his coach at UCLA. He had forgotten, and I had to get on him about it. Since he knew that I strove for perfection as a player, for some odd reason he put me on a pedestal in his mind, assumed that I never had to face any of the issues, either professional or personal, that he was wrestling with (or might have to wrestle with), that I was somehow an exception. When he discovered I wasn't perfect, far from it, that I was just like him—filled with insecurities, self-doubt, and, in his view, "not a happy camper"—he was relieved, though somewhat disillusioned and saddened too.

Karen and Jamaal's wife, Valerie, became close and then worked together at the travel agency Karen owned. For as long as I have known him, Jamaal has been quiet; he prefers to let others have the limelight, and he always looks like he's about to fall asleep. Even in his thirty-seven-point game against Philadelphia in Game Six of the 1980 Finals, the game that clinched the championship, he was overshadowed by Magic Johnson, who played center in place of Kareem (who was injured), poured in forty-two points, grabbed fifteen rebounds, dished out seven assists, and became the only rookie ever to win the MVP Award of the Finals.

When we made the ultimate decision to waive Jamaal, five years later, after a serious knee injury cut short his season (in 1985, the first time we beat the Celtics), I was distraught for days afterward.

In reflecting back on this, Jamaal said he felt it might have been harder on me than it was on him. He also said that he always admired my candor and directness in dealing with him, that he was always struck by how I "could be like a little boy, always with that little glint in his eye, always wanting to know, 'What are you up to? Where are you going?,'" and how I always seemed vulnerable, forever wearing my heart on my sleeve.

There were many things I loved about these players, and the others who couldn't make it that day in Springfield. They were like a Ferrari; that car, with its incredible power and inimitable sound, was going to beat your car up and down the court. (I used to drive my teammate Keith Erickson home after road trips, often at two in the morning, and his wife still talks about how she could hear us coming down San Vicente long before we ever got to his house.) These guys were so competitive that every practice was like an actual game. They went at one another, and Pat fueled the fire, inspiring them, motivating them, single-mindedly driving them harder and harder (until, eventually, he drove them away from him and drove himself out of a job). The trainer called me so many times to tell me that Kurt Rambis and Mitch Kupchak had to be pulled apart and the number of stitches he'd had to give them, it was absurd. The more stitches they, or any of them, had, the more they considered it a badge of honor. It got so bad—and not just between those two—that I dreaded hearing Gary Vitti's voice on the phone, knowing I was about to get the latest injury report.

They were a great group of guys to be around, guys who genuinely liked one another, liked doing things together after practice and after games: movies, barbecues, clubs, you name it. The entire city of Los Angeles loved them and they knew it, savoring the adoration and returning it in kind. Every year in mid-April, the team would attend the birthday party that Jack Nicholson would throw for Kareem and Michael Cooper, at a club he and the music impresario Lou Adler owned called On the Rocks; it was above the Roxy Theater and, according to Jack, was "the only truly private club in town."

Earvin was the glue for it—for all of it—one of the best natural leaders I have ever been around. When the Lakers boarded the plane going to Philadelphia for Game Six of the 1980 Finals and left an injured Kareem behind, the first thing Earvin said was "Never fear, Buck is here" (the nickname many of his teammates used to refer to him). Some people are put here on earth for a reason, I really believe that. Earvin always found a way to pick everyone up around him, to make sure they understood their roles.

The electricity and fervor and color of Showtime was not just confined to the court. In many ways, Showtime was just like what many people consider the era of the 1980s itself—overflowing with excess, with the notion that more really was more, and that boundaries were meant to be crossed. And in a place like Los Angeles, there is always that extra layer of star power and glitz, the elements that James Worthy initially struggled with. In the words of the great singer Sam Cooke, "Let the good times roll," and they did. Jerry Buss, often wearing his jeans, denim jackets, and cowboy boots, liked to party with his players, particularly Earvin, and there were young girls everywhere you looked, at the Forum Club and elsewhere, willing, it appeared, to do anything and go anywhere, and Earvin, in particular, eventually paid the price for his many assignations with the devastating announcement in November of 1991 that he was HIV positive.

I knew something was wrong when the insurance company wouldn't renew the policy on Earvin, but I didn't know what, not at first. What I do know is that the events of that confusing period are as vivid and tragic to me as if they occurred five minutes ago,

∧

especially going into my bathroom at home and sitting on the floor and just sobbing, wondering whether Earvin would live or die, basketball the furthest thing from my—or anyone's—mind.

Earvin's condition, as it turned out, was really the final death knell for Showtime, but oh, what a time it was. It began with Kareem's retirement in 1989 and it continued with Pat's departure the following year. He had won Coach of the Year in 1990 but he had lost the players.

The roundtable discussion was supposed to be about Pat, and that was why he wasn't present. But for whatever reason the former players who were there talked a lot about me. Earvin spoke about my "intricate thought process" and his belief that I possessed the smartest basketball mind of anyone he knew (he insists that my knowing Kurt Rambis would be valuable for us and signing him was perhaps the greatest decision I ever made, and a much, much harder one than deciding who to pick in the first round), but what mattered most to him, he made clear, was our personal interaction over the years. He said that I was his "support system for life," that the first call he received for any news, bad or good, was from me, and that I had always been straight with him. A couple of months later, he reflected back on the roundtable with Jonathan and said it was a perfect example of my receiving the one thing that he feels I not only can't do without—a special sort of affection he calls "basketball love"—but shouldn't do without. Earvin apparently is convinced that when I am not officially connected to an NBA team it is far worse for me than the stress and anxiety I encountered on a daily basis in running the Lakers. He says this because he is troubled by my seeming inability to find and sustain happiness when it doesn't involve basketball and feels that my impatience with life in general can make me hard to be around at times, especially since I have "success," "a beautiful family," and "money." Though Earvin thinks of himself as a perfectionist, he feels that I take it "an extra step." When he first joined the Lakers in 1979, he told me that he and his friends tried to emulate me growing up, but that instead of making "the right shot in the clutch," he was always trying to make "the right play." He was very glad that Jerry Buss bought the team from Jack Kent Cooke, especially since Cooke, before the deal was finalized, "scolded" Earvin at his first lunch at the Forum Club for not knowing what Pacific sand dabs were. I remember sitting there with Chick Hearn and thinking that was so typical of Cooke. Here was this young man from Michigan, about to leave college early and join the Lakers, and the soon-to-be-former owner was giving him a hard time about not knowing about something that was both a delicacy and barely familiar to anyone outside of California. Cooke went ahead and ordered the sand dabs for Earvin anyway, but as soon as he had his first bite, he asked if he could have a hamburger or some pizza instead, and Cooke was offended.

Earvin asked me all sorts of questions when he first came to the team, and I did my best to answer all of them. I liked that he didn't come in with the attitude that he knew everything. He wanted to know "how to play in the NBA" and what the essential difference was between the pros and college. One time, early on, I noticed how he would be up in the air trying to make a pass, and I told him that he needed to stay on his feet and stay down. If he was short on his shot, I pointed out ways for him to get it up a bit.

But it is Earvin's darkest hours that he thinks about most when he reflects on our relationship. When Paul Westhead was let go in November of 1981, Earvin was blamed for it and booed by the fans, and he said that I was able to bring him out of it. "I think Jerry knew I needed a hug and just a shoulder to lean on and he became that shoulder every day, saying some words to uplift me and giving me a pat on the back." In the 1984 Finals against the Celtics, who won in seven games, Earvin made a number of mistakes, and I was seriously worried about him that summer, worried how—or if—he was going to be able to bounce back and recover from being derided as "Tragic Magic." "It was the worst summer I had ever had," Magic said. "I had never failed like that in a pressure situation before, in a championship series. I didn't come outside much, and beat myself up much like Jerry does. But he was there for me, gave me things to think about, and I was so glad to get another shot the following year and redeem myself when we finally beat the Celtics in 1985." But the moment that Earvin remembers best is when he came into my office to say he was retiring—and meaning it—and "we both just cried like babies," he said. "That was probably our greatest moment. Just sitting there, the two of us. It showed me how much he cared about me, and it was just so personal." Earvin being Earvin, he had one more thing to say: "I am glad Jerry is doing this book. He needs therapy, and I have to believe that doing this is good therapy, that it could really help him."

Byron Scott recalled the time he was playing in Tempe at Arizona State in a pickup game, a game in which he was guarding Dennis Johnson, who had played for Phoenix and the Celtics for many years, and I suddenly showed up. He hadn't been planning to participate that day, but he was glad he did, because we wound up trading for him—the fourth pick of the 1983 draft, to the San Diego Clippers—during training camp later that year. We parted company with Norm Nixon, an extremely popular player whom I had coached for two years. (Jack Nicholson not only lobbied me not to trade Norm but wore black in mourning when we did.) I was tough on Norm, as I mentioned earlier; then again, I was tough on all the guards who played for me. But in 1983 there was a conflict and it needed to be resolved. Norm wanted to handle the ball as much as possible, but we needed Magic to do that. Magic without the ball was merely Earvin, a Monet without his brush. When Magic was out for a period of time with an injury, it was difficult for Norm to give up the ball when Magic returned. And it was nearly impossible for Norm to prevent his unhappiness from becoming known.

Byron grew up in Inglewood, blocks from the Forum, and it was his dream to play for the Lakers, just as it had been for Jamaal Wilkes. Byron likes to tell the story of how he was on his way to work out when I called him early one morning—his negotiations with the Clippers were stalled—and said we were trying to make a deal for him but that if I didn't phone back by two that afternoon, it wasn't going to happen. "I was nervous, excited, looking at the clock, looking at the phone, hoping for it to ring," he recalled. "I remember distinctly, at about ten minutes after two, the phone hadn't rung, and I told my mom, 'I'm going to work out. He's not going to call, so the deal's not done.' My mom was in the kitchen and she was calm. She kept saying, 'He's going to call, don't worry, honey,' and I'm like, 'No, Ma, he's not.' So I walk out the door at fifteen minutes after two. The phone rings and she calls me back in and Jerry West says, 'Congratulations, son. You're now a Los Angeles Laker.' Oh, man, it was the happiest day of my life." We arranged a press conference for the next day, the trainer called to get his sizes and find out what number he wanted to wear, he came to a game the following evening, I introduced him to the players, and he reported to practice the morning after that.

At first, the players—Magic and Michael Cooper in particular—were very cool toward Byron, because he was replacing their close friend. Also, he was a rookie, and who knew, who really knew, how he was going to perform? He certainly got worked over in practice—"The players couldn't take it out on Jerry," Byron said, "so they figured the next best thing was me"—but Byron was a tough kid, and before long, he and Earvin and Coop got so close that they became known as the Three Amigos.

In his rookie year, Byron recalled (just as James Worthy had) that I would occasionally come down to the floor during practice. I tried to do that when a rookie or new player joined the team. Most of the time, if I watched, I would watch from a greater distance, from Portal 27, my habitual spot at the Forum. I didn't want Pat to feel that I was hovering (though he says he never minded my being there). But if I saw something I didn't like or something I thought could be improved, I would occasionally come onto the court and demonstrate what was bothering me, though I would do it at an appropriate time. Sometimes I would send word, but often through an intermediary—similar to what I do with Gary Colson and others in regard to my family—and often in the middle of the night. Gary Vitti, the trainer, received, and delivered to Pat, a lot of such messages over the years. Gary laughs about it now, but it probably wasn't all that funny at the time.

With Byron, I would frequently say, "You're doing a great job, young man. Just keep up the good work." I realize now that the way Pete Newell would talk to me as a young player had formed the way I would speak to players—except that he always called me "lad" instead of "young man." I also told Byron what I told all new players—if you need anything, or if you need to talk, you know where to find me. Byron was always amused that I seemed to know what was going on with him off the court at all times. In Byron's view, "The thing I ended up finding out with Jerry is that he had people all over Los Angeles who knew about *everything*. He knew when I went out at night and where. Not just me, *everybody*. He had eyes all over L.A. It's not so much that he was trying to find out things. It's just that people would see us out and report back to him. It's as if he were not only the GM of the Lakers, but the head of a spy organization."

I always stressed that he (all our players, for that matter) needed to plan for a life after basketball and that what he did with his money and whom he invested it with were crucial. The *hardest* thing for these players to learn was that if they were making three million dollars a year, they were really only getting half that.

Ten years — and three championships — later, I had to have a different conversation with Byron. We weren't going to re-sign him. As soon as he came into my office and we began to talk, we both became emotional. As it turned out, the Indiana Pacers wanted someone who could lead and be a teacher for their younger players — and I told Donnie Walsh, their GM at the time, that Byron would be perfect. Byron later said that he had been in L.A. all his life, so this gave him an opportunity to venture out and attempt to do something special somewhere else. "I did everything I could in L.A. and played with some of the greatest players to ever play the game. I felt I had the experience to help younger guys to hopefully become champions, to give them some of the things that Magic and Coop and those guys taught me and to make them better."

Three years after that, in 1996, Byron returned to the Lakers because he wanted to retire with the team he had begun his career with. We gave him a one-year contract and he was extremely helpful to the rookies on the team, especially Kobe Bryant. Over the years, as he has coached the New Jersey Nets (whom the Lakers defeated for the 2002 championship), the New Orleans Hornets, and now the Cleveland Cavaliers, he has continued to seek me out for personal advice.

A. C. Green, the "Iron Man" who played in 1,192 straight games and whom I never had to worry about off the court, talked about how "Mr. West"—which he continues to insist on calling me—took a chance on him out of Oregon State and how he never dreamed he would be "playing with guys I used to have breakfast with on my Wheaties box."

Bill Bertka, Pat's assistant coach, was there at the roundtable, and he said that one of the things that made this group so great was their willingness to subordinate everything to be successful. Today, with the salary cap and the midlevel exception and the collective bargaining agreement and the luxury tax, you couldn't do what we did during the 1980s—essentially keep this band of brothers together for ten years. It's not the way the league works now and it is a shame.

For all the players who were there, one player's absence in particular was conspicuous: Kareem Abdul-Jabbar. Michael Cooper, whom I had first met when he was a teenager and came to Camp Clutch, couldn't be there because his WNBA team, the Los Angeles Sparks, was in the playoffs. Norm Nixon and Mychal Thompson couldn't make it for various reasons. But Kareem wasn't there because his relationship with Pat was strained. When Kareem retired in 1989, they were barely speaking. Kareem felt Pat's demands on the players were unreasonable, that he had pushed them over the brink. Pat was the one who'd predicted a repeat win after we got the 1987 title, then came up with the term *threepeat* after the 1988 one, boldly raising the bar higher and higher.

Whenever I think about Kareem, I regret the way I dealt with him as a coach. To this day, I feel bad that I said he didn't play hard enough. He and I laugh about this now, and we are very close (something he is not with many people; some feel he is difficult and aloof, but they don't really understand how shy he actually is). What I couldn't see or, I guess, accept is how easily the game came to him, how effortlessly. To say he is a student of the game doesn't even begin to tell you the story. He is like a Rhodes scholar. He corresponded with Wilt Chamberlain at Kansas when he was in fourth grade. He knew that his coach at UCLA, John Wooden, had been known as the "Indiana Rubber Man" when he'd played, which was long before Kareem ever stepped on the court at Pauley Pavilion. I first met him when he was Lew Alcindor, a ninth-grader at Power Memorial in New York; his school's gym was the one we often practiced at when we came to play the Knicks. Perhaps because he was so heavily recruited—in 1965 he was the most sought-after player in the country since Wilt Chamberlain, a decade earlier—he dealt with the press in a unique way: he wasn't going to be anything or anybody other than who he was. He was very precise in everything he said, and he hated stupid, obvious questions. He may have been aloof, but he was never disrespectful. Never. Beginning in the fifth grade with some drills the great Laker center George Mikan used, he developed and perfected the most unique and effective shot in the history of basketball, the Sky Hook. Why no other big man has ever really learned to do this remains a mystery to me.

When I think about players, especially great players, I primarily think about their basketball IQs. I think about what kind of play a player will make when the game is on the line. About whether he will be more precise, be less likely to make mistakes. Kareem didn't make mistakes late. He might miss a shot or something, but he wasn't going to make a mistake. And yet I would look at the stat sheet after the game and check Kareem's rebounds and turnovers, and wonder why, with all that ability, he didn't get more rebounds. Why couldn't he do that? At the end of the 1976–77 season, he wound up averaging 26.2 points a game and 13.3 rebounds, but I would still look at him—I'm not talking about a player, I'm talking about *an extraordinarily gifted player*—and say to myself, *My God, this guy could do so much more. He could do so much more if he only had a little bit more pit bull in him* (and I am not forgetting the times he got into fights).

But I was wrong, really wrong. I should simply have accepted Kareem as he was, and what he had in him. He was graceful and he was one of the most unselfish players I have ever been around. When I coached him, it took me a while to realize that we had too many people playing with him who did not complement him. As a result, he was carrying an enormous burden, which I didn't appreciate at first because he was such an unstoppable force. I mean, over an eighty-two-game schedule, he rarely had a game that he didn't play well. But it was those close games when I felt, *My God, if he could do just a little bit more.* . . . Winning the close games is what separates good teams from great ones, and good players from great ones. And if you have one of those players on your team, that one person can drive the others to enormous success. Kareem was able to do that with Magic, and he was able to do that with Oscar (who also felt Kareem could have been even better than he was) when they won a championship together with the Bucks, but that was not consistently the case during the three years I coached him; we simply weren't good enough. I alluded to this earlier, but don't think I emphasized it enough: When I took the job of coaching the Lakers in 1976, if anyone had asked me to write a play on a blackboard, I couldn't have done it; I wouldn't have known what the hell to write down. I wasn't a student of the game in terms of watching what coaches did. As a player, all I tried to do was implement what coaches wanted. That's why I hired Jack McCloskey and Stan Albeck, two guys with experience who knew what the hell they were doing. Frankly, it was the smartest thing I ever did, because they saved me time after time. What I did know a little about was defense, and I knew the tough-minded concept I wanted us to have. But when somebody asked me about offense — "What are you going to do for Abdul-Jabbar?" — I didn't have a clue. I soon learned that we could run any offense and he was going to shine.

That first year of coaching was probably one of the best times of my life. The team had not made the playoffs the previous two seasons, but we did that year (in fact, we not only won the Pacific Division title but also had the best record in the league at fifty-three and twenty-nine). And this despite making only one personnel change: bringing in Don Chaney, a free agent, whose one knee was so bad he could hardly get up and down the floor. But he gave us a stability and a toughness that we needed. He wasn't the same player he had been with the Celtics, but he was a tremendous addition.

Portland won the 1977 championship, with Bill Walton, but we got the best of them during the regular season. Had it not been for two key injuries — to Kermit Washington and Lucius Allen — it could have been a miracle story for us.

I had tried to persuade Jack Kent Cooke to pursue Julius Erving when the ABA folded, but he wouldn't hear of it. As far as he was concerned, anyone who played in the ABA had to be inferior. To this day, I can't believe what an unbelievable opportunity we squandered. With Dr. J. complementing Kareem, maybe we could have won a championship. Or even more.

*　　*　　*

"When I first met Jerry, it was interesting because it was like he wanted somebody to talk to," Kareem said to Jonathan at his agent's office one day in Long Beach. "I was this very shy guy and I am looking at these professional players and they are who I want to be and I am in awe. Wow, he wants to talk to me. I had seen him play already. He was a rookie and I used to go to the double-headers at the Garden, which was only twelve blocks away. I was at the game when Elgin got seventy-one points in 1960. I was thirteen. I wanted to be Elgin, but I didn't have his athletic talent. Jerry might not even know I was at that game.

"Jerry just wanted to know what my life was like, what I was doing. I was a tall, skinny kid and he just asked me about me. It was very natural, it wasn't difficult for me to talk with him. At that age it is hard for you to talk to adults, especially people you are in awe of, but it was the total opposite with Jerry. The one thing I remember most is that Jerry didn't think they were using Bobby Smith in the right way. Felt he should be playing more than he was. You see, Bobby Smith was quick, he could mix it up under the basket, really fast, athletic, he could shoot it, played good defense on the perimeter, a perfect small forward. But in those days the book was that guys who play the front line had to be six nine, and Jerry didn't agree with that and here he was, talking to me about it, a freshman in high school. He was complaining, but in hindsight I can see he had the ability to assess talent even then, he understood what worked on the court and what didn't. For Jerry, to play with somebody who could keep up with him, the quick open-court game where he could get those open jumpers, Bobby Smith would have been perfect. But management didn't see it. They had Rudy LaRusso, who was a good power forward. Frank Selvy. Ray Felix. Guys like Wilt and Bill Russell used to eat Ray Felix alive.

"I knew about Jerry from the 1960 Olympic Team. That to me was the real Dream Team. They were awesome. Jerry and Oscar over the years: the competitive fire, the will to win, the basketball IQ. Sometimes I wish I could have not been playing just so I could watch.

"I didn't tell Jerry this when I met him, but I was a Celtics fan, partly because the Knicks were so pathetic then. I had already gotten to meet Bill Russell — he was a great role model for me — and Red Auerbach not long before I met Jerry.

"I think it is unfortunate that Jerry has never been able to make peace with his losses to the Celtics and can't fully appreciate his own extraordinary achievement as an athlete. I will never forget listening to Richard Pryor make jokes about how Jerry would light up the black players who were supposed to be so superior. Jerry West killed all of that myth on a regular basis. Anybody who could make the black players have to work hard to keep up must be one hell of an athlete. That's what Pryor was saying.

"I didn't see Jerry again until I came to UCLA. But it wasn't until I joined the Lakers and began to have extended conversations with Jerry that I really understood why I thought he was cool the whole time: he was a great fan of Joe Louis. He told me how, one night, he was listening on the radio and Louis was losing and a storm set in on West Virginia and knocked out the power and how he couldn't sleep all night not knowing the outcome.

"Being on the team when he was coach, you are with him all of the time. I could see, as the game approached, he became withdrawn and he would get very uptight. When we won he was relieved, and when we lost he was very, I won't say depressed, but it ate at him. I felt for him because he had to deal with the press and he had to deal with Mr. Cooke, which wasn't easy. I knew that they had a number of screaming matches. I was never in the room but it is easy to imagine, because Jerry had his own personal line of integrity, and he didn't like it to be crossed.

"I only learned recently, to my amusement, that I frustrated Jerry when I played for him. One of those years, I think it was '76–'77, I won MVP for the second year in a row and I was in the top five in scoring, rebounding, and blocked shots. Anybody that can do that and Jerry thinks he is not playing hard? I guess that is one time where Jerry's powers of observation were playing tricks on him.

"I was very happy that Jerry was the GM because he had a sharp eye for talent and he always got the right guy for the team: James Worthy, Mychal Thompson, A. C. Green, even Milt Wagner for the '87–'88 team. When I had a variety of personal troubles—including a fire at my house and death threats and so forth—Jerry was always there for me. I actually wanted to retire after the 1987 championship—I was forty and Pat just kept trying to manipulate people and press their emotional buttons and it got really tiresome—but Jerry convinced me to stay on for two more years. I was really satisfied with my career, but he convinced me that we couldn't win another championship unless I did. I just really appreciated the fact that I was being appreciated, because Earvin had the spotlight and everything, but Jerry said, 'No, you are the guy that makes things happen here.' It was like a friend talking to me, not like some CEO. So I stayed and he gave me a generous contract and we won again the next year and I retired the year after that.

"When Jerry left the Lakers, I honestly did not sense it coming but I wasn't surprised because Dr. Buss does have a tendency to take people for granted. Dr. Buss is not like Mr. Cooke, who was interfering and pompous, but I don't think the Lakers appreciated Jerry. Given his qualities as a human being, there is no way they could reciprocate because there is nobody there who understands what I am saying well enough to put that type of effort out to deal with someone like Jerry as they should. If Jerry can hear from you your appreciation and respect, you have a friend for life. No question. The Lakers, they are not like that. They may say they are, but you don't feel it."

Mitch Kupchak came to the Lakers in 1981 from the Washington Bullets, where he had won a championship, but his playing career with us never panned out due to a serious knee injury. Mitch was so determined to recover, though, that he took to posting the phrase *Yes, I can* wherever you looked. Every time I saw Mitch's declaration of American optimism, I silently said to myself, *No, you can't.* I knew how nearly impossible it would be for him to become the player he'd been when we acquired him, but I couldn't help but notice his incredible work ethic in trying to make it back.

I had first met Mitch when he was in high school in New York, and Bucky Waters, the Duke coach who was recruiting him and a good friend of mine, brought him into our locker room when we were playing the Knicks at the Garden in the 1972 Finals. (His first real awareness of me, he loves to tell people, is when I hit that sixty-three-foot shot in the NBA Finals in 1970, the shot that merely tied the game, which the Knicks then won in overtime. "I was a Knicks fan and I am sitting at home," Mitch recalled. "It was well past midnight in New York and Jerry hits the shot and I suddenly start screaming. In fact, I was screaming so loud that my father, who was fast asleep and who had to get up for his construction job early each morning, came running downstairs to find out what the hell had happened. Was someone trying to kill me, that sort of thing. I am not very vocal to begin with, so for me to be yelling like this was very unusual and disturbing.") When Mitch joined the Lakers, nine years after I met him in New York, he seemed very surprised that I remembered how we first met.

I knew that Mitch had begun taking classes at UCLA so that he could get an MBA. This was exactly the type of forward thinking I encouraged all players to have—to plan for a life after basketball—and I spoke to Jerry Buss about the possibility of bringing Mitch into the front office with me. (I had told Mitch that he didn't have to keep doing this to himself and that whenever he decided to hang it up, I could use his help.) I told Jerry that I could see Mitch eventually doing many of the things I had little patience for—handling the pesky financial details of deals, understanding the fine print of the collective bargaining agreement, the salary cap, the luxury tax, the midlevel exception. I knew that more and more expertise of this kind would be necessary, and I also thought Mitch's calm would be a great balance to my high-strung nature.

I might have thought that, but that didn't mean he would. No sooner had he joined me in the front office than the possible trade of James Worthy to Dallas erupted. Mitch relishes the story of being in the men's room when I came in, red-faced and fuming, and said, "Mitch, I've had it. I can't take this crap anymore and I am going to damn well quit and recommend to Jerry Buss that you take over ASAP." So, according to Mitch, he is standing at the urinal and is thinking, *I have only been on the job a month and now Jerry is walking out and how in the hell am I supposed to take over?* He had never really seen this side of me, and I've only recently figured out—or think I have—why I threatened to resign so often. If it was just frustration or irritation, that would be one thing. But it really was much more than that. The job totally consumed me and I cared way too much about every little thing. It wreaked havoc on every aspect of my life, and it was what I imagine being addicted to drugs would be like. The only way to survive, and live with any chance of normalcy, was to get away from it entirely.

I couldn't do it — at least not then — and yet Mitch's presence gave me a chance to better cope with things. It enabled me to get out of the office — I was too antsy to be there all the time anyway — knowing that he was fully capable of dealing with whatever might come up and that he could reach me easily (even though this was well before cell phones). I trusted Mitch completely.

We often had lunch together at Tito's Tacos, a little Mexican place not far from the Forum where you stood in line and ordered, or at Little King. I introduced Mitch to golf, but he played so slowly and methodically that it drove me crazy and he knew it. I tried to show him some things, but it was hopeless. I recently learned that Mitch, who thinks of me as "peculiar," had made up his own rules regarding how to deal with me on a daily basis. The basic ones are these: *(1) Let Jerry drive and follow his own route. Understand that he is superstitious and will avoid traffic lights whenever possible. (2) Let Jerry pick the restaurant and let him order. If Jerry says the food is no good, don't try to say otherwise. Eat fast or he will act so irritated that you will wish you had. (3) Don't be late. Accept that he is always in a hurry to get somewhere, and that once he's there, he's in a hurry to leave.*

Another story Mitch delights in recounting is of an evening in Hawaii during training camp when we were having dinner at Ruth's Chris Steak House with a number of the scouts and others from the front office, there must have been fifteen of us altogether. Now, I happen to know a lot about steaks because I am in charge of cooking them for large family dinners, which we have nearly every Sunday night in the summer at our home in Bel Air. So on this night at the restaurant, my steak came out and the minute I cut into it I could tell it was raw. The second time it was well done, and the third time it was raw again. I told the waiter not to bother trying anymore, that I would eat it the way it was. The manager said he wasn't going to charge me, and I said that not only did I want them to charge me for my meal but I would never come back again if they didn't. I didn't want them to cook me a new steak because my instinct told me that on this particular occasion they weren't going to get it right. When the bill came, I grabbed it, as I always do, and despite what I'd told them, I couldn't believe they'd charged me for the steak. I suddenly got up from the table and walked out. No one knew if I was coming back or not. I left the restaurant and was gone for about five minutes. When I reappeared I had four brown paper bags with me. In each one was a cheesecake I had gotten from another restaurant, and I spread them out on the table, which I am pretty sure is not even a legal thing to do. That, I guess, was my weird, defiant way of getting back at Ruth's Chris for screwing up my steak. Is that a rational thing to do? No, of course it isn't. I am sure something else was bothering me, and I misdirected my feelings about it toward the steak house.

To this day, I am told, whenever the words *Ruth's Chris* and *Hawaii* find their way into the same sentence at the Lakers' offices in El Segundo, everyone simply smiles. And even if you find this hard to believe, I do too.

6

Kobe, Shaquille, and the Summer of 1996

Shaquille O'Neal and Kobe Bryant

The stress of acquiring Kobe Bryant and Shaquille O'Neal in the summer of 1996 sent me spiraling downward and into the hospital for exhaustion for a few days. The elation of what should have been — and eventually was — one of my greatest accomplishments as general manager simply did not last. When I returned from Atlanta and the press conference that announced the signing of Shaquille (he was there to play in the Olympics), Karen and my sons had made up signs that welcomed me home as if I were a conquering hero. I was excited, that's for sure, and even went so far as to say that, aside from the births of my children, it was the happiest day of my life. But then I experienced such an emotional letdown, and my depression, which has plagued me all my life, reared its ugly head once more.

The whole process of acquiring those two players had been tedious and nerve-racking. In the case of Shaquille, it felt as if we were being teased all the time, that a carrot was being held out that I couldn't quite grab hold of. As if someone said to you, *If you are able to do this, we'll let you have that set of golf clubs or a free trip to Bora Bora.* I was on the phone constantly, at all hours of the day and night, trying to clear cap space, my son Ryan by my side. Shaquille was upset that Orlando and its citizens didn't seem to think he was worth $100 million (the team took a poll, and the results were overwhelmingly against), and he was aware that Alonzo Mourning had just gotten a new contract for $115 million from Miami. The problem was that the best we could offer was $98 million (and Orlando went up to $99 million), and yet I had the sense that Shaquille wanted to come to us, and also have the opportunity to be in Hollywood and get into the entertainment business. Every time we thought we were reaching an accord with Shaquille's agent, Leonard Armato, another roadblock emerged, something else seemed to be conspiring against us. Eventually, though, with the full support of Jerry Buss (who essentially told me to do whatever it took) and our eleventh-hour success in persuading the Vancouver Grizzlies to acquire Anthony Peeler and George Lynch, we were able to make the deal for seven years for $120 million. In order to get Kobe, which we'd done first, we gave away our starting center, Vlade Divac, a crazy thing to do and a point of personal sadness to me. We had drafted Vlade in 1989 based on reports coming out of Europe and our watching his Yugoslavian national team play the Celtics, first on television and then, repeatedly, on film. All of our scouts were opposed to drafting Vlade, thought I was nuts, but Vlade turned out to be a terrific player—his hands were like a spider's web—and an even better person. I will never forget picking him up at the airport. He had two brown duffel bags full of personal belongings and little else (reminding me a little of myself when I'd gone off to college). Vlade turned out to be the embodiment of the American Dream.

I've already mentioned this but it can't be emphasized enough: trading a player—one asset for another, or two or three others—or releasing a player was the thing about my job I despised the most. You become attached to the players, you get to know their families. In an ideal world, a deal benefits both sides. Sometimes that was the case, but often it was not.

In any event, the deal for Kobe almost didn't go through. Mark Fleischer, Vlade's agent, suddenly announced that Vlade was going to retire. Bob Bass, the general manager of the Charlotte Hornets (who were going to take Kobe with the thirteenth pick), phoned to say that they were backing out. "Bob, we have a deal, goddamn it," I told him. "Vlade is not going to retire. Trust me." I got Mitch involved because I was so irritated that Bob would go back on his word and I didn't want to deal with it any longer. I'd had it, and so I asked Mitch to carry on. There was also a future first-round pick we were supposed to get, which very few people know about and which we never got anyway. Vlade did not want to leave the Lakers, and eventually, Vlade's wife talked him out of retiring; when he later played for the Sacramento Kings, he made our lives miserable.

But Vlade wasn't Shaquille. Nobody was.

The thing that angered and upset me the most in the Shaquille situation was the growing suggestion — from Orlando Magic executives — that we had tampered with him. When I learned that the commissioner's office was investigating that possibility, I considered resigning. I was interviewed on *Charlie Rose* that November and said as much. I had been at Leonard Armato's Santa Monica office and he'd been at my house only when we were allowed to begin talking, and not one second before (just as would happen in 2010 with LeBron James, when teams had the official green light to trek to Ohio and make their case). How in the hell is that tampering? When the All-Star Game was played in Cleveland in February of 1997, the fifty greatest NBA players of the league's first fifty years were honored, and I didn't go. I had recently had surgery on my nose for a deviated septum and didn't feel up to attending. At least that is what I said, and my family was angry with me. The real reason was that I was still upset about the tampering allegation, the notion we had done something illegal. If you work for Jerry Buss, you are not going to cheat. So to be accused of that and for them to want an investigation, I just couldn't believe it. I'd always loved Red Auerbach — hated him too — but I never loved him more than when he came out and said it was sour grapes. It may not have been reason enough for me not to attend, but I still didn't go, and David Stern, the commissioner, and other people in the league office were not happy about it. The other two players who didn't show up were, ironically, Shaquille (who was injured) and Pete Maravich (who was dead).

The deal for Kobe Bryant could not have been completed, would *never* have gotten done, were it not for Arn Tellem, Kobe's original agent and my close friend. When we had the sense that the New Jersey Nets might take Kobe with the eighth pick in the draft, Arn helped persuade them not to; basically, he told them, and had Kobe's parents tell them, Kobe had no interest in playing for New Jersey. I didn't need to watch much of Kobe's workout at the Inglewood YMCA, going one-on-one with Michael Cooper (even though he was forty, he was still in good shape), to know that he was someone I coveted, that we had to have him. Earvin Johnson said he had never heard me more excited about a prospect. In fact, I thought that Kobe was possibly better than the players we had on the team at the time. Never in my life have I seen a workout like that. When I said I had seen enough, I meant it. I knew who he was, and just from looking at his eyes, I knew what he wanted. Even though he was only seventeen years old, Kobe was a once-in-a-lifetime player who could cast his shadow on the franchise for years to come. His fierce competitive drive was innate, could not be purchased on the street or in a store or anywhere. You need to possess more than a little nastiness to play basketball at the highest level, and Kobe had that in abundance. You need to have the cold-bloodedness of an assassin, and he possessed that too. He clearly modeled himself on Michael Jordan, which was fine. But I had no idea how long it would take him to mature and develop, and I did worry that it might take him a while to fit in.

Since Kobe had lived in Italy, he loved coming over to the

house for Karen's spaghetti and meatballs. He and Ryan, just a year younger, became friendly, and I think it is fair to say that I became a father figure to him. I tried to talk to him about the importance of patience, which is funny because I am the most impatient person I know. I told him that he couldn't impose his will on every situation he faced on the court, that he needed to learn to trust his teammates. (I knew he was going to piss people off, and he did, repeatedly. In the 1998 All-Star Game, in only his second year, he basically told the veteran Karl Malone to move his pick-and-roll ass off to the side so that he could go one-on-one with Michael Jordan.) I also kidded him that he wouldn't have been able to beat me one-on-one in my prime, that he would be too eager and too anxious.

He and Shaquille were going to need to find a way to coexist—it pained me to see how much of a struggle it was for them, how unwilling Kobe was to defer to Shaquille in any way— and I had to do my part to make sure that happened, make sure that these two guys understood what it would take for them to win. I would often talk to both of them and try to get them to real- ize what they had at stake and how much success they could enjoy. I even wrote each of them a letter (which Shaquille apparently still has). Kobe's demeanor couldn't have been more different than Shaquille's. Whereas Shaquille was a big kid, blowing kisses to everyone, the way Magic did (if Shaquille and I had been in high school together, he would have been my best friend), Kobe was young and immature. He had a showboat style and a bottomless reservoir of drive that fueled him; he wasn't content just to beat people, he had to embarrass them, even players on his own team. He still lived with his parents and was detached in much the same way that Kareem Abdul-Jabbar had appeared at times to his team- mates. Shaquille felt that I coddled Kobe too much, that I was too protective of him, and maybe I was. (What many people don't realize, though, is that Shaquille occasionally was too. After Kobe had fired three consecutive air balls in the playoffs against Utah in his first season, Shaquille was the one who told him to shake it off and not to let it get him down, even complimented him on his courage to take those shots as a rookie.) He said that partly because I would have "serious discussions" with Shaquille if he did something stupid or poorly—which he said he didn't mind because of the strict discipline his father had imposed on him as he was growing up. One time, he slapped Greg Ostertag of the Utah Jazz before the first game of the 1997–98 season for no reason other than he was tired of his mouthing off. Another time, after a game we lost to Dallas, Shaquille recalls my coming into the locker room wondering why he would be taking fadeaways against their reed-thin center Shawn Bradley instead of just backing him down and powering over him. "You gotta be kidding me," I said. "Shooting fadeaways against Shawn Bradley? What the hell were you thinking?" And then there was the time I came into the locker room after a bitter playoff loss at the Forum and found him literally dismantling the place—ripping out the sinks and the urinals—and told him that he needed to calm his ass down.

In retrospect, all I can say is that these two guys—Shaquille and Kobe—could play, they could *really* play, and that, ultimately, is what mattered. We were rebuilding a franchise that needed an infusion of star power (in the wake of Earvin Johnson's "final" retirement) because that is what the league is based on, has always been based on, even if the Celtics of the 1960s and the two Knicks championship teams of 1970 and 1973 stand as relative exceptions to that notion. But star power means that you have someone who can be the foundation for a team, someone you can build around. We had a lot of really good pieces to start with, in Eddie Jones and Nick Van Exel and Cedric Ceballos, but getting Kobe and Shaquille meant that we could put some glamour back into the franchise, and we could see the enthusiasm immediately in our season-ticket sales.

And yet the whole effort had taken a big emotional toll on me. It brought me back to 1972, after we won our first championship in Los Angeles (and my only one as a player), and reminded me of the Peggy Lee song "Is That All There Is?" I say that because the first few years did not result in the sort of achievement we had hoped for. When you have a personality like Shaquille's, one that essentially requires him to be the focal point, the Big Diesel (as he called himself), I know he got frustrated. I know that Kobe got frustrated because he wanted to play more and more (I hadn't forgotten how I felt my rookie year) and that was the main reason we eventually traded Eddie Jones. (It was somewhat similar to the Norm Nixon situation back in the early 1980s in that Eddie too was very popular with the fans, but we needed Kobe to play, just as we needed the ball to be in Magic's hands.) Nick Van Exel was a tremendous player and was team captain the year Kobe and Shaquille arrived. I liked Nick personally, and he became more than just another player to me. I empathized with his tough upbringing, and I did everything I could to help him alleviate the problems he always seemed to run into, with officials, his teammates, and his coach, Del Harris. I even tried to enlist the other players' help (as I would do with Rick Fox for Kobe and Shaquille), but nothing worked. Nick was just too angry. Ultimately, we traded Nick — for Tyronn Lue, a player who wasn't as good — and I hated doing it.

I know it is a cliché, but doing what's right isn't always popular (trading Eddie Jones), and doing what's popular isn't always right (trading Nick).

* * *

A players' strike had started in the autumn of 1998, and it continued until late January of 1999. A few weeks after the shortened season began, Jerry Buss phoned me and said he wanted to make a coaching change, a change I was not looking forward to. Del Harris had been our coach since the autumn of 1994 (he had been named Coach of the Year in his first season, at the same time I was named Executive of the Year), and he was a close friend of mine. Del was essentially old-school, believed things should be done a certain way, and the players were tuning him out, not unlike what had happened ten years earlier with Pat Riley. This is something that often happens about four or so years after a new coach comes in — not always, but often. Calling Del in was extremely difficult. He was a great teacher and no one in basketball was more prepared than he was. But chemistry is such an intangible thing, in all relationships. It was year three of our attempt to win another championship, to see if Shaquille and Kobe could lead us back to where we hadn't been for more than a decade, and Jerry Buss was clearly getting anxious. We decided to promote Kurt Rambis and make him the interim coach. Kurt was an integral part of the organization. He had been on the championship teams of the 1980s and had his own crazy following in Rambis Youth. (The group consisted of eighteen kids who came to games wearing the horn-rimmed glasses with a strap on the back that had become Kurt's identifying feature, and these kids both confounded and delighted Kurt.) His wife was best friends with Jeanie Buss, Jerry's daughter. Like Del, Kurt was not going to be outworked by anyone. He too had had his share of problems with the players, but we wanted to see if he would pan out and become the permanent head coach.

That did not happen. Dennis Rodman joined the team for a New York minute. Jerry Buss thought he would be a good addition. I was wary of Rodman, thought he would be another distraction in a season that had had more than its share of them. He was a great rebounder and defender and one of the smartest players ever to play the game, a future Hall of Famer, but he played one week and then essentially wanted two weeks off. Exit Rodman. The last thing this particular group needed was more controversy.

I forget exactly when I brought up the name of Phil Jackson. Jerry and I felt that we needed someone of his stature to come in and put an end to the musical chairs. Phil's accomplishments spoke for themselves. After six championships in Chicago, he left the Bulls, along with Michael Jordan, after the 1997–98 season. Jerry Krause, the Bulls' general manager, who used to scout for the Lakers at one time, told me in no uncertain terms that Phil was trouble, that we should stay away from him. Phil, for his part, made no secret of his dislike of Krause.

I had played against Phil when he was with the Knicks, and he'd contributed to their success. He had a large ego, Krause stressed, and Jerry was certain we would clash. But I had always prided myself on being able to get along with anyone, and so I flew to Chicago to meet with his agent, Todd Musburger, and then I spoke with Phil by phone. I told him that we had a talented team, but the players—especially the young, immature ones—needed the kind of leadership and discipline his Bulls teams had had. If he could provide that, I said, this was a group that could win championships.

Phil was eager to get back into coaching after traveling all over the world on his motorcycle and licking his wounds over his departure from the Bulls. I happened to know that Jerry Reinsdorf, the owner of the Bulls, had his own issues with Phil, but there was no denying the success he had had. He'd felt underpaid in Chicago and had told Krause back in the early 1990s that the era of the million-dollar-a-year coach was fast approaching. Krause did not think so, apparently, but as it turned out, Krause was very wrong.

In the middle of June, a press conference was held at the Beverly Hilton in Los Angeles, and Phil Jackson, wearing sandals, was anointed as the next coach of the Lakers. His salary would be six million dollars a year for five years. He and Jerry Buss had not met in person until Phil arrived in Los Angeles.

Kurt and Linda Rambis were furious with me, and they had good reason to be. They felt I had made a promise to support Kurt's continuing as coach, and I did feel he deserved a chance beyond a strike-shortened season to prove his worth. But Jerry Buss wanted a big-name coach, as did I, truthfully, and Jerry Buss owned the team. So we went with Phil, and Kurt reluctantly agreed to stay with the organization even though Phil wanted to bring in his own staff. Phil added Kurt as an assistant coach once he got to know him better, but it would be ten years before Kurt got a head coaching job, joining the Minnesota Timberwolves for the 2009–10 season.

Not long after Phil became head coach, he began dating Jeanie Buss, who did a great job overseeing the business side of the operation and with whom I worked very closely on the planning of the Staples Center. Their relationship became a cause of great concern to me, and I expressed that to Jerry. I knew how important and fragile a team's dynamic could be, how one little thing could upset it, but Jerry didn't share my concern. He said they were both adults, that Phil was a consummate professional, and that he didn't see it as being a problem in any way.

An even bigger problem, to my mind, was this: I had always viewed the Lakers as a family—in conflict at times, to be sure, as most families are—and had, as I've said, always tried to instill a family atmosphere in the office. If in the course of a season you lose thirty games, you are going to be miserable for a day or two until the next game, when hopefully you win. Knowing that, I would try to make things in the office as pleasant as possible, strive to treat

Karen was the most naturally beautiful woman I had ever seen.

Our favorite photo from when we were dating, 1976

Our wedding at the Beverly Hills Hotel, May 28, 1978, with Mark, Michael, and David—the first and last time I ever wore a tuxedo *(Portraits by Merrett)*

With Pat Riley, Ken Jones, and Bill Bastien *(Portraits by Merrett)*

Leaving for our honeymoon *(Portraits by Merrett)*

Doing one of the things I love best, particularly on Sunday nights, with my good friend Gary Colson, who introduced me to Karen

At my home in Pacific Palisades, 1979, needing to get my gardening in before taking Karen to St. John's Hospital, where she gave birth to Ryan

That I don't swim is a secret I have never revealed before. With Ryan.

With Magic Johnson and Pat Riley, during Pat's first month as coach of the Lakers *(Los Angeles Times)*

In my office at the Forum, wearing one of my many Missoni sweaters and having my eightieth call of the day *(Wen Roberts/ Photography Ink)*

With Bill Sharman and Jerry Buss in the Forum *(Bob Seidemann/LA Times Magazine)*

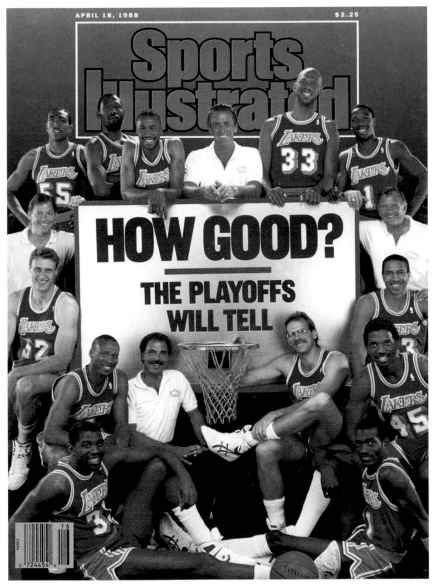

In Jack Nicholson's opinion, the Showtime Lakers provided the best entertainment to be had anywhere in the world for a whole decade. *(Lane Stewart/Sports Illustrated/Getty Images)*

With Rafer Johnson and Oscar Robertson, on a visit back to Rome in 1996

Ryan, Karen, and me, with Jonnie above

Ann Dinardi's surprise ninetieth birthday party in Morgantown, 1996. Rod Hundley is between Ann and me.

I have always viewed Kobe Bryant like a son.

Kobe celebrating the 2001 championship in my old jersey, which he asked to borrow

Without Arn Tellem, I could never have brought Kobe to the Lakers.

If Shaquille O'Neal and I had been in high school together, we would have been best friends. *(Wen Roberts/ Photography Ink)*

Many people forget how much fun they had together. *(Andrew D. Bernstein/NBAE/ Getty Images)*

Phil Jackson, Mitch Kupchak, Shaquille (with his 2000 MVP Award), me, and Jerry Buss *(Andrew D. Bernstein/NBAE/Getty Images)*

Cutting up with Bill Russell *(Wen Roberts/Photography Ink)*

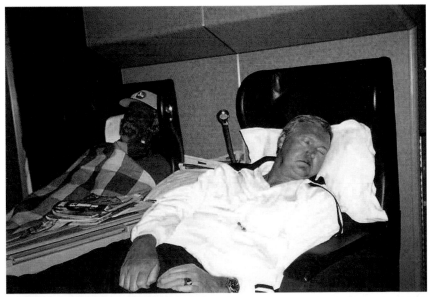

Winning a sleeping competition with Bill on our way back from the 2000 Olympics in Sydney *(Karen West)*

Dedication of parts of Beechurst Avenue as Jerry West Boulevard, with Ann Dinardi and Governor Cecil Underwood (holding sign), August 2000

Outside the Coliseum in Morgantown, 2007 *(ALL-PRO Photography/Dale Sparks)*

With Bootsy Collins in Memphis *(Joe Murphy/NBAE/Getty Images)*

Sharing a private joke with Jack Nicholson at the Staples Center, 2009 *(Kevork Djansezian/Getty Images)*

With Chuck Yeager, guide Wayne Leong, and Barron Hilton in Alaska

My number one "stray"—Bobby Freedman. We eat lunch together once a week and he makes sure I always know my place. *(Marc Sidoti)*

With Karen and her sister, Mary Belton

Turkey hunting with Jim Justice,
owner of the Greenbrier

Jonnie, Mark, Michael, Ryan, and David

Always happy to see Michael Jordan; at the Hall of Fame, 2010 *(Andrew D. Bernstein/NBAE/Getty Images)*

And to have my sons Ryan and Jonnie with me, even though I ruined their weekend

Patricia, Charlie, Hannah, me, and Barbara, October 2010, in St. Albans, West Virginia

Jonnie—playing for my alma mater but very much his own man *(West Virginia Illustrated/Howie McCormick)*

Senior Day, 2011, with Willie and Linda Akers, Jonnie, Ryan, and Karen *(ALL-PRO Photography/Dale Sparks)*

At the end of a long
and sometimes
complicated journey:
Jerry Buss and me,
February 17, 2011
(Garrett Ellwood/
NBAE/Getty Images)

Standing guard outside
the Staples Center,
February 17, 2011
(John W. McDonough/
Sports Illustrated/
Getty Images)

JERRY WEST
LOS ANGELES LAKERS
1960 - 1974

everyone well. (The playoffs are a different matter altogether because everyone's tense. *Everyone.*) I never sat in my office for more than fifteen minutes. I had restless energy; I wanted to go see other people, take everyone's pulse. Hell, I spent more time in Joan McLaughlin's office (Joan was our director of human resources, the mother hen of the Lakers, and someone whose wrong side I *never* wanted to be on) than in my own. That's how you find out things. Elgin Baylor gave me a lot of nicknames, but the one that irritated me even more than Zeke from Cabin Creek was "Louella," after the famous gossip columnist Louella Parsons. Karen says it is fitting, and Mitch Kupchak says he has run into people who have run into me, people I don't even know, and I have shared with them my deepest and darkest worries about the team, that I have essentially told them *everything*. I am not sure how true this is, but this much I can tell you: I do like to know what is going on and I care about people and I ask a lot of questions and sometimes I talk too much.

So, yes, I would go and see Joan, and Claire Rothman, who was in charge of all scheduling for the Forum (like Mary Lou Liebich, Claire and Joan were women I felt I worked for, not the other way around), and I would drop in on Joe McCormack, the chief financial officer, and Jim Perzik, our counsel (who had met me in Atlanta in the middle of the night when we signed Shaquille), and John Black, the head of public relations, and Bob Steiner and Lou Baumeister, both of whom worked closely with Jerry Buss, and I spent more time than anyone ever realized with Lee Moore, who had worked for the Lakers since the 1960s, starting out sweeping floors at the old Sports Arena and rising to a position in security (though, as I never stopped reminding him, he wasn't able to prevent me from being robbed outside the Forum in 1992). Lee was from the same hometown as Bill Russell—Monroe, Louisiana—and he always had advice for me about this ballplayer or that. He would watch players warm up and give me his opinions, strong ones, on what kind of game they were likely to have that night. He would suggest trades to me and he would share gossip. Lee is one of those people I treasure. The sort of person whom everyone else might ignore—John Black was stunned to discover we had a relationship—but whom I looked forward to seeing each and every day. He reminded me of the security guard at Mountaineer Field House who would always say, "Good luck tonight, Jerry," the moment I came in the door. For someone like me, who is a ball of twisted coil before a game, I can't tell you how comforting that was. (When I went to Memphis to run the Grizzlies, Lee always tried to get together with me when he came to town for the national convention of Baptist churches, and whenever I could, we did.)

So one of the problems I had with Phil was this. His office was right near mine and when he would arrive in the morning, he would walk right past and never even bother to wave or duck his head in to say hello. He would later say that he felt the need to stake out his territory, that on top of that he was "a wack job," but I am sure it was more than that. I had had some experience with things like this. More than ten years earlier, Pat Riley, wanting more and more autonomy and power, even wrote a letter to Jerry Buss suggesting that he could coach and do my job at the same time. The reason I know about the letter is that Jerry showed it to me. The difference was this: Pat and I were close and had a long history together; Phil and I had no relationship. None. He didn't want me around, and he had absolutely no respect for me—of that, I have no doubt. (Tex Winter, who created the triangle offense and coached with Phil for years, has spoken about this in an oral history of the team.) In fact, Phil even threw me out of the locker room once, an incident that no one other than Bill Bertka and Mitch and Tex really wants to talk about. After a game, Mitch and I would wait outside the locker room until the coach was finished talking to the players, and then we would go in and I would talk to them individually. On the occasion I speak of, I honestly thought Phil was finished addressing the team, and so I walked in. As soon as I did, Phil barked, "Jerry, get the fuck out. I'm not finished here yet," and I immediately backed away, red-faced. I have never intruded on a coach's territory in that way, never, and I vowed that I would never go in there again, and I didn't. With my personality, I wasn't going to have a confrontation with Phil. I wasn't going to lower myself and get into a pissing contest with him. (Phil's recollection is different; he says he didn't know who it was, that he didn't call me by name, but this is my version — corroborated by Tex, Bill, and Mitch — and I am sticking to it.)

My decision to leave the Lakers at the end of the 1999–2000 season, the season we won our first championship since 1988, was not tied in with, or about, any one thing. I didn't leave because of Phil Jackson and my nonexistent relationship with him (though if I had known the degree to which he didn't want me around, I would have left shortly after he arrived). I didn't leave because of a disastrous meeting that had been held in a hotel in Santa Barbara at the beginning of training camp the previous autumn, a meeting involving Glen Rice and his agent that not only revealed a distressing lack of communication between Jerry Buss, Mitch, and me (which had never happened before in all my years as an executive), but crystallized the moment my incredible feeling for the Lakers began to wane. I was never the same after that. Never. I didn't leave because of Jerry Buss's detaching himself more and more from the day-to-day operations and allowing his son Jim, whom Jerry had asked me to mentor, to have greater involvement in running the organization. I didn't leave over not being paid more money and having to negotiate my contract with Jim Perzik instead of with Jerry directly as I always had done. Though each of these things certainly may have played a part, and together may have created the perfect storm, I left the job because it was not only providing me with zero joy but also affecting—ruining, really—every aspect of my life.

People close to me were worried about my health—my physical, emotional, and mental health—and so was I. After one particularly harrowing weekend in Phoenix in April of 1999, Karen wrote Jerry Buss a letter, a letter I didn't know she had written at the time and only recently learned about.

April 17, 1999

Dear Jerry,

 However inappropriate this letter may seem I am not one to keep silent. I think that you need to be aware of what is going on in the West household, whether it matters to you or not. I just spent the three most painful days of my life with Jerry in Phoenix.

 As I am positive that you know, my husband is a very tormented individual. The greatest source of his torment in the last few years has been the Lakers. That I am sure you also know. But he seemed to have overcome that torment when the two of you worked things out over last summer. I made him promise that he would be happy staying with the Lakers before he agreed on a contract extension and he responded that he had a renewed enthusiasm and that he knew that the correct decision was to stay. He was raring to go. As long as Jerry was happy, I was happy.

 Well, everything has gone to hell. He is a man that if he were suicidal he would be gone. The fact that some major decisions have been made that he did not agree with and that this once most-respected team is now, as he says, the "laughing stock of the league" has put him in a downward spiral that is almost as self-destructive as Rodman.

*I left Phoenix yesterday morning knowing that my life would never be the same. On Wednesday Jerry told me that the only things that he cares about in the world are our children, me and the Lakers. On Thursday evening after the Rodman release he told me that when he got back to LA that he was leaving the Lakers, and he was leaving us. As much as my children live and die for the Lakers and how the Lakers have been our life, I don't care if I ever hear another word about them. I have been hearing for two years from Jerry that he was going to resign, that he can't take it anymore and it basically goes in one ear and out the other. But in our 21 years of marriage he has **never** said that he would leave this family. NEVER.*

I love my husband very much and I love my family very much and he will just devastate us if he leaves. He is on such a self-destructive war path and I don't know where it leads. I think that you and he need to sit down together for a long, friendly talk. Just thought you should know.

Sincerely,
Karen

This letter says as much about Karen as it does about me. Karen will do anything to protect me and our family and she is steely enough to not back down from me when I become totally unreasonable (which is often). She is not one of those wives who always agree with their husbands. She has strong opinions and will air them—even more readily than I will, as a matter of fact. It has not been easy living with me, I know that. When she says she would not pay much attention every time I threatened to leave the Lakers, that was smart of her. If you ride every emotional up and down with someone as crazy as me, it will only make you insane.

The force of her letter doesn't surprise me. That she wrote the letter and never told me doesn't surprise me. But that Jerry Buss never responded to her letter not only surprises me, it disappoints me. It was a delicate time in our relationship and he has expressed since how worried he was about my overall health and well-being.

I hate to talk about money. It is easier for me to ask for money on someone else's behalf than it is for me to ask for myself. My good friend Rod Thorn, who played after me at West Virginia, against me in the NBA, and is now president of the Philadelphia 76ers, thinks I have a coal-mining, company-store mentality, born out of the state we both grew up in: that if you are doing well, the company will reward you. But there's no point in asking because it would be un-Southern and ungracious, and besides, they have all the power anyway. I think there is some truth to what Rod says. Jerry Buss believed that my salary was fair, that I was making (he later told Jonathan) two to two and a half times what any other head of basketball operations was making. But the worst and most hurtful part, honestly, was this: hearing from others during that last year that Jerry had some resentment toward me, that he felt that I got—or took—too much of the credit for the success of the organization, that people tended to forget there was another Jerry around.

I may be many things, but a braggart I am not. That is *not* who I am, and that was never the case. Ever.

7

Wilt and My Urge to Disappear

On the move with Wilt, 1972

During my last year with the Lakers, the death of Wilt Chamberlain in October of 1999 hit me particularly hard. Wilt was only two years older than I was, and when I got word that he was dead, I didn't believe it. In fact, it took nearly fifteen phone calls of my asking people "Is it true?" before I grudgingly accepted that it was. How could someone that strong and that athletic and that imposing be dead at the age of sixty-three? For as long as he played, Wilt was generally considered the greatest athlete in the world. He was also the most sensitive and insecure person I had ever been around. I thought I was sensitive and touchy, but Wilt took sensitivity to another level, constantly feeling unappreciated. As he always loved to say, "Nobody loves Goliath."

I have been around a lot of big men in my life in professional basketball, but Wilt stood out as always being primed for an insult or a slight. He constantly complained that he would give parties at his hilltop home on Mulholland Drive and invite everyone — actually, he would have two parties in an evening: one for married couples and a much later party for singles — but that he often would go uninvited in return. In his book *Wilt,* he singled me out on more than one occasion as being one of the culprits, but I can promise you that Wilt ducked his head in the front door of my home in Brentwood, just off Sunset, on a number of occasions in the early seventies. He often expressed the opinion (as Oscar did) that the media loved me, that in their eyes I could do no wrong, but that he was seen as a villain.

I have so many memories of Wilt, and nearly all of them are

funny ones. I remember during his beach volleyball period that he would arrive in his Rolls-Royce convertible at the Forum right before a game or practice with his light blue nylon shorts on and his flip-flops and sand in his hair. I never understood how he thought he would have enough energy to go out and play, but that was Wilt and he never felt he had to explain or justify anything (he could easily go for days without a real shower, blithely ignoring the deodorant and soap we would put in front of his locker, settling for a sponge bath instead). He of course insisted he was the greatest beach volleyball player of all time, but our teammate Keith Erickson, who actually played volleyball in the 1964 Olympics, said that while Wilt might have been the biggest and brightest star on the beaches of Santa Monica, he wasn't a great player.

He was, however, a great eater. Perhaps the most vivid memory I have of Wilt is from Kansas City, when we were playing the Royals. I got a call from Wilt asking me to come up to his room, but he did not say why. Once I got there, I found him sitting like some sort of Buddha in those blue shorts, wearing nothing but a towel around his neck, and literally surrounded by food from Gates Bar-B-Q—slabs of ribs, pulled pork, one-pound brisket sandwiches, French fries, onion rings, collard greens, hush puppies, sauce, bread to soak it all up with—and two liters of 7-Up, his favorite drink. He wanted me to join him, and I was flattered, but since I knew that I couldn't even get through half of one of those sandwiches, I politely said no. (But if I had joined him, my competitive spirit would have driven me to out-eat him, just as I "raced" Bill Russell to sleep—and won—when we flew back from the 2000 Olympics in Sydney.) That image of Wilt, alone in that hotel room, has never left me, and it is one of the reasons I think of him as perhaps the loneliest person I have ever known.

As for all Wilt's claims of having slept with twenty thousand women? That is such a joke, because he was with me a lot of the time. When his sister Barbara would stop in unannounced to see him, she would go searching for any sign that a female had been there, but she could never find anything, not an article of clothing, not a photograph, nothing. She even asked him about it. "Dippy," she said, "you say in your book that you slept with all these women, but you could have fooled me. I can't find a thing."

When Bill Sharman became coach of the Lakers in 1971, he wanted to institute what he called the morning shootaround—he had the radical notion that he could persuade the team to actually practice on the day of a game. When Bill played for the Celtics, he found himself so restless on game day that he would go to a neighborhood school and shoot baskets in order to relax and stay sharp. He felt the key to getting the team to agree to this was Wilt, who often didn't get out of bed until the afternoon. If Wilt could be convinced that it was a great idea, then it would happen. Bill was right, although Wilt made it clear that if the team started losing, he might have second thoughts. That was the year we won thirty-three games in a row, and the morning shootaround, much as the players dreaded it, became standard practice for all teams. Bill also felt it was important to ask Wilt if he wanted to be co-captain of the team, along with Elgin—that it would have great meaning for him—and asked my opinion. I told Bill that I thought it was a good idea, and it was, but I have often wondered why I was never captain of the Lakers before I retired.

Wilt's funeral made me think a lot about my own mortality. I was having problems with my racing heart. My upset over that meeting in Santa Barbara one month earlier continued to gnaw at me. I was no longer just standing during games; I was leaving them early or watching at home. It didn't matter if we were twenty points ahead or twenty behind. Some nights I would drive up and down the freeway, just like I had after I retired as a player and after the Finals defeat to the Celtics in 1969. One time, I left Staples Center and wound up going to see *Gladiator*, happy to be alone in a dark theater.

I had enjoyed such a close relationship with Jerry Buss, but once we moved to Staples from the Forum, he wasn't around as much, stayed home a great deal of the time, and, frankly, it wasn't as much fun. The close nature of our relationship began to change, and not only did I feel more and more unappreciated, or underappreciated, but my personal demons, rooted in my childhood, were threatening me. The Lakers had been home to me, unlike the home I had grown up in and felt apart from. But now that home was feeling less and less hospitable, and I was sensing that I didn't belong, or wasn't wanted, there anymore, that I had stayed too long at the fair and it was time for me to go.

I don't mean to sound like a crank, but, frankly, it's a shame that so many people coming into basketball today think they know it all. When Jim Buss expressed the opinion, in a *Sports Illustrated* piece about the Buss family, that being a general manager didn't seem like that hard a job, I hardly knew how to react to that, so I didn't. Still, I found the comment laughable and naïve. For nearly every executive coming into basketball now, if a few good things happen, all of a sudden they think they know something their competitors don't. Well, let something bad happen and see how much they really know. In reality, there is so much luck and good fortune involved in running these franchises. So much depends on the people you're working with, on the talent that has been assembled. So many little things make the difference between success and failure, and there's no damn formula. None. It drives me crazy, drives me absolutely crazy, when I read the phrase *this is a model franchise.* Because if you lose one particular player—a player you were fortunate enough to acquire in the first place and build your team around—we'll see what kind of *model franchise* is there. It's also condescending to the other people in the league who work just as hard or harder than they do but don't have the same success in terms of a win-loss record. Every year the NBA crowns a champion. In 2008 it was the Celtics, and everybody talked about what an incredible job they had done, which they had. But what happened to them in the twenty-one years before that, when they didn't win a conference title? After they won the championship in 1986, nothing seemed to work for them. But then, in 2007, the team brings in two veteran players, Kevin Garnett and Ray Allen, to go along with Paul Pierce—most people didn't even know how great he was—and all of a sudden they win it all and they are the smartest people. Hell, they are pretty much the same damn people who were there all that time, and they struggled. Call a franchise *well run,* but get rid of the word *model.*

There have been teams that won the championship that don't even make the playoffs the next year. That's how fragile basketball is. Football too. You lose the wrong one or two players, to injury or retirement (the one opponent no one ever beats is Father Time), and you're common. I have never ever tried to look down on another team and something they may have done because no one really knows the inner workings of a franchise. We may have our own private thoughts about a deal that everyone thinks was particularly one-sided, but publicly you can't be critical because you don't know. In many cases owners have such incredible input that the people who work for them are nothing but caretakers.

I think of Mark Cuban, owner of the Dallas Mavericks, who has done a superb job of building a team and a brand in that city. He challenges the league office, which I think is very important, but I'm just not sure that he's the basketball expert he thinks he is. In fact, there are no "experts"—the most you can hope for is to make the best educated guess. Mark has spent tons of money, as many owners have, but he didn't win a championship—that frustratingly elusive prize—until 2011.

If I knew anything while running the Lakers, it was this: we were always one misstep away from disaster.

On the morning after the Lakers won the 2000 championship against the Indiana Pacers, after a night of not going to the game at all and driving on the Ventura Freeway all the way to Santa Barbara, a hundred miles north (I told my friend Bobby Freedman only to call me if there was good news), I was in my office early, staring blankly, the only light coming from a small Tiffany lamp, and wanting to be anywhere but there.

I didn't attend the press conference two months later, in August of 2000, that announced my departure. It was too emotional a time for me, and much as I liked many members of the media, I didn't feel like answering the inevitable, repetitive questions. A large part of me (and this has always been true) just wanted to vanish into thin air, just wanted to get away from being "Jerry West" and, like Huck Finn, light out for the territory, where I could drift lazily along the margins, anonymous in America. So I took out an ad (in the form of a letter) in the *Los Angeles Times* and headed to Alaska to go fishing.

August 7, 2000

Dear Lakers Fans:

This is a difficult yet happy time for me personally as I retire my position with the Los Angeles Lakers and enter another period of my life, one that will allow me more freedom

*to enjoy my friends and particularly my family, unburdened
with the pressures of the professional athletic business.*

*We have experienced much success and many happy
moments and I would like to thank you for 40 years of support.
There should be many more wonderful moments for the Lakers
franchise to enjoy.*

*My gratitude goes to Shaquille and Kobe for their belief in
the Lakers.*

*A special thank you to all of my teammates, coaches, players,
and associates, particularly Jerry Buss, for allowing me to
continue my association with the Lakers for so many years.
The Lakers have brought me a greater appreciation of all
things in life.*

*I have been blessed with the privilege to play for and work
for the best athletic franchise in all of sports and I will always
treasure the experience. As I watch their progress with great
interest and pride, I will remain their biggest fan.*

Very Sincerely,
Jerry West

I didn't watch the video of that press conference until recently.
John Black, the team's public relations representative, made a few
remarks, and then Mitch was left to face the press alone. Jerry Buss
was not there.

"It was the oddest thing," Mitch told Jonathan not long ago in his
office, "but as well as I think I know him, I don't try to figure him
out and I don't know why he is the way that he is. Not really. It
didn't surprise me in the least that Jerry wouldn't be there—public
environments make him uncomfortable—but I did find it strange
that Dr. Buss wasn't there. I found myself announcing Jerry's

retirement, but I didn't think it was my place. I kept expecting Jerry to walk through the door at any moment, but he was gone. I didn't feel inadequate, but I did feel alone. It was weird, knowing that Jerry wasn't coming in the next day, or the day after that. The funny thing is, I was never really officially told that I would be getting the job. Dr. Buss never called me up and said, 'Mitch, as you may have heard, Jerry's leaving and I would like you to take his spot.' I tried to get him to say that, but our conversations were more like it was assumed I would be taking over. I had other opportunities, but Jerry West always told me not to take them, to be patient.

"I don't think there's anybody that's had a greater impact on my life than Jerry. To this day it's just hard for me to fathom that I have the relationship with him that I do. To this day I don't exactly know why Jerry thought I was the right person to work with him. Yeah, I was going to school, but that doesn't mean you'll be any good at business. Maybe if I was able to say 'I've been scouting for five years,' it would have made more sense. I used to kid Jerry that they needed a roster spot, but they could have cut me and paid me. They didn't have to offer me the job. Maybe Jerry figured, the guy goes to class, you know, he'll show up at the office. I don't really know. What I do know is that Jerry processes information really quickly and makes snap decisions. It took me a while to learn that I had to be really organized because I might only get less than five minutes. I did all the things that he did not have the patience to do—all of the mundane business stuff. He was the kind of guy that had a notepad and would scribble and negotiate and once he was done negotiating, there it would be on a little piece of paper. He was much more of a big-picture person, so I thought we complemented each other very well. From day one, he never tried to protect his turf. He kept on giving me projects and encouraging me to take on more and more responsibility.

"I don't remember him ever expressing disappointment over anything I did. I am sure he had it and he talked to Karen about it, but he never came in and said, 'Mitch, I need to talk to you about something.' When we had that meeting in Santa Barbara with Glen Rice, it was tense and anxiety-filled and nothing was really accomplished. Jeff Wexler, the agent who worked with David Falk, tried to pit me against Jerry, Jerry against Dr. Buss. It was a meeting we should probably never have agreed to.

"When Phil Jackson came to the Lakers, it was not a good mix between him and Jerry. He had just come from an environment where there was an incredible amount of distrust with the GM and great separation, where he had bonded with the players against the world. Phil can be abrupt, but it didn't bother me as much as it bothered Jerry. I guess you could say I had gotten used to that with Kareem, who could walk past you in the airport at six thirty in the morning as if he didn't know you.

"In regard to the whole locker room incident, there is no doubt it set a tone for their relationship. I can't recall *anybody* ever telling Jerry to get out of the locker room.

"Toward the end of that year, Jerry seemed to lose interest and those 'bathroom episodes' didn't happen as much. The flip side to Jerry is that he can get very quiet—which I hadn't seen before—but I really began to notice it in the spring of 2000. He didn't talk about quitting so much, whereas over the previous fourteen years I had heard it fourteen times. From my perspective, knowing Jerry, it could have been something as simple as 'I am not needed here much anymore. This team is set for ten years.' Shaq was twenty-eight, Kobe was twenty-one, you got Rick Fox and Derek Fisher, whom Jerry had drafted the same year we got Shaq and Kobe, and Brian Shaw. All of this is in place and suddenly the challenge is not there. The job was completed, the cupboard was full. Maybe he thought, *I don't want to sit here and not be challenged. They got a coach who has been through it all and doesn't need me to come in and sit and talk about the game and give him my advice.* That's not Phil's way. He'd already won six championships. So maybe that was part of it: the other coaches were always in his office and he was used to giving his advice. Phil didn't need Jerry's advice and wouldn't have wanted it anyway.

"Even though I said at the press conference I would call Jerry to consult with him and he would need to return my call, I wound up not calling him on purpose, other than to periodically check in, because I was always concerned with the direction the conversation might go. I know it bothered him, but I said to myself, *Mitch, if you start calling Jerry every week, it is going to be as if he is running the team and the same problems he experienced a year ago with his anxiety and his health, he will just be experiencing them at home.* So when I did call, I tried to keep the calls generic; otherwise, he would be right back in the middle of it and that is one of the reasons he retired — to get away from it. The other thing, too, is that when you talk to Jerry, it is hard to get a word in edgewise because he does most of the talking. I do remember calling him about Isaiah Rider and tried to keep it simple: 'Jerry, give me the plusses and minuses of this player' — as opposed to saying, 'Do you think we should do this?' And part of not calling was that I wanted to try to do it on my own, even though Jerry set it up nicely for me. But in my mind, I kept thinking back to the morning after the championship and he was in his office with just his Tiffany lamp on and it was dark in there and he was not in a good spot.

"I knew he had the heart thing and that he was taking medication but he didn't really want to talk about it. He would mumble something under his breath about his heart racing around, or his nerves, or his anxiety.

"The hardest thing I had to face after Jerry left was how to deal with guys like Kobe and Shaq on an equal or better-than-equal basis. Jerry was able to do that because he brought them both here. I was okay as a player but how do I relate to Kobe Bryant, you know what I mean? I can try to, and maybe if I talk long enough he will get part of what I am saying, but I am not Jerry West. The fact that he is who he is, and that he brought them here to L.A., he could have worked through most of the issues of those players after he left, and there were lots of issues."

As I sat there in Springfield on the day of Pat Riley's induction into the Hall of Fame, I looked at Mitch and was reminded again how he was thrust into a difficult situation. The team went on to win two more championships, but he didn't have the rapport with Shaquille and Kobe that I did. Had I still been with the Lakers, I would like to believe I could have prevented Shaquille from publicly antagonizing Jerry Buss to the degree that he had. I would have told him that if someone is paying you $120 million, you can't denigrate him like that in the press. If I could have done that, there is a good chance Shaquille wouldn't have left the Lakers after the 2004 season. But I don't know that for sure, much as Mitch and others, including Shaquille (who continues to insist that if I had still been there, he would have still been there), seem to think otherwise.

When Kobe had the encounter with the woman in Colorado in the summer of 2003 and was arrested, Rob Pelinka, his new agent, called to tell me. I will never forget the night in July when that happened, over the Fourth of July weekend, I believe. We were back home from Memphis and there was a lot of family over and no sooner had the news come on the television than the phone rang, changing the evening from festive to somber in an instant. I hadn't contacted Kobe or Shaquille since I'd left for Memphis the year before, because it is considered unethical to stay in touch with players if you are with another team. But there was nothing to prevent them from reaching out to me. That call from Pelinka, telling me what had allegedly occurred and that Kobe wanted to speak with me, reminded me of the time twelve years earlier when I'd learned Earvin Johnson was HIV positive. Then and now, basketball was the last thing on my mind. All I cared about was Kobe's well-being. I told Pelinka to get it settled as quickly as possible. I am not naïve about things like this, but to this day I feel he was set up.

When the tension between Shaquille and Kobe appeared to be at its worst, I recall thinking that this is what I would have done: I would have appealed to both of them and said, "Hey, this does not make either of you look good." If their response had been, "I don't care," I would have said, "No, you should care, because this will affect your future. It will affect your ability to be paid the kind of dollars that you want to be paid. You guys *can't* make this personal." I would have spoken with them both individually and then in a room together. I would have bluntly asked them, "What are you guys trying to accomplish here? Tell me what the hell it is. Do you guys really dislike each other? Is this professional jealousy? What's this about?"

Players of that magnitude have to be praised, and they cannot be pitted against each other. They have to be financially rewarded. That has to be in place. The owner, the coach, and the GM all have to be in full agreement about how the press is going to be dealt with. As much as possible, this kind of thing has to be handled behind closed doors.

But that isn't what happened. They continued to feud and

snipe at each other through the press (Kobe through Ric Bucher of ESPN, Shaquille through the people he frequently spoke with), and the result was Shaquille being traded to Miami at the end of the 2004 season. Phil Jackson was not re-signed and left the team—getting his own comeuppance—but he returned a season later, after having published a book, *The Last Season*, that was highly critical of Kobe. I couldn't have done what Kobe did, but he is more thick-skinned than I am. If I had helped my team win three straight championships, I couldn't have played for a coach who vilified me the way Phil did Kobe in his book. I knew as well as (if not better than) anyone that Kobe could be a handful, but why Phil would do that is beyond me. During the time Kobe and Shaquille played together, Phil would talk about the Lakers being Shaquille's team, and he would say that Kobe had to adhere to that, and then he would start talking (as did Kobe) about how big and out of shape Shaquille was. Phil likes to needle people; he likes to stir the pot a little bit. Some of that is fine, but with two strong personalities like Kobe and Shaquille, I am not sure that was the best approach.

At the end of the 2007 season, a year after Shaquille had helped Miami win a title, Kobe again took his dissatisfaction public and in a different direction, lobbying for my return and being viciously critical of the way Mitch was running things. I would never have gone back to the Lakers under such circumstances— not that Jerry Buss would have wanted me back anyway—and I would never have done anything to undermine Mitch, who, to his credit, remained stoic in the face of Kobe's relentless criticism of him and his demands to be traded.

In the end, I was glad I went to Springfield. I was glad to see that Kurt Rambis hadn't lost his sense of humor or his sense of how perfectly he fit his role during those Showtime years (even if he remained angry that I hadn't fought harder to have the "interim coach" label removed when the decision was made to go for Phil Jackson). After all, he was a guy who could easily have not been in the league at all. He was a guy who, with his friends, used to go up to Wilt's house on Mulholland and knock on the door and be a pain in the ass and do everything he could to get Wilt to come outside. But he battled and he scraped and did the dirty work and made himself invaluable; he swallowed his pride and stayed with the organization. Kurt may be weird, but then again, as my son Ryan has pointed out, so am I.

In the months after his induction in Springfield, Pat Riley and I exchanged some heartfelt letters. He was so grateful I had come that his gratitude bordered on being embarrassing, but that's okay. We are both at very reflective points in our lives.

In his Miami Heat office some time after that, looking back over his nine years of coaching the Lakers, Pat expressed to Jonathan that he should have acted more humbly overall.

"I let our success go to my head, me thinking I'm better than God, and I had actually forgotten that Jerry was the one who made it possible for me to be there, and he was always there for me. He was the one who convinced Jerry Buss that I was the right choice, that the 'interim' label should be removed. He was the one who said, 'It's you, Pat. It's you. It's your opportunity.' I know he didn't like that I promoted one of my books during the playoffs one year, and I suspect my being on the cover of *GQ* also gave him some pause. He and I were nonconfrontational with each other, but I knew.

"The truth is, I had gotten too full of myself, too big for my britches, and the players didn't like it either. At the end of the 1990 season, even though I had won Coach of the Year, it was time for me to go. We got beat by Phoenix in an ugly series and I was at my all-time worst. I put a fist through a mirror. I was trying to get my team fired up, but I was doing more yelling and screaming than I ever had, and I could feel the whole thing slipping away and could feel the players' indifference to me. I didn't want to accept that it was time for me to go—you always want to be a member of 'the club,' to be inside the protective bubble of the Laker family—but it was, and nobody was telling me otherwise.

"My sense is that this is what happened with Jerry ten years later. But unlike with me, that should *never* have happened. Jerry and Chick Hearn were the taproot of the Lakers. He had been there since 1960. Everything good that happened there Jerry had a hand in. He built two championship teams—ours and the ones with Kobe and Shaq. And in between, he put a competitive team on the floor, bringing in guys like Sedale Threatt, Nick Van Exel, Cedric Ceballos, Elden Campbell, and Eddie Jones. His pursuit of Shaq in 1996 and his getting Kobe Bryant (not to mention Derek Fisher and Robert Horry and Rick Fox) was unbelievable. He knew, having lost to Bill Russell so many times, that getting a dominant center like Shaq was crucial, the linchpin. He needed to feel appreciated for what he had done, and I don't think he did. Frankly, I feel they disrespected him and I think he's still really hurt, disappointed, probably even angry at what happened with the Lakers. How did they let it end? Perhaps he created such a negative feeling with the Buss family or with Phil or with 'I'm going to quit' so many times that they eventually threw their hands up in the air. But in the end, I don't think he was taken care of in the way he should have been taken care of. I don't know what he was earning, but I believe the guy did something unprecedented that should have really been rewarded. He did it. It was *his* vision, *his* mind. Jerry West is the person who for forty years was synonymous with L.A., not only as a player but as a general manager and an architect of two championship teams.

"When I think of Jerry, I think of all the times we used to sprint up and down the steps of Fourth Street in Santa Monica, right off San Vicente, getting ready for the next season. He was a 1990s player in the 1960s: he had big legs, great leaping ability, long arms, big hands. I think of how hard he took losses, of how he would be so fucking miserable that, one time in Kansas City when he was coaching, we were out on the balcony of our hotel, fifteen floors up, and he was looking over and I simply said, 'Don't do it.' I have never seen anyone more competitive in my life. If he was good at something, like golf, he thought he should be better at it. He held the course record at Bel-Air for the back nine, for the longest time. *Twenty-eight.* He could have played the pro tour, but he didn't think so. I will never forget him saying to me, 'There's no way I could ever have made it, because I act too crazy, too emotional, have this thing *in me,*' whatever that *in me* was that could not tolerate anything else but being perfect.

"I think of the times after the morning shootaround, when we would go in the back door of Westwood Drugs by UCLA, where Hollis Johnson ran the lunch counter, and we would sit on those milk-carton crates in the back and eat cream custards and hamburgers, just hanging out. My wife, Chris, and I used to do a lot of things with Jerry and Jane, were often over to their house on Bristol, got to know their three sons. To me, it looked like the ideal marriage, seemed like they had everything anybody would ever want. He had this incredible game and this fame and this marriage and these children and this wonderful house and this absolute, universal respect as a player, but, obviously, there was something wrong there. After he sublet my house on Bowling Green the year I was in Phoenix, I came back and found, in the little guesthouse behind the house, an absolute mound of stuff—clothes, old uniforms, memorabilia, pictures, golf clubs, a golf bag that had his name on it—some of the stuff that Jane had dumped in the driveway. I asked him what he wanted me to do with it and he said, 'I don't care what you do with it. Keep it, throw it away, sell it, I don't care.' So I kept it for a long time, up in our attic. Now I think it is in one of the storage bins I have here in Miami. One day I have to go down there and look at it and give it to him. He might like it. It could be worth some money. In that respect, Jerry and I are very different. Every one of these basketballs in my office—*every single one of them*—has meaning to me because of all of the people involved in the different situations over all of the years. I am not saying that Jerry cares any less than I do, I am not saying that at all. He may be less sentimental when it comes to personal mementos, but we are both addicted to the game and it is a very hard thing to walk away from."

8
The Dark Spot in the Wood

Scouting in Las Vegas, December 1998

W hen I left the Lakers in the summer of 2000, it felt like the greatest relief in the world and was similar to how I felt when I retired as a player: that I was escaping confinement, that I was free. For a long time, I didn't watch any NBA games, just needed to be away from it, all of it. Wanting to have some sort of daily routine, though, I became a chauffeur for my youngest son, Jonnie, taking him to school in the mornings. We would sit and listen to Howard Stern on the radio and laugh our asses off. The pure simplicity of those moments felt good—to be that unburdened, to reconnect with my family.

But it didn't last.

The Lakers were the only thing I had ever known. I worked for a franchise that had given me opportunities to do things that I never dreamed I could do. I never had a clue that I could be successful at anything other than being a player. That Jerry Buss showed such confidence and trust in me is something that, on some level, still touches me and amazes me. I never really thought about anything other than winning. And I was just so caught up in winning that I didn't even enjoy the winning. Because as soon as you win, you immediately start worrying about next year. And winning in Los Angeles is not like winning somewhere else. You are not only expected to be in the playoffs, you are expected to contend for a championship. It takes, as I have said, a lot of good fortune and a lot of good timing; things have to work a certain way before you can get to that level. I had been to the NBA Finals nine times as a player and had only won once. So I knew.

These were dark times for me. Very dark. Beyond feeling

unappreciated or underappreciated, I could see, as I reflected back, that I also felt unacknowledged. Just not being verbally acknowledged for my hard work and dedication to what I cared most about. I now know it is one of the reasons I threatened to walk away so many times—that I, unfairly, not only expected other people to care as much as I did, but I also cared about their approval too damn much. It is also possible that even if it had happened, even if I had gotten the verbal acknowledgment I am talking about, it wouldn't have been enough, given my earlier comment and sad realization that I have a hole in my heart, a hole that can never be filled.

The word I keep coming back to is *addicted*. I was addicted to what I did. Too much so. And I just didn't know any other way of life. The way I sort of protected myself was through this enormous passion I had for what I was doing—trying to be an athlete, then running the team. And I think anyone who participates in things to this degree needs to understand that there are certain things our bodies are addicted to. And if it's the wrong addiction, you're screwed. The only cure for it is to go cold turkey.

I think we all take different approaches to living our lives. My life has been about different passions, but the one great one, the one that has driven me, has been basketball. It's a sick passion, but it's a passion. Sometimes when you feel so isolated from your family, where do you go to seek satisfaction? Where do you go? You go inward. Other people can help ease tensions, can help ease some things in your life, but ultimately they don't resolve your problems. You have to do that yourself. And if you don't, you're stuck. I have never looked to someone else to fix my insecurities. It's no doubt one of the reasons I have never been serious about pursuing any sort of therapy.

At Karen's urging, I went a few times, but I felt there was no way that any therapist could understand my particular torment and also felt in some respects they were sicker than I was. I didn't feel comfortable there. I was exposing myself to somebody I didn't even know. You hope to build a relationship with the person, but they don't know you. I felt awkward and it felt futile, that no particular good was served by me going there, that it was too difficult to try to unscramble something by mere talking. I know people who have been going for years, and I don't see any difference in how they feel about themselves. Doesn't seem like it has been any magic elixir for them. I also felt it was a crutch, something I should be able to handle myself and get through. The problems were almost always related to sports, almost always related to basketball. Very little to do with me personally, but then again, who knows? I'm never sure what the real answer is.

There are these protective devices that we use in our lives. Professional athletes, people who compete, have their minds wired a certain way. We are not people who are always joyous or happy. The thing that separates all of us, not just athletes, is our individual traits, the things that hold our interest, the people we feel good about. I love people. I do. But I also don't make friends easily. I wish I could. I hear people say, "Oh, here's my friend here, here's my friend there," and I never completely understand it or trust it.

In terms of down periods in my life, it's interesting what I have had to experience to get through them, how often I wake up in the morning and feel as if I don't care if I live another day (as I did that time in Phoenix, which in part prompted Karen to write that letter), and I wonder why I feel that way. Into the darkness, that's where I go, into the darkness, and then trying to get through these minefields is an intriguing battle in and of itself.

In the course of doing this book, I began reading William Styron's *Darkness Visible: A Memoir of Madness* to try to get a better understanding of—and insight into—what I have struggled with since childhood. You feel as if you are alone, you feel like things are hopeless, you feel lost. Sometimes I don't even know how I function. I don't. It's like I'm fighting an enemy I can't even see. And the real enemy is myself. Obviously it's about self-esteem, at least some of it. Why would someone like Ernest Hemingway kill himself? Why? Because he was a tormented soul. I have known families in which someone kills himself and the surviving members say, "How could he do this to me?" How could he do it? I can see where it would be easy to do it. People say it's a coward's way out. I say just the opposite:

> Of the many dreadful manifestations of the disease, both physical and psychological, a sense of self-hatred—or, put less categorically, a failure of self-esteem—is one of the most universally experienced symptoms, and I had suffered more and more from a general feeling of worthlessness as the malady had progressed.

When I read this, I thought back to the confrontation with my father when I told him, "This is going to stop," and to the time that David died, and to my starting to have feelings that weren't what you would consider normal, for someone of that age anyway. Utter despair. Wondering if I am going to make it through the day, or how am I going to make it tomorrow? This is something that followed me for my whole life—as an athlete, as an executive, and personally. This whole mix of self-hatred, failure, and low self-esteem plagued me even when I was playing at a high level and getting pleasure from it. It's something I coped with, and something I still cope with.

I loved David, but the fact that he was held in such high esteem in our household made me feel that maybe I didn't measure up. I wasn't jealous of him, but it was a lot to live up to. David was like calm water, and I am anything but. To watch how he conducted himself and handled himself, to see someone that young be that mature, was pretty amazing. It was as if he had an aura about him. You *wanted* to go and talk to him. He had such an easy way about himself. He was going to do the right thing, not the wrong thing. I, on the other hand, was quite defiant, but I didn't start off that way. Circumstances had a lot to do with my becoming like that.

I used to ask myself all the time, *What did I do wrong? What did I do wrong for this to happen? Why?* I almost felt like I was being picked on — for what reason, I don't know. I didn't bother anyone. If my parents wanted me to do something, I did it. I was busy all the time doing what boys do — hunting, fishing, playing basketball — like one of those Rocket Boys that Homer Hickam wrote about in his book of the same name, a book that I completely identified with when I read it (later made into the movie *October Sky*). What on earth is wrong with that?

Kids should be playful. They should have some joy in their lives, and that certainly wasn't the case in our uncertain household. I knew things were difficult financially, and I wondered how we were going to survive, especially when I looked around and everything seemed so bleak and I felt this despair, felt forlorn. I felt it as an adult even when my life was good. But I learned how to get through the dark times.

Years later when I went to New York to accept the award for being the MVP of the 1969 Finals, my sense of self-worth was so low I didn't feel entitled to it. I didn't care how I had played; we hadn't won. I would *never* have voted for myself. I must have done something right, but it was still embarrassing to me that I received it.

Styron wrote of going to Paris to accept an award that he felt he didn't deserve. What came with the award was a check for $25,000, which he lost, and left him wondering if he had intentionally lost it as a result of not feeling worthy to receive it.

I believe in the reality of the accidents we subconsciously perpetrate on ourselves, and so how easy it was for this loss to be not loss but a form of repudiation, an offshoot of that self-loathing (depression's premier badge) by which I was persuaded that I could not be worthy of this prize, that I was in fact not worthy of any of the recognition that had come my way in the past few years.

When I become depressed, Karen stays clear of me. I am barely able to function and am only able to keep going because of the enormous drive I have always had. But trying to concentrate—what Styron calls "the luxury of concentration"—is almost impossible, it's ridiculous. I have to get away from the noise and the chatter of daily life. But what often brings me out of it—and, boy, does it feel good to snap out of it—is basketball, the one area of my life where I have always felt most comfortable and most engaged. And yet what I find so daunting is my inability to function and find that same sort of peaceful place in other areas. Playing golf, playing cards, and being alone in the woods come closest. Or the times in my childhood when my neighbor Francis Hoyt would take me on trout fishing trips, trips that felt like journeys to the moon. My father certainly wasn't going to take me. He had no interest in what I did with my life. None. My brother Charlie would take me to lunch in Charleston every so often (he worked there and I would take the bus to meet him), and a friend named Butch had a TV and I would go over and watch boxing at his house on Friday nights.

While I was able to rise and function normally during the earliest part of the day, I began to sense the onset of the symptoms at midafternoon or a little later—gloom crowding in on me, a sense of dread and alienation and, above all, stifling anxiety.

In the mornings I would go to work and feel really refreshed. Both when I was playing and as an executive, if it was a game day, I would follow a strict, unvarying routine of taking a nap and eating at a specific time and then taking my own route to the arena, avoiding lights whenever possible, my own form of "blue highways." Particularly as a player, game days were special; my concentration was most acute and nothing disturbed it, *nothing*. Even if it seemed like the whole world was exploding around me, I was able to block everything out. But when I was no longer playing, the evenings at home seemed like the darkest periods to me. My home should have been just as much a sanctuary as the court was, but it often wasn't. When things should be fun and exciting, when things are going good, hell, I might have a stretch of melancholy that engulfs me and lasts for two weeks. I do know this: if I'm completely idle, if I'm not engaged in something or feeling that I am contributing to something, that's a dangerous spot to be in for someone like me. That's why I often feel like a man on the run, fleeing something that is always trying to chase me and hunt me down. It might be a mean dog or it might be the Manson Family or a job that's become all-consuming, but in reality, I have come to see, it really is myself. The high opinion others may have of Jerry

West, whoever they may think he is, has never been shared by me, not in any consistent or self-satisfied way. I don't allow it.

For as long as I can remember, people have either wondered why it is that I don't seem as happy as perhaps I should, as content as perhaps I should—or they have expressed the outright hope that I could "find happiness," find some form of peace. On Jerry West Night at the Forum in March of 1971, Bill Russell made a surprise appearance, something I have still not gotten over forty years later, and said that that was his ultimate wish for me—to be happy. Elgin Baylor told me not long ago that he hopes I can find peace, that I shouldn't be too obsessed with my own mortality, which I adamantly feel I am not. Michael Jordan said that even he, whose competitiveness was greater than anybody's, was able to come to terms with losses by viewing things in a religious vein—that "it wasn't my time." Everyone always thinks that it is the six Finals losses to the Celtics in the 1960s that is a permanent emotional albatross around my neck, an albatross that I have never been able to rid myself of. I always felt as if there were something more I could have done and should have done, a remark that I realize sounds very egotistical, a remark that Bill Russell always reacts to in the same way: there was nothing more the Lakers could have done, the Celtics were the better team and we were not going to defeat them. He doesn't just say it flat out. He says it flat out and then he cackles, perhaps the most recognizable sound in all of sports. He knows how to push my buttons, but I try not to let it show (and probably do a bad job of it). Bill is the greatest winner of all time, bar none. Eleven championships in thirteen seasons. You got to be kidding me.

When the Lakers won the championship in 1985, *in Boston, on the parquet floor* (a mantra that Bill Bertka never tires of repeating, huge grin on his face), that victory probably meant more to the franchise than any before or since; the championship ring of 1985 is worn by more players from the Showtime era than any other, and five were won in all, from 1980 to 1988.

Quite a few demons were extinguished that day. I was back home in Los Angeles—I hardly ever traveled with the team and hadn't since 1983 because I was convinced I would bring bad luck, another superstition and quirk of mine—but the joy I felt is, like depression, ironically, almost impossible to put into words. Nonetheless, this dilemma of mine—of not being able to find a resting place for the losses to the Celtics in my era, of constantly feeling there was something more I could have done to produce a different outcome—was something I even talked to John Wooden about when I went to visit him at his condominium in the San Fernando Valley (a place so chock-full of stuff and mementos it could be a damn museum, for Christ's sake). I asked him why he thought this was, why I couldn't put those defeats in some sort of perspective.

John and I met not long after I came to Los Angeles and joined the Lakers in 1960. We were introduced by Hollis Johnson, and we used to have breakfast or lunch from time to time, sitting on the same milk-carton crates in the back of Westwood Drugs where I would later sit with Lew Alcindor, Pat Riley, Gail Goodrich, and others, two small-town, everyday guys shooting the breeze, not quite believing our good fortune, always knowing it could end tomorrow. I have always loved hanging out in places where I can just be Jerry, and this place, and Hollis (whom I often went fishing with, along with Darrall Imhoff, one of my teammates), became very important to me.

My West Virginia team had played UCLA once, and I had even yelled something profane at John during the heat of the game (which I felt he'd provoked me into doing, by the way), something that was very uncharacteristic of me, but we weren't really introduced, you could say, until we started going to Hollis's.

"Jerry," he began slowly, his Midwestern accent still evident after nearly a century of life, his eyes peering out from behind his professor's glasses like a wise old owl's. "When your team won," he wanted to know, "did you take all the credit?" "No, Coach, of course not," I immediately said. "Well, then, Jerry, when your team lost, there is no reason for you to take all the blame."

"I hear what you are saying, Coach," I said, "but when I look at this wall in front of me" — filled with framed photos of the ten UCLA championship teams in twelve years he had been in charge of during his nearly thirty-year tenure at the school, "I don't see a lot of losses up there."

He smiled at that.

What Coach Wooden said certainly made sense. He was a sensible, logical guy. But whether I, who didn't really fit that category, could ever come to terms with, and accept, his straightforward point of view was another matter.

When I start reliving the past, it seems like such a miracle that somebody from my background would be able to be in the NBA, function, and make a lifetime career for himself. And so my experience in Los Angeles was about trying to grow up and trying to be someone, to do something that I loved to do as a kid, something that empowered me to feel good about myself: I was playing against the best players in the world and I was playing effectively. It was a feeling of euphoria.

Retracing my steps in California, as I did not long ago, was a poignant experience and an interesting parallel of sorts to the trips I took in West Virginia. Jonathan and I drove to the Sports Arena, where I'd first played in the Los Angeles Classic less than a year before coming to the Lakers (the team stayed at the Ambassador Hotel, the same place where Bobby Kennedy would be fatally shot less than a decade later), and found two guys in an office on a slow Thursday afternoon.

"Hi," I said, "my name is Jerry West. I used to spend some time in this building a long time ago. I was wondering if it would be okay if we looked around."

They didn't say anything at first, but then they smiled. I don't think they knew what to make of my sense of humor.

"Sure, Mr. West, go right ahead," one of them said.

The arena where John F. Kennedy became the 1960 Democratic nominee shortly before I came to town was, at one time, state-of-the-art, with escalators and such quirky touches as an attendance counter, affectionately known as the Crowd-O-Meter. Now the place was run-down and ghostlike, and so dark it was hard to see. I expected them to turn the lights on, but they didn't. As we made our way around, it all came flooding back. The Crowd-O-Meter was still there; it had counted around four thousand or so fans when the Lakers first came to town. Pretty paltry. I don't think there is an athlete alive who doesn't like to go into buildings where there is excitement, and what brings excitement is the fans, their involvement with the team, their enthusiasm for the team, but when we first arrived in Los Angeles, there wasn't much of that. All anyone cared about were the Dodgers (who had come west from Brooklyn two years earlier and won the World Series in their second season) and the Rams, both of which played right next door at the Coliseum and overshadowed us. We were on the last page of the sports section. A lot of people who came would root for the other team — particularly for the Celtics or the Knicks, as there were so many transplanted Easterners here. In order to drum up interest, the players would drive up and down the city streets in an open flatbed truck (if there had been hay in it, it would have been like a hayride), coaxing people on a loudspeaker to come out and watch us play, or we would give clinics at Sears using makeshift baskets, and Jane and our first child, David, would occasionally come along. Slowly but surely, the numbers on the Crowd-O-Meter crept higher and higher, and celebrities such as Pat Boone and Doris Day began coming on a regular basis. But the real reason for the spike, in my opinion, had less to do with our performance on the court than with the hiring of Chick Hearn to do the play-by-play in March of 1961, right in the middle of our playoff series against the St. Louis Hawks. Before you knew it, four thousand became fifteen thousand, and we slowly made our way to the front page.

I haven't said much about Chick Hearn so far because I've been saving the best for last, as the saying goes, for near the end. There is no question that Chick had so much to do with enriching the image of the Lakers, but he was also responsible for further elevating Elgin Baylor's career and helping enormously to make mine. Even if Elgin Baylor was the one who came up with Zeke from Cabin Creek—I say *if* because I have never been entirely sure— Chick was the one to give it currency. He was definitely the first one to call me "Mr. Clutch." And he was the one who said he had never seen a player take a loss harder or allow it to linger longer. He didn't think I would last very long as a coach. He felt that I would be extremely impatient and would hold my players to an unreasonably high standard. As it turned out, he was right about all of that.

Chick (his given name was Francis Dayle) was from the Midwest, from Aurora, Illinois, and he never lost his common touch and his common sense. His work ethic was second to no one's; he would be at the arena at three on game days and was preparing at home well before that, often rehearsing in front of a mirror. He came up with expressions—Chickisms—that were unique and made everything about the game even more special: *Air ball. He got caught with his hand in the cookie jar* (a reaching foul). *Finger roll. It's garbage time! Throws up a brick. Throws up a prayer. The game's in the refrigerator, the door is closed, the lights are out, the eggs are cooling, the butter's getting hard, and the Jell-O's jiggling. Triple-double* (in terms of points, rebounds, and assists in a single game). And perhaps his most famous: *Slam dunk!*

But Chick was far more than the play-by-play Voice of the Lakers, the Godfather of Talking, perched at the Forum in his Chick's Nest where he had "a word's-eye view." He had a hand in personnel decisions and was a vice president. When I played and coached, he made our road trips special, joking and carrying on and playing cards and keeping everybody loose. If he had a few drinks, which he liked to do, he was one of the funniest men I ever met (along with Richard Pryor and Don Rickles). We traveled commercial back then, in coach. One time Chick was sitting next to a much older lady who could hardly hear, and he started lying to her that he was a war ace who had shot down a hundred German planes, and she said, "My God," and he said, in a whisper, "You can't hear a word I've said," and she again said, "My God, what an incredible man," and on and on it went. There was nobody, I mean *nobody*, who didn't come in for kidding, but he wasn't so thin-skinned that he couldn't take it in return. Like me, Chick was secretive and humble (which didn't mean we didn't have healthy egos) and ever the escape artist. In fact, we often competed to see who could exit from some function first without being conspicuous about it (even if the event was honoring one of us). We had private arrangements with all the parking valets. If I saw him the next day, he might say, "I beat you last night, didn't I?" and I would respond, "Next time you won't."

We were, for better or worse, company men, lifers; he lasted two years longer with the Lakers than I did. In Chick's case, in my opinion, he sacrificed his career for the Lakers. He was with NBC for about ten years, but he could have been even bigger than he was, like Keith Jackson. His relationship with Jack Kent Cooke was better than mine, although his wife, Marge, said he threatened to quit a number of times but Cooke wouldn't let him. He once went to visit Cooke in Washington (Cooke also owned the Redskins) and Cooke asked him how much money he was making. When Chick told him, Cooke said, "My God, Chick, that's all they're paying you?" "Mr. Cooke," Chick replied, "you signed me to this contract."

It was priceless.

As I continued to make my way around the sports arena, I was pleased to see that the Wall was still there—the one where Lou Mohs, my first general manager, would measure the reach of those players with long arms, guys like Bill Russell and Wilt Chamberlain and Nate Thurmond and myself—though the marks had long since vanished. I walked some more and suddenly I detected, as if it were yesterday, Fred Schaus's voice, saw myself stewing on the bench as a rookie, heard Fred stomping his foot on the ground (the reason he was called the Stomper) and arguing with the referees (he was also called Big Beef because his nose would get so red while doing so). I played in this building for seven and a half seasons, slightly more than half of my pro career, and I remember how much fun it was to have my son David be one of the team's ball boys, something that would never happen today.

Once we left the building, I drove through neighborhoods that have always been predominantly minority. When the Watts riots in 1965 took place, not far from there, a lot of the buildings were burned to the ground and there was a lot of looting.

I drove on to Mar Vista, the neighborhood where Jane and I bought our first house, on the corner of Rose and Butler, and I can't get over how minuscule the house looks. At the time, it seemed so large, even for a family of five.

A few minutes later, I pulled into the parking lot of the Forum, the "Fabulous Forum," as it was popularly called, the House that Jack Kent Cooke Built, one of the best and most intimate arenas you could ever imagine. From the end of 1967 until the fall of 1999, when the team began playing at Staples, this was my home away from home (with the exception of the two years after I retired and before I became the coach). Six championships were won during that time, the first being the 1972 team that I was on in the twilight of my career.

I come into the building and walk into the arena, and the memories come rushing back. I still see those balloons up in the rafters in May of 1969, and the USC marching band, who were all ready to play "Happy Days Are Here Again" but never did. I see the area where Cooke and then Jerry Buss would entertain friends—Jerry's playpen, filled with every stunning young girl in town—and the staircase which would lead down to the owner's office. I walk into that office and remember the time I told Mr. Cooke (who once described his life as "better than any F. Scott Fitzgerald novel") to go screw himself and slammed the door. I was coaching then, and he kept demanding that I play the players he wanted me to play. I also recall the time he phoned down while a game was going on and told my friend Lon Rosen, a Laker intern then, something similar, and I told Lon to relay this message: go to hell. Even though I have had my share of problems with authority figures, beginning with and mainly because of my father, I always try to be respectful (even when I don't really feel like it), but when I feel a line gets crossed, I speak my mind.

Thinking more about my tempestuous relationship with Cooke takes me back to a night in December of 1977, the night that Kermit Washington punched Rudy Tomjanovich of the Houston Rockets, a moment so traumatic and momentous that John Feinstein wrote an entire book about it. I didn't see what happened, it occurred so quickly. Kareem Abdul-Jabbar, to this day, reminds everyone whenever the subject is raised that it was Kevin Kunnert who started the fight in an encounter with him, that Kermit was just defending himself. (In fact, earlier in the season, Kareem and Kent Benson of the Milwaukee Bucks had gotten into it, and Kareem wound up with a broken hand.) There was a lot of fighting in the league at that time—as well as a lot of drug use. A lot. It was one of the reasons that fans got turned off to the NBA during that period and why the entrance of Earvin Johnson and Larry Bird into the league in 1979 was considered the beginning of a new era.

But what happened that night stood out from everything else. Rudy's blood was everywhere and he was lying on the floor, unconscious, his skull fractured. I had never seen anything that awful and sickening in my life. Karen's parents were sitting across from the Laker bench and saw everything. My face went ashen when I looked at Rudy and when I got home that night, I phoned Karen and told her that I didn't want to coach another game. I had just gone through an awful divorce and now I wanted to divorce myself from basketball.

Kermit, whose game had improved immeasurably by working with Pete Newell, was a great kid, one of the hardest-working players on the team. I never had to get on him. He played tough defense, was a fierce rebounder, and took a lot of pressure off

Kareem. He was immediately suspended for sixty days, but I knew that Mr. Cooke would get rid of him as soon as possible, regardless of the facts, and he did, less than three weeks later. It was going to be a public relations nightmare and Cooke was not going to stand by Kermit. If Kermit had been white and Rudy had been black, would it have been a different story? I often wonder about that. The Lakers were sued and I had to give depositions in Houston and the team wound up settling with Rudy for a large amount. I always found it ironic that Rudy wound up coaching the Lakers for a year, the year that Phil Jackson's contract wasn't renewed after the 2004 season.

Red Auerbach acquired Kermit for the Celtics (his daughter knew Kermit's wife in college) and my admiration for Red, which was always great, only increased. Kermit continued playing, and playing well, for a number of teams after that, and he now oversees a program that does tremendous work in Africa, in schools in the slums of Nairobi (long before the NBA Cares program ever came into being), but that night at the Forum, sadly and wrongly, will be the thing that most people think of when they hear the name Kermit Washington.

One of my biggest regrets is that I didn't take more of a stand against Cooke on Kermit's behalf when this happened. And I regret that I never told Kermit how I really felt, that for me it was one of the lowest points of my career in basketball. I hated the fact that people formed an opinion of Kermit and they didn't really know him. They didn't know him at all. I felt helpless at the time, because no matter what anyone said or did, it wasn't going to make a difference. In everyone's mind, he was guilty, guilty, guilty, and yet I didn't make enough of an effort to talk to Cooke. I resented Kermit's being described as someone out of control, a thug, when I knew him to be so different, as did Pete Newell. You couldn't defend what had happened, but the aftermath seemed so predetermined. He never came to practice after that. He disappeared.

It's funny, strange even, how this one building came to symbolize so many things in my life. A year after the 1969 Finals, I made that sixty-three-foot shot against the Knicks that, as I have mentioned, only tied Game Three of the Finals, a game we then lost in overtime. Had the three-point shot been in existence (which didn't happen until 1979), maybe we would have won and gone on to win the championship. But things are as they are.

When they held Jerry West Night in March of 1971 at the Forum—something that had been planned well before I sustained a serious knee injury and was lost for the remainder of that season—I was on crutches, and my mother and my brother Charlie flew out from West Virginia. I wasn't sure why Jack Cooke was doing this, as I wasn't even retired yet. Letters and one particular telegram came in from all over and I was overwhelmed and embarrassed by all the attention. The telegram was from the president, Richard Nixon, who said he "found it easy to see why your professional career brings such pride to the city that honors you. But it is even easier to understand the special place you have won in the hearts of your fellow citizens for the way in which you have enhanced your skill in the game by an equally admirable reputation for service to others." Ronald Reagan, then governor of California, sent a letter, as did the governor of West Virginia and its two senators. But the letter from Jack Cooke, even now, is hard to read:

Dear Jerry,

Apart from the magnificent contributions you have made to the success of the Lakers through the years, I count it as one of

*the great good fortunes that our association, rather than that
of player and owner, has been more a relationship between
friends.*

*You have been and always will be a real pro, Jerry. No
athlete I have met could pass you in deportment, on and off
the court, in competitive zeal and in dedication to the game
and the team. You have been an inspiration to the Lakers,
an inspiration to our fans, and an inspiration to me.*

*This is your night, Jerry. I know it embarrasses you, all
this fuss. But no Laker ever has been more deserving of such an
honor. You have earned it, so enjoy it.*

*You have been something extremely special to basketball
and to the Lakers and will continue to be in the years to come.*

As ever,

Jack Kent Cooke

The letter pains me because there is such a disconnect between
what he wrote and what our relationship became just two and a
half years later when I held out. His final insult to me—in the
form of another untruth—was in 1979, the year he sold the team,
the Forum, the Los Angeles Kings, and a thirteen-thousand-acre
ranch to Jerry Buss for millions upon millions of dollars, a deal so
complicated that the best financial minds are still trying to untan-
gle and make sense of all its elements. I had just stepped down
from coaching and was helping to advise the team about the
upcoming draft. We had the first pick, the result of a deal a few
years earlier that had sent Gail Goodrich to the New Orleans Jazz.
Everyone was talking about Earvin Johnson and Larry Bird, but I
thought that Sidney Moncrief of Arkansas was pretty impressive
as well. Still, I knew, as I wrote earlier, that players had to be
viewed as assets—basketball was a business, and it could be a

cruel one—and that you couldn't be so enamored of one player that you didn't consider a lot of other factors. I liked Earvin Johnson, I liked him a lot, as did everyone. He played with a personality and a flair that was impossible to resist.

But I *never* said that I didn't think the Lakers should take him with their pick—which is what Cooke didn't tell the truth about, especially when he was talking with Jerry Buss, who wanted me to stay on as coach, giving Earvin the sense that maybe the Lakers had some doubt about him. I simply suggested that we should keep all our options open to the end. No one could know for sure that a player of his size would be the perfect fit at point guard. Hindsight is always a wonderful thing. A genius one minute is a dumb-ass the next. There is a whole group of guys I like to call the After-Drafters, the guys who take no notes so there is no evidence of what they really thought about a particular player and why.

But in the end, it didn't matter: Jerry Buss was adamant that the Lakers take Earvin because Jerry wasn't buying just a basketball team, he was buying the Lakers as a form of high-level entertainment, Hollywood-style, including scantily clad Laker Girls and Dancing Barry. By centering on a player whose infectious smile was so unique, Jerry was certain the team would draw people from miles around. Had Jack Kent Cooke balked at this, the deal would not have gone through and there would have been no Showtime.

Depression runs in families. My sister Barbara suffers mightily from it; my sister Patricia became depressed as a result of a terrible marriage; and my sister Hannah was deeply affected for a time by all that she had to confront. And yet my brother Charlie seems up and bubbly all the time. Do I think he could ever be depressed? No. He seems to be the happiest person in the world. I envy him.

Loss in all of its manifestations is the touchstone of depression—in the progress of the disease and, most likely, in its origin.... I would gradually be persuaded that devastating loss in childhood figured as a probable genesis of my own disorder.... I felt loss at every hand.... One dreads the loss of all things, all people close and dear. There is an acute fear of abandonment. Being alone in the house, even for a moment, caused me exquisite panic and trepidation.

I read this passage of Styron's and I not only think of David but I think of my mother, whom I considered strong but who had a breakdown and was lost to me when David died, lost to her own grief and to her anger toward my father over his infidelity. But at least I had basketball to turn to.

And as I got better and better and met with more and more success, I realized there was an incredible driving force within me, and that it was present all the time. Reading that Styron lost his mother at thirteen, the same age I was when David died, he goes on to say that a trauma like that at such an early age can create "nearly irreparable emotional havoc," that you are faced with "incomplete mourning," that it is nearly impossible to achieve "a catharsis of grief," and that you are practically doomed to carry within yourself through later years "an insufferable burden" of which rage and guilt and unreleased sorrow become "the potential seeds of self-destruction."

It was often hard to derive any joy from winning because I knew how hard I had pushed myself and I eventually realized what it had done to me physically, mentally, emotionally. But while you are doing it, you don't really know because you are so damn committed. I realize now that part of that commitment was trying to provide my mother with joy and something to be proud of—me, her youngest son, Jerry—and maybe give her a slightly rosier picture of life despite what had happened to her true pride and joy, David. So when I stopped playing, and when I stepped away from the Lakers as an executive, I was able to ask myself, *Why did I have to do this? Why did I have to be so committed?* And one of the reasons has to do with that couple back on the porch in West Virginia who didn't think I would amount to anything. They had a lot to do with that angry, emotional chip on my shoulder, that attitude of *I will damn well show you.* But, I see more clearly now, it had even more to do with Cecile West, with helping to give her a better reason to live.

I never mean for anyone to take it personally when I go into a shell and don't talk and want to be left alone, but I understand how hard it is for Karen (and was for Jane) not to feel it as a direct rejection. We all react differently to things that are stressful or unpleasant. Some people lash out; some don't. Others are able to laugh things off. But deep down there is anger or sadness.

> When we endure severe discomfort of a physical nature our conditioning has taught us since childhood to make accommodations to the pain's demands—to accept it, whether pluckily or whimpering and complaining, according to our personal degree of stoicism, but in any case to accept it.... The pain [of depression] is unrelenting, and what makes the condition intolerable is the foreknowledge that no remedy will come—not in a day, an hour, a month, or a minute. If there is mild relief, one knows that it is only temporary; more pain will follow.

I went through a lot of physical pain in my career. A lot. Didn't even compare to the emotional pain I felt. Didn't even know what it was. Because I was so self-critical, was so all over the place, that's real pain. People tell you that you will heal, but how in the hell are you going to heal something you don't know anything about?

> The sufferer from depression…finds himself, like a walking casualty of war, thrust into the most intolerable social and family situations. There he must, despite the anguish devouring his brain, present a face approximating the one that is associated with ordinary events and companionship. He must try to utter small talk, and be responsive to questions, and knowingly nod and frown and, God help him, even smile.

I don't let many people get too close to me, even though I try to be cordial to everyone. I don't seem to be capable of having a lot of friends in my life, and even for those who are, I am guarded with them. If I feel someone getting too close, I back up and go inward, probably out of fear, fear to expose myself and show some of my real feelings. Sometimes I don't even know how I function in the world. Over and over, seclusion and time, as Styron wrote, can be of great help in the healing process, but that is not always true for me. I am a tough nut to crack in that way. But depression, Styron pointed out, extends to the sufferer its "only grudging favor—its ultimate capitulation." I wondered early in this book what made Abraham Lincoln so great and so accomplished, and after reading about him in Styron's book, I have a better understanding of his background. He lost his mother when he was nine and then his sister ten years later and he contemplated taking his own life. I knew none of this. Lincoln was a man for the ages, and Styron was a great writer, and I, hell, I was merely a basketball player. But somehow, like them, I have been able—so far at least—"to vanquish death through work honored by posterity." Which helps me answer, to some extent, the lofty question I have always wondered about: Did I, consciously or not, set out to be a hero, or was this some notion that was thrust upon me by others?

On a simpler level, what I do know is that I played in order to try and feel good about myself when everything else in my life was confusing and frustratingly unexplainable. And my often wanting to take the last shot, I see ever more clearly, was a desperate need for control on my part—when the rest of my life was in chaos—a fierce desire to write my own ending.

9

Rebirth and the Difficulty of Becoming Elvis

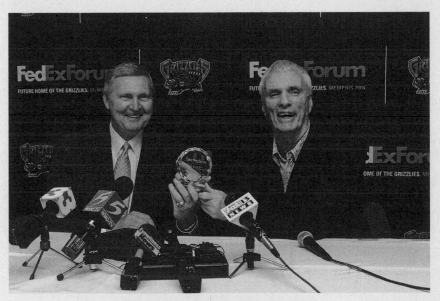

With Hubie Brown in Memphis, 2004

The kind of poverty you see in West Virginia and even in Los Angeles looks far different from the grinding poverty I was shocked to see when I first arrived in Memphis in late April of 2002. In the world I grew up in, we had very little, but there was food on the table and a clean place to live, so I never thought of myself as poor. But as I drove around the downtown area of Memphis, I had the sinking feeling that the opportunity for a better way of life was being denied to nearly everyone everywhere I looked.

After nearly two years out of work — I was handsomely paid as a consultant by the Lakers but, for whatever reason, was never consulted — I agreed to become head of the Memphis Grizzlies, a franchise that had moved from Vancouver the previous year. There were many things I enjoyed about my free time but I couldn't fill up my days just driving Jonnie to school and laughing at Howard Stern's bawdy humor and reading and playing golf and gin at the club. As always, I needed a new challenge, something to fully occupy me, though I worried what effect this decision would have on my health and my irregular heart.

I had been talking with the Atlanta Hawks, and Karen was all set to look at houses there, but the deal never got done because Time Warner in New York kept struggling with how to define *talent* in terms of how much my contract should be worth.

Then Memphis came calling. Mike Heisley, the head of Heico, a Chicago company that purchases failing businesses and rehabilitates them, was the owner of the Grizzlies. He phoned and said he wanted to come see me and then flew out to Los Angeles. Mike can fly on private planes whenever he wants but feels it is important to fly coach whenever possible so as not to seem extravagant and send his employees the wrong message. He is a billionaire who enjoys driving himself to work each morning.

Mike is short and stocky and forceful and we are about the same age; our backgrounds were similar in that we both had to work our way up. After I picked him up at the airport, we sat in my living room talking for a number of hours, and he told me how much he wanted me to become involved with the Grizzlies (and how much he had enjoyed watching me as a player when he lived in Los Angeles and had Lakers' season tickets). Having me come to Memphis, he insisted, would give the franchise just the lift and credibility it needed in a new town. He asked me to write down on a piece of paper everything I wanted. If it was agreeable to him, I would need to come right away. There would be no negotiation.

Now this was new to me, the idea of making a wish list, with no back and forth. When Mike left for the airport, Karen did some research, and we learned that he was someone who apparently could be difficult to work for, that he could be volatile and lose his temper. Since I was no stranger to losing my temper at times, that didn't particularly bother me, and yet I decided to make this one of my conditions: *If you ever raise your voice to me, I will be out the door before it has a chance to shut.* I also wrote down that he could expect me to abide by this too.

Before sending my list to Mike, I spoke with both John Wooden and Jerry Buss about the prospect (for some odd reason, I felt as if I needed Jerry's blessing). In no time at all, it seemed, Mike said yes to everything I had requested. I had asked for an amount of money that I was sure he would find unreasonable, but he didn't. I was stunned, but part of my being stunned was in realizing that Mike felt I was potentially more valuable to the Grizzlies than I had been to the Lakers. So within two days, Gary Colson (who would become my chief assistant) and I flew to Memphis and there was a big press conference.

I had been with the Lakers my entire professional life and now I was moving to a new area, a move that would mean a different way of life for me and for Karen and for Jonnie. Karen in particular felt it would be good for us to get away from L.A. She felt it was hard for me to be in town and "retired" and not connected to the Lakers on a daily basis. She knew how restless I got when I was not fully immersed in something, and she felt that Jonnie would benefit from an environment that was less pressured and more relaxed.

Mike had made it very clear that he was going to let me run the team as I saw fit and that he was not expecting me to consult him on things the way I had become accustomed to doing with Jerry Buss. He was there if I needed him and there were certain things, money-wise, he would need to sign off on, but he and his attorney, Stan Meadows, were going to stay in the background. I told Mike I appreciated that but that I would be most comfortable with keeping them apprised, just as I had with Jerry.

Gary's wife, Mary Katherine, and Karen were not going to come with us right away (though they were at the press conference, along with other family members), so we wound up staying at the Peabody, where ducks famously come down on the elevator in the morning and make themselves at home in the lobby during the day. Our offices were right across the street, at the Toyota Center, and it was both odd and uncomfortable, frankly, to walk that short distance accompanied by the Memphis police.

The expectations of me were enormous and I was treated as if I were Elvis, back from the dead, though people in Memphis are convinced he is still alive. I wanted the spotlight to be on the play-ers and the coaches, not on me—just as I had in Los Angeles. (That is the main reason I have never appeared in one team photo as an executive. Not one.)

In coming to Memphis, I was, in a way, coming full circle. Just as when the Lakers had come to Los Angeles in 1960, getting the city interested in the team was crucial. I would need to do far more than just run the Grizzlies. I would have to go out into the com-munity and forge relationships with the city fathers and the fans, make them believe that we were going to do and be something special. One of the things I had always done as GM of the Lakers was to continue scouting players myself. I liked to get out and beat the bushes if necessary to see someone play, and I would tolerate any sort of weather, or bad food, or inconvenience to do so. I just loved to evaluate talent and find out everything I could about a potential prospect, and form some sense about his character— what he liked to do when he wasn't playing, how much sleep he got each night, what he ate, who his parents were, who his friends were, what he hoped to do beyond basketball. But I was simply unable to do that my first year there.

Since Memphis, I quickly discovered, is a very family-oriented city, which I greatly respected, there were certain days—Sunday and Wednesday—when it was extremely difficult to draw people downtown to a game because of religious obligations. And the majority of people who could afford to come to a game lived east of town, nearly a half hour away. I was coming to a city that rabidly supported college basketball—the Memphis Tigers—and we were also up against that.

A few short weeks after I arrived, right before our wedding anniversary, I wrote Karen a letter on Peabody Hotel stationery:

Dear Karen,

Being away from home and the family has been a most difficult time for me. I can't tell you how lonely I've been, our boys and you have brought a stability to me that I never dreamed possible, but the reality is that I'm here and you guys are there.

I took this job for two reasons only, one the challenge and two the family. I don't want anyone to live a life without some of the comforts I didn't have. This is going to be a huge task to build something that I will be proud of when I leave, they simply don't know what it takes to build a winner. Gary has been a real blessing for me, his attitude and contribution have been great so far. But the pressure on me will be enormous to turn this franchise around. I really think I'm going to make a huge difference.

I'm really sorry that our anniversary will be spent apart but I'll be thinking about our first time that we were able to be together. Remember Laughter in the Rain, I'll never forget how special you made me feel. I know that there have been some rocky roads in our years together but on balance this has been a great meeting of a special woman and a very strange man. It's hard to believe we have shared 24 years together. We have been so blessed in many ways but our boys make me so proud, they are just the best.

Maybe something special will be in store for our 25th. Hopefully it won't be spent apart. Can't wait to see everyone, this really isn't fun being away from everyone.

> Happy Anniversary,
> Love you,
> Jerry

I have always enjoyed writing notes and letters by hand. Even when I was a player, I tried to write back to everyone who wrote to me. As an executive, I would often stay late in my office at the Forum and do the same thing. I don't use a computer. I don't write e-mail. I don't text anyone. I don't Tweet on Twitter (even though Elgin Baylor called me "Tweety Bird" because of my high-pitched twang when I first joined the Lakers). If I send an e-mail, I do it through Karen. She loves technology. I don't. I may be old-fashioned in the way I do things, but I am actually very modern at the same time. I just like to do things as personally as possible.

The situation I came into Memphis had the potential to be awkward. Dick Versace, who had been with the Pacers for many years, was the president of the Grizzlies, and his family had long-standing ties to Mike Heisley's. I knew Dick might be unhappy that I was being brought in as president and that he would become GM, but I wanted to make Dick feel he was a valuable part of what we were trying to do: essentially change the culture of the organization, get everyone to believe we could have a winning team.

I have never liked the concept of "managing people." Ideally, you work with people, you don't manage them. I knew that people would wonder why I wanted to come to Memphis in the first place, that they would question my sincerity, and even speculate how long I would stay before frustration drove me away.

But unless you have worked with me, you don't know me. I went around the organization and tried to get acquainted with everyone, to understand them as people, what their dreams and aspirations were. I wanted to create the same family atmosphere we had in Los Angeles. When my first assistant, April Nichols, left after a year, I hired a young woman named Laura Glankler, who had drive and ambition but was being underused. I got personally interested in the lives of all of our employees, and I did my best to be supportive of them. Dick Versace eventually left the organization, which came as no surprise to anyone, but he was not pushed out. I brought my son Ryan in as a scout because he is very knowledgeable about the game and has a great work ethic. It was wonderful to have him working with me (though he stayed on the West Coast), but he received no special favors—*none*—and was treated the same as everyone else. Sidney Lowe was the coach when I arrived. Personally, I liked Sidney very much, but he was not the right person to take us forward. We caught everyone off guard—particularly Mike Heisley—by hiring Hubie Brown, who is smarter about the game of basketball than perhaps anyone I know but who hadn't been a coach since leaving the Knicks in 1987. I would watch Hubie's practices and learn something each and every time. I thought I knew the game, but I didn't know anything compared to Hubie. Everything he had the players do at practice—and I mean *everything*—had a purpose and was timed down to the second.

Being with the Lakers for so many years, I never gave the draft lottery (which came into existence in 1985) much thought because we were hardly ever in a position to really benefit from it. It is my strong opinion that once the first pick is awarded through the luck of the bouncing ball, the order should follow in terms of the worst record (which was how it was done for two brief years in 1985 and 1986, though they used envelopes then). I have made this case many times to David Stern and other people in the league office, but I have gotten nowhere. I am sure they think I act like some crazy relative (I have certainly been outspoken at league meetings over the years), but I couldn't care less. David claims he views me as his mentor, and perhaps he does. He also says that when he gets a call from me and I say, "It will only take five minutes," he settles in because he knows it will probably be an hour. If that's true, and it might be, at least he has St. Patrick's Cathedral to gaze at through his upper-floor window.

Seriously, though, had we been able to get LeBron James or Carmelo Anthony or Dwayne Wade in the 2003 draft, or a player like Al Horford to go along with Pau Gasol, what a difference that would have made, to say the least, and what a luxury for a coach to have.

After a difficult first year, the Grizzlies made the playoffs in the next three, winning around fifty games each year. At the conclusion of the 2003–4 season, Hubie was named Coach of the Year and I was named Executive of the Year. The night he was given that award—the night of the Grizzlies' first-ever home playoff game—was my proudest moment in my long career as an executive. The arena was packed, and the city was excited, and we were building something.

Unfortunately, we didn't win a game in that playoff series, and I hadn't come to Memphis just to get into the playoffs. I wanted more, much more. Mike Heisley would tell people how thrilled he was—giving me generous gifts like a golf trip to Scotland with his friends and business associates to demonstrate how he felt— but I knew he wanted more too.

No sooner had the next season gotten under way than I got a phone call from Tony Barone, one of our assistant coaches. I was in Europe scouting at the time, and Tony informed me that Hubie wanted to quit. I was shocked over the timing of this and wondered why the hell Hubie wasn't calling me himself and why he couldn't wait the two days until I returned. We were just hitting our stride and we were playing in a new arena—the FedEx Forum, a state-of-the-art facility.

I knew he had concerns about some of the players and whether they were the right fit, but more important, Hubie had legitimate concerns about his health—he had fainted not long before this—and I was the last one who would be insensitive to an issue like that.

Hubie agreed not to announce his resignation until I got back, right before Thanksgiving, and it was pretty somber in our household. My favorite holiday was ruined; Karen's brother, Joe, who was visiting from Los Angeles, felt as if someone had died—a similar feeling to what he had had a year earlier when I got the call about Kobe's arrest in Colorado. In the retail business, Black Friday is what the day after Thanksgiving is called. Well, that was the day the press conference was held and it is precisely what it felt like for the Grizzlies organization—along with bizarre and strange. You would have thought we had fired Hubie when in fact we desperately wanted him to stay on. I have attended a lot of press conferences, but this one was different, let me tell you—even surpassing the one Jerry Buss had in 1981 to announce that I would be co-coaching the Lakers with Pat Riley, then my getting up there to say I wouldn't.

We needed to find somebody to take over and eventually settled on Mike Fratello. We went again to the playoffs that year and the year after but still did not come away with any victories.

Aside from Hubie's leaving, the first four years in Memphis were wonderful, probably the most satisfying of my life. I felt rejuvenated. Karen and I loved where we lived, a golf course community called Southwind, and I became involved with the city in a different way than I had in Los Angeles. I got to know the mayor, Willie Herenton, and I got to know the local businesspeople who had a stake in the team—brothers Staley and Andy Cates, Pitt and Barbara Hyde (all very philanthropic members of the Memphis community), Charles Ewing, and Fred Jones. I also had the good fortune of renewing my association with Gene Bartow, the superb college coach who had tremendous teams at Memphis and UAB and who had the "misfortune" of following John Wooden at UCLA. Gene and I loved to kid that I took him to lunch 267 times and he never paid. Speaking of food, I found an Italian restaurant—Ronnie Grisanti's—that reminded me a lot of Dan Tana's and Valentino's in L.A., two of my favorite spots, places where I could go and pretty much be left alone and still kid with the owner, have the sort of relationship where I can be myself and affectionately tell the owner to go to hell. These things may seem trivial, but they aren't to me.

When I was not at the office, I often stopped by James Davis, an upscale clothing store, where I not only purchased items for myself but would often suggest to other customers outfits and accessories that I thought would look good on them. I laughingly told the owner, Van Weinberg, that he didn't have to pay me. I simply loved doing it because I love clothes and have strong opinions about them, and I became so close to the salesman who took care of me, Monte Stewart, that I invited him to my suite at the arena on many occasions. (Monte would later joke that he'd "fired" me without my being aware of it because he was convinced that nothing pleased me and that I always thought I was right. I don't think that's true—at least I hope it isn't—but when I did point out once that one sleeve on a suit was one-sixteenth of an inch shorter than the other sleeve, Monte, sure I was wrong, snapped that perhaps I could do his job better than he could.) I cared for Monte a great deal. When I eventually left Memphis, there is no question that he was one of the people I sorely missed.

Other people who would come to the suite for games included Ken Jones, my old roommate from Los Angeles who lived nearby in Jackson, Mississippi; Simon Hewitt, a friend and Titleist representative from Little Rock; Laura Glankler's mother (she and Laura loved the dessert tray, but she was not always happy about the amount of foul language she heard if I saw something on the court that did not please me); and Bill Lucchesi, who had a wine warehouse on Montrose where I would often go after work to read, have a glass or two, a meal, and just relax with a wide assortment of people. Just as James Davis had, Bill's warehouse became a hangout for me, a second home.

I have always enjoyed the company of different types of individuals. Strays, I call them, and I don't mean it unkindly; I mean it in the best sense. The sort of friends who make the world go 'round. (In Los Angeles, Bobby Freedman fits into that category. Bobby—who is more connected than God—and I have been having lunch nearly every week at different restaurants around Beverly Hills for as long as I can remember. Whenever we get together, we laugh our asses off and he heckles me the whole time and I love it. I would trust Bobby with my life.) In Memphis, it was Jimmy Cross. Jimmy owned a liquor store, Jumpin' Jimmy's, and could easily have stepped out of the pages of *To Kill a Mockingbird* or *Deliverance*. He reminded me of people I had grown up with. Jimmy was someone (along with his sons Bradley and Greg) with whom I hunted and could completely be my unvarnished self; and someone who managed to do the nearly impossible with me — pick up the check before I did. When Jimmy came to the suite, he tried to convince everyone that the suite was his and that the rest of us were *his* guests. (You never knew who was going to be there for each home game because Gary Colson, who has never met a stranger he didn't like, basically invited the world and made it into America's living room.)

Karen became friendly with Jimmy's wife, Debbie, and we would go over to his house for dinner on many Sunday nights.

Much of what I know about wine I know from Jimmy. Of all the people I met in Memphis, Jimmy was the one whose friendship became the most important. There was eventually a break in our relationship, for reasons I will not get into, and I miss him still.

For Karen, the move to Memphis was everything she had hoped it would be. She found the people she met were, by and large, friendlier and more genuine than in Los Angeles. She missed her family, but she loved Memphis's slower pace. I may be biased, but it is impossible not to like Karen, and she is welcoming to everyone she meets. She had movie night once a week at the house with a number of women, and Jonnie thrived at his new school, Lausanne, where he was teammates with Marc Gasol (Pau's brother), who now plays for the Grizzlies.

I made a number of mistakes in Memphis — drafting Drew Gooden instead of Amar'e Stoudemire was one; signing Brian Cardinal for the midlevel exception was another — but I was fortunate enough to bring to the team its second future star in Rudy Gay. (Pau Gasol had been Rookie of the Year in 2002, the year before I arrived, but he suffered a major injury that prevented him from playing for the Grizzlies in the same consistent, passionate way he had played for Spain.) That meant trading one of my favorite players on the Grizzlies — Shane Battier, who also did so many good things in the community — which was not an easy thing to do. Shane was a very solid player and a great defender but he was not a star, and a team needs at least one, and ideally two. It may not have been a popular move — even Jonnie took a lot of flack because Shane's wife taught and coached at his school — but it was the right decision.

Weird, unsettling things happened too. I became the object of a couple of stalkers and needed a security guard. One woman even went so far as to buy a wedding dress for the happy life she envisioned we would have together.

The problems I had with Mike Fratello had to do with the type of offense he wanted the team to run—a very slow, controlled game—and I tried to tell him that he needed to reconsider this. I warned him, "Everyone is killing me, Mike. The agents with players' complaints, the fans, the press. This is *not* what we should be doing." But Mike was very stubborn; he was *convinced* that his approach was correct. As an executive, you need to support a coach as much as you can, get him the players he feels he needs to win (I still remembered how frustrated and angry I would get when Jack Kent Cooke obtained or traded players without consulting me), but this was not working. It was *not* working. One morning, after a game in which he did not call a timeout that I thought he should have, I called a meeting, a meeting I will never forget. Mike had three cell phones, and he put them on the table in front of him: one was for business, one was for friends and family, and one was for "personal reasons." One after another, the phones started ringing. Not only was I furious that he hadn't put them on silent, I was even more enraged that he would then take the call. Finally, I had had enough. "Mike," I said, steaming, "if you answer one more of those calls, I am going to smash those goddamn phones." I have always liked Mike personally, but this was business, and I felt another change had to be made, even though it is usually not a wise thing to do in the course of a season.

Jimmie Mancell and Dana Davis. Of all the people associated with the Grizzlies, the two I probably became closest to were them. Jimmie was the team doctor and he became mine, but he was far more than a doctor to me. He was someone I could confide in, and I confided in him a lot—not just about my ongoing concerns with my atrial fibrillation but about anything and every-thing on my mind. Jimmie has a patient bedside manner about him I found very comforting. He knew how to help me calm down.

Dana Davis, whom we promoted to vice president of basket-ball operations, does everything and knows everybody. He is a fixer, an arranger, in the way Bobby Freedman is. No one can say no to him. It is impossible. He is short and compact like a bowling ball, and has more warm-up outfits than any man should (or even that the law allows), and he uses his stature to his advantage. No one in my professional career has given me a harder time than Dana. No one is able to get me more worked up. Whatever but-tons I have, Dana knows how to push every one of them and I love him for it. He makes me laugh my ass off (his own laugh goes on forever), and he keeps things loose. Mike Heisley would trust his life to Dana, and so would I. Dana is the rare sort of person who would do anything for you, anything he possibly could. He is a constant presence in my life. Even if I manage to disappear after this book is published, I'm afraid he would find me.

Sometimes you can stay too long. During my fifth year in Mem-phis, Mike Heisley considered selling the team, a potential deal that was a huge distraction and that ultimately was not made. No matter what we did, we couldn't seem to increase the revenues and put enough fannies in the seats. I had to be much more mindful of spending than when I first took the job. (The obstacles facing small-market teams like Memphis are enormous, especially in light of how dramatically the country's economic climate changed in 2008. In the autumn of 2010, the New Orleans Hornets were taken over by the NBA when their owner, George Shinn, couldn't find a buyer. I have always felt the league would be better off with fewer teams; having the kind of business model that works for *all* teams, not just the ones in large markets, could ideally bring about a much more competitive balance.) In their own odd way, these challenges took me back to the awful feelings and frustration we had in trying to beat the Celtics. In the Grizzlies' case, the team was beset by injuries. We were going in the opposite direction from where we wanted to be. I felt completely responsible and personally disappointed that we couldn't seem to improve.

Normally, as I've written, I am very adept at dealing with the press, but the local paper, the *Commercial Appeal*, had two reporters—Ron Tillery and Geoff Calkins—whom I liked personally but who really tested my patience and who, I felt, could have been much more supportive of what we were trying to achieve. I became totally unprofessional with them on more than one occasion. I understand the job they have to do, but I felt Ron and Geoff were frequently wrong in what they wrote and that they took some perverse delight in seeing us struggle, that they didn't want us to prosper.

My years in Memphis were not as successful as I hoped they would be. Mike and I certainly had our share of "spirited discussions" about what needed to happen for the team to go much further than just getting into the playoffs—but at no time did I ever feel he wasn't behind me. (In fact, he even financed a sculpture of me as a college player that stands in front of the Coliseum in Morgantown, a gesture on his part that I was completely unaware of and am still amazed and humbled by.) I sadly came to the conclusion that I would not, in the end, be able to do what I had set out to do—win a championship—and so, at the end of the 2007 season, Karen and I moved back to Los Angeles. I had taken the job with the hope that I would somehow be able to do it in a less frenzied, less manic way than how I had run the Lakers, but I had just been kidding myself. You take yourself with you wherever you go.

Not long before we left town, though, Laura Glankler arranged a surprise birthday party for me at the Westin Hotel. What Laura didn't know is that I hate surprises of any kind. As soon as Dana Davis and I walked into the room and I saw what was in front of me (including a disloyal team employee I had no interest in being around), I turned and walked out. I insisted on paying for the party, but it was too late: the damage had been done, and my offering to pay for the party only added insult to injury. Laura had put a lot of effort into planning that party and it took her a long time to forgive me, a very long time.

For someone she considered the best boss she had ever had (and who becomes emotional whenever she is asked about me), it was not one of my prouder moments.

10
The Ride to Rancho Santa Fe, 11/17/08

Pete Newell with me and other Olympic teammates at West Point, 1960

The drive from my home in Bel Air to Rancho Santa Fe takes about two hours, a fairly straight shot south on the San Diego Freeway. I wanted to leave the house at eight fifteen sharp that morning so we could get there by ten thirty. I hadn't seen Pete Newell, my Olympic coach, mentor, and the general manager of the Lakers in my later years as a player, for about six years; he was ninety-three and not doing well but sounded eager to see me. I was going to visit him at the home of one of his former players, Earl Shultz, who had been on the 1959 California team that defeated West Virginia by one point for the national championship. Pete was being looked after by one of his four sons, Roger, but Earl and his wife, Karen, were responsible for a large part of his care. Earl was a doctor and he bred racehorses, and anyone who knew anything about Pete knew that he loved the track.

There had been fires throughout Southern California for the past few days and there was evidence of destruction nearly everywhere I looked. If you live in the area long enough, as I have, you might get used to the fires, especially in the autumn, but you never get used to the destruction — at least I don't, because so much of it seems preventable. If they would just have burn areas in some of these canyons, it would make it harder for the fires to spread.

Speaking of fires, it just so happened that I was on the phone with Emily Barker, one of my researchers, and she told me that when my family's house burned, in 1962, a neighbor was able to salvage some of my athletic trophies by putting them into his refrigerator. She knew someone whose family knew the Chelyan neighbor who had done this. This was the first I had heard of it;

my parents and Jane had prevailed upon West Virginia University to replace the trophies that had a connection to the school, and the school was able to do that with some of them. It was strange that I hadn't heard about this before, and I doubted that it was true. In any case, the fire, I told Emily, had miraculously spared the two things that were most important to me: my Olympic Gold Medal and uniform.

Emily was recovering from a torn ACL, and talking with her reminded me of the many, many injuries that I had suffered throughout my career. I told her about one of them, a very bad groin pull not long before I retired. Jim Bush at UCLA ran the best track-and-field program in the country at that time, and after the injury he put me through three grueling months of exercise. In basketball everything is quick starts and stops, and it was very disturbing to realize that I might not be able to regain my ability. Jim believed in running up and down hills, all sorts of inclines, and he believed in interval training: run 100 yards as fast as you can, walk 100, run 100. Then you'd run 220, walk 440, and run 220 again, and then start running for distance. It was a scary time, I told her, not knowing if I would be able to resume doing what I loved.

On the way there, all kinds of thoughts were filling my mind. So many of the major decisions I'd made in my basketball life I had discussed with Pete first. He was a father figure to me and a counselor. Little did I know that a year or so after the 1959 NCAA championship game, Pete would be my Olympic coach. I played so badly at first in the trials that I was sure I wouldn't make the team. In fact, I was walking aimlessly around the streets of Denver, dejected and sullen, and who should suddenly appear but Pete. "Young lad," he said, "if you're not going to Rome, I won't be going either."

Pete knew how to reach me and he knew how to help me relax. Despite my being a two-time first-team All-American at West Virginia, I still was not brimming with self-confidence from day to day. I still was plagued by a lot of self-doubt. What made Pete a great coach and teacher was his ability to find that one thing, that small needle in the proverbial haystack, that motivated me, that enabled me to do what he needed me to do. And Pete also had the ability to poke fun at my thin skin without making me angry. He knew how to make me laugh. When the Olympic squad trained at West Point, he and I were talking one day and he suddenly blurted out, "For Christ's sake, West, speak English!" I knew that my high-pitched twang was hard to make out, but no one had ever teased me about it publicly before.

I was so busy thinking about random things and talking with Jonathan that I missed the damn exit. I told him that John Stockton was perhaps the most underappreciated player ever to play the game. And that as much as I admired Larry Bird as both a player and a competitor, I wasn't sure that Rick Barry hadn't been just as great. Because Rick seemed to be so disliked personally, I don't think he got the acclaim he deserved professionally. I was thinking about Stockton and Barry as players who had never really gotten their due because Elgin Baylor had been very much on my mind.

A few weeks earlier, Elgin had left the Los Angeles Clippers, where he had been general manager since 1986 and, in my opinion, poorly paid and poorly treated by the owner, Donald Sterling. He had either resigned—the Clippers' version—or been fired, which was Elgin's. The whole thing upset me and made me sad, and I said that to any reporter who called and asked my opinion. As great as Elgin was as a player, I didn't feel that he got his just due either, and not just because he'd retired nine games into the

1971–72 season, the year the Lakers finally won their first championship in Los Angeles. Like life, sports can be particularly harsh and unforgiving; the fact that Elgin wasn't there when we hoisted the trophy is a perfect example of that. But what is also interesting—and cruelly ironic in its own way—is that I have often wondered if we would have won the championship had he still been on the team. We already had two aging stars in Wilt Chamberlain and myself. I had had to change my role that season and become more of a playmaker, and I suspect that Elgin would have had to change his as well. We had had our opportunities, in 1969 and 1970, to win as a trio, and we didn't. What's to say that we could have done it in 1972?

"I hope you make it soon, Jerry. We're losing him."

I had called to say we were almost there and wasn't prepared for what Earl Shultz was telling me. It was a glorious November day, and we were a few minutes away. It was too pretty a day to die.

"I hope you get here," he said. "I really thought he wanted to see you so badly that he would rally and this would be his last hurrah."

Goddamn, I thought. *This might be my last chance to say good-bye to him. He was so excited that I was coming.*

A few minutes later I pulled up in the driveway, and before I could even get out of the car, Earl and his wife had come out of the house.

"He's gone, Jerry," Earl said, tears in his eyes. "About ninety seconds ago."

We made our way into the house and there, in the kitchen, sitting slumped in a wheelchair and facing the window, sunlight streaming in, was the man whom I had known and loved for nearly fifty years. I went over to him and put my left hand on his right shoulder and gave it a squeeze. He appeared small and frail and not at all as I remembered him. I needed to remember him as he was—strong and vibrant and tough-minded and demanding but always kind, and always humble. I looked toward the ceiling and silently said something to Pete that I prefer to keep private.

I was so stunned I could barely move from that spot. It was as if I were waiting for Pete to give me some piece of advice, just as he had in Rome before we went out to face the Russians. Earl and his wife asked if we would join them in the living room and watch a video of Pete's being inducted into the Breitbart Hall of Fame in San Diego earlier that year. Bobby Knight had flown in to introduce him.

There was no separation between the living room and the kitchen, and every few minutes I would turn my head slightly to see if Pete was going to get out of the chair and join us. The whole thing was surreal. Over the years I had gone to hospitals and nursing homes to visit people who were dying. I remember going to see my Laker teammate Happy Hairston every day until I simply couldn't go any longer. I remember the time Mitch Kupchak and I were asked to come to the morgue because officials thought that one of the Lakers, Duane Cooper, had been shot and killed. But it wasn't Duane; it was someone who had robbed Duane's house and stolen his ID and then been shot later that night. And I will never forget the day nine years earlier when I heard that Wilt Chamberlain had died at his home on Mulholland Drive and I refused to believe it. Or the day six years earlier when Chick Hearn died and I flew home to Los Angeles from West Virginia to eulogize the man who epitomized the Lakers and had done so much to elevate Elgin's and my careers.

But I had never experienced anything like this before. All I kept thinking was *Oh my God, I can't believe this is happening.*

I watched the tribute to Pete but couldn't really concentrate on it. Earl and his wife offered me something to drink, but I didn't want anything. What I wanted was for someone to come and remove the body. I am a passionate watcher of every kind of crime show you can imagine, and this felt too much like a crime scene to me. Perhaps because Earl was a doctor, none of this seemed odd to him. He was used to being in the presence of death.

"You know what's interesting," I found myself saying. "Being involved with sports brings out the best in people and the worst in people. But with Pete, you never saw the worst. He was compassionate, and he was loved by so many. He was a giver, and he never cared about being paid."

Aside from being one of the game's greatest minds, he was probably best known for running his Big Man Camps, and nearly every "big" came to him for training at one point or another. Pete understood, better than anyone I have ever met, the fragile psyche of big men — how they are self-conscious about their size and often never make eye contact — and he knew how to reach them. Having a fragile psyche myself, I marveled at his genius and his patience.

Earl was saying that Pete had wanted to die, that once a person decides to give up the ghost, it's over. I told him I understood that. "The vitality of a person is the most important thing, particularly in a man," I said. "Pete was always a real vital person. To hear that he was excited about my coming down to see him, obviously that made me feel good. Come here and walk in and there's a dead body, my God."

"I knew it was going to be soon," Earl said. "In fact, I was pretty sure you would be the last visitor he would have. You hold — *held* — a very high position for him. You and Bobby and Mike Krzyzewski. And then teammates of ours at Cal, and Jerry Colangelo."

"He and I had a special bond," I said softly. "In some of my most down times—look, I'm a depressed person, always have been, always will be. Pete was a real mentor to me, he understood me. When it came to basketball, he knew how crazed I was about winning. I mean, I was obsessive. Winning was the only thing that mattered. And when we didn't win that game against you guys, it just crushed me because I didn't feel like I did enough. He truly *got* that part of me. Where most people say, 'Get over it,' Pete understood the part of me that couldn't. People will ask, 'When does the healing begin?' and I say it *never* begins."

I told Earl that I'd always had the sense that Pete and John Wooden had a testy relationship, even though Pete had never said anything derogatory about him.

"No, he never did," Earl said, laughing. "Pete loved John when he was beating him and he knew that it drove John crazy that Cal won the last eight times they faced each other, before Pete stepped down in 1960 and became athletic director."

Talking about Pete and John's fierce rivalry with Earl reminded me that someone from UCLA (not John himself) had tried to recruit me. Success begets success, of course, but being the curious person I am, I always wondered if players from all over the country had come to UCLA because of the prominence of the program, or solely because of John, or whether there were other reasons, or a combination of all three. (When I was being recruited, a number of schools offered me money—more than my father was making—and other things that they shouldn't have before I officially settled on West Virginia. One coach, Kenny Loeffler, who had coached Tom Gola at La Salle, was so desperate for me to come to Texas A&M that he gave one of the greatest performances I have ever seen: He sat on our front porch, broke down in tears, and said he would see to it that I could go home whenever I wanted, that I got a car—which would have been of little use to me, because I didn't know how to drive—that I married the richest girl in Texas, and that I wouldn't have to wear a military uniform, among other enticements.)

Earl and I laughed about Pete's completely nondescript lifestyle, about his never wanting to be singled out and recognized, about how being "just one of the guys" was so important to him. We also laughed about his absolute unconcern with his appearance, and the orange socks he loved to wear. In a way, I envied that about him; I am always matched. Even when I didn't have anything, I was like that. My kids call me Cement Head because I never have a hair out of place.

There was a knock at the door, but it wasn't a priest and it wasn't someone to take away the body. It was the husband of one of Pete's nieces. And then Bobby Knight called. Earl's wife had left him a message. Bobby was down at Duke doing a clinic, helping Mike Krzyzewski, who played for him at Army, get his team ready for the season. Bobby had retired from coaching; he was the winningest college coach of all time (until Mike surpasses him) and without doubt one of the finest, most prominently at Indiana. A lot of people who don't know Bobby don't like him because they think he's crazy. He's not. If he likes you, he embraces you. You'd want to go to war with him. If he doesn't like you, you know it. People see all the outrageous things he's done, and I'm sure, in the back of his mind, there are some of those things he wishes he hadn't done. You know, there's a lot of different approaches to climbing a tree. And Bobby was going right up the tree regardless. He didn't give a damn what obstacles were in the way.

Earl's wife said that Bobby wanted to speak with me, and I took the call outside. It was nice to get out of the house. It had been some time since I had talked with Bobby and we were both emotional. The game had lost a giant, but we had lost a close friend. I told Bobby that Pete got to know what a sick competitor I was and that I was pretty sure that was one of the things he liked about both of us. If the family needed or wanted any help with the funeral arrangements or anything else, Bobby and I agreed that we would do whatever we could.

When I came back in and was sitting there, I began thinking of my admiration for Japanese culture and its reverence toward older people. In America, we don't feel that way. We think that they contribute nothing. But can you imagine when Pete was at a point in his life where he could articulate things, the things he'd seen, the wealth of information he had? If you knew this man, as I had, if you knew him and if you knew what he stood for, you would know that he could write a book that would transform his wonderfully complex thoughts into words that would capture the absolute essence of what he was thinking, words that anyone could understand.

Sadly, we try to explain away everything in this world we find too painful to look at. But there are some things you can't explain away. There are some things that are just predestined, are like the mountains where I grew up. "I was so excited about seeing him today," I told Earl, "and you walked out and you say, 'He's gone.' You told me that he was not going to make it till Christmas. You told me that. And so I am thinking, *Oh my God, was this the way I was supposed to end with him?*

"Wise old men like Pete, they've seen it all. They've seen changes in cultures; I mean, every change you could see in a lifetime. I've seen a lot of changes. Yet someone like Pete has seen far more than me and he's experienced far more than me. I've led a much more sheltered life. He was much more of a people person than me. And the people he's touched. Oh my God."

My mind returned once again to Rome and how fair Pete was with all the players. He was demanding, but he was demanding in the right way. He believed in me at a time when I needed it most. When Oscar Robertson and I went back to Rome together in the mid-nineties for a documentary about our Olympic experience, we talked about Pete and how much we benefited from staying in the Olympic Village (an experience that the 1992 Dream Team never had) and laughed about the dollar a day we received for incidentals.

I had no idea in Rome that Pete would eventually be connected with the Lakers. As general manager, he was the one responsible for bringing Kareem Abdul-Jabbar to Los Angeles from the Milwaukee Bucks in 1975. He was there when I walked away from the game a year earlier, and there when I began coaching, which was one of the reasons I took the job. One of the many things I loved about Pete — and that we shared — was a dislike of people who talked about themselves all the time. Perhaps *dislike* is the wrong word; *would never associate with* is probably better. That wasn't me, and it wasn't Pete.

I honestly didn't know how much longer I could sit there. I am a restless person under the best of circumstances, and this was the most unsettling feeling I had ever had. For the life of me I couldn't understand why somebody didn't come for the body or a priest didn't appear.

Pete was a son of Loyola Marymount University and he would be laid to rest near there the following week, and a memorial service would be held in a month's time. Ryan had gone to college there and the Lakers had practiced there for years, and now Pete

Newell would be returning home. Even though Karen can't stand it when I say that I am in God's waiting room, I certainly felt like that as Pete lay dead in the next room, waiting, it almost seemed, for the Lord to come through that large bay window and embrace him.

I told Earl that we were going to head back up the highway.

"Not really the inspirational visit you had hoped for," he said quietly.

"I'll tell you, I've had a lot of unbelievable things happen to me in my life, but this is the most unbelievable. I need to say good-bye to him once more."

And so I slowly made my way back into the kitchen, put my hand on Pete's shoulder one last time, and then I was gone.

11

Self-Recrimination

With Chick Hearn, in his Nest at the Forum

I was disoriented and upset and angry, mainly at myself. If I had only left my house when I had planned to, Pete would have been alive when I got there. Though now that I think about it, that might have been worse—to see him and speak with him and then have him die right in front of me. In any case, I was angry yet again about something else: that I don't tell people clearly enough how I feel about them before it's too late.

As soon as I got in the car, I left a message for Karen and then one for John Black at the Lakers to call me, but I did not say why. When Karen reached me and I told her what happened, she could hardly believe it and she also couldn't understand why the body hadn't been removed or the priest hadn't come.

I had planned to see Marge Hearn on my way back home, and Karen knew that. "We are only going to spend an hour or so. The day has been filled with enough trauma already."

"Well, give Marge my love," Karen said.

I reached Marge by phone and got the directions, but I had a hell of a time finding her place. She had recently moved into an upscale retirement community near Fullerton, which was more or less on my way back, but it sure didn't seem that way. On the drive there, my friend Dana Pump phoned; he had somehow heard about Pete. I wish I could say I was surprised, but he and his twin brother, David, are so connected throughout the sports world, they know things practically before they happen. I had spoken to Dana on the way down, and now he was phoning to see how I was doing. John Black phoned back from the Lakers and he knew about Pete because he had just spoken with Karen. I asked him to let other people with the Lakers organization know, especially Bob Steiner, who worked closely with Jerry Buss and who went all the way back to Cal with Pete (Bob had been the sports information director there). I suspect he already knew because they had never lost touch. John said he would let Mitch Kupchak and Phil Jackson and Jeanie Buss know, and I couldn't think why he needed to tell Phil. Phil had no real connection to Pete that I knew of.

Driving to see Marge naturally made me think of Chick. In fact, it was nearly impossible to think of one without the other; they were inseparable.

When Chick died, in August of 2002, at the age of eighty-five, his funeral was televised in Los Angeles and flags were lowered to half-staff on all city property. I could barely get through my eulogy, partly because his and Marge's life had already been marked by the tragic deaths of their two children, Gary and Samantha.

When I finally arrived, it was impossible not to notice how beautiful the place Marge lived in was, but I would rather live in a tent and ride out my days in the wilderness. The idea of living in any sort of communal way with people I didn't know would not be my idea of a good time, no matter how nice the accommodations were.

Marge was happy to see me and she was shocked by the news about Pete, about the circumstances. She and Chick had known and liked Pete and his wife and family, and Marge knew all too well, as did I, how the children of a prominent parent can face a whole array of challenges and obstacles that other kids might not have to confront.

"I almost think they're in competition with their parents," I said, "I really do. They don't feel like they measure up sometimes."

(At the same time, I am a firm believer that actions have consequences and that each of us is responsible for those actions, no matter what our particular family dynamics might be.)

I have five sons and I have never forced them into basketball or made them feel as if they would be disappointing me or making a mistake in not playing. All I wanted was for them to take their schoolwork seriously and work hard toward being successful, and, despite some missteps here and there, they have done that. David, Michael, and Mark—my three sons with Jane—have succeeded in business and are happily married, and I am extremely proud of them, as I am of Ryan (who now scouts for the Lakers) and Jonnie, who received his MBA in 2011. As I've mentioned, Jonnie played basketball at my alma mater. That was his desire and choice, not mine. In fact, I worried that it would place an unfair amount of pressure on him, but he wanted to go there. He didn't wind up playing much, but that is another matter, something that was much harder for Karen than it was for me. I understand how these things can go. Jonnie was recruited by one coach, John Beilein, who left and went on to Michigan, and Jonnie wound up being coached by Bob Huggins. Jonnie can shoot the ball and is a very gifted jumper and possesses a high basketball IQ. But I didn't feel he was competitive enough, and I couldn't teach him that. That meanness and nasty streak had to come from him. He didn't do enough extra things to stand out in practice and, to some extent, was just happy to be there. Is the fact that he had been given so much in life part of the problem? No question, and for that both Karen and I can accept some of the blame. I wanted my kids to have things that I didn't, and I realize that that can dampen one's raw desire. Having said all that, what is most important is this: Jonnie's a terrific kid and everyone likes him and likes being around him. But Karen protects and spoils him and Ryan too damn much and doesn't really allow me to have an equal voice and influence. I should probably be more assertive, but I detest conflict. The one time I can recall doing so was the night before Jonnie left for college, when in front of everyone at the dinner table, I badgered him about the importance of being competitive. He wound up telling me, "Dad, shut the hell up," which I secretly admired him for doing. At least I got a rise out of him.

Marge had made some notes. "Anytime the Lakers lost," she said, "Chick would say to me, 'Let's get out of here. Jerry's down there going crazy again.'"

It's true. I detested losing. It tore me up. Not long after Karen and I were married, when I was coaching, there was a period when I didn't speak to her for several days. She was a young bride and had no idea how to react, no doubt wondering what she had done or gotten herself into. She spoke with her mother, who told her not to take it personally, that I would snap out of it. Which I did, until it happened again.

If you ask Karen if I am happy, she will tell you that by nature I am not, and she will also tell you that she is convinced that if, for whatever reason, I ever decided to end things and leave her, I would move forward and not look back. All I can or will say in response is this: If a person—*any* person—ever decides they need to leave, then they should go. I know that sounds harsh, but that's how I feel. (I am not sure I really believe this, though, and I imagine my expressing this is merely a form of self-protection, but I can't say for sure.)

It was funny to hear Marge relate how I would react to losses, because I always thought Chick took Laker losses much harder than I did. He prided himself on not being biased, which used to make me laugh, especially once I stopped playing and heard his broadcasts. I would always say to him, "If you really know yourself, you would know that you're the most unbiased biased person on earth." The other thing about Chick was this: he was as loved, if not more loved, than any player who ever played for the Lakers. "He truly was a celebrity," I told Marge.

She was quiet for a moment, then said, "It's such a shame he never knew that."

"He didn't want to know that," I said. "He didn't think of himself that way." When Chick was inducted into the Hall of Fame in Springfield the year after his death, I presented him posthumously.

Marge wanted to talk about the sudden way that Chick died. I had already experienced one death that day, and I knew the story, but she needed to relive it. "We were just sitting on the porch," she recalled. "We'd just gotten home from Vegas the night before. And there was a plant by the pool, from here to there"—she gestured—"not even that far. And Chick said, 'You know, that plant should be turned around. The sun isn't hitting it.' So I went into the house for something. He walked over and turned the plant and it was on the steps that went down to the pool, and he slipped and fell and smashed the back of his head."

"I'll never forget when you first told me that," I said.

"And what made me go back out there so fast? I think I just walked past the kitchen door and I saw him lying out by the pool. But I'm blessed that he never really came to. They operated on his brain three times, trying to do whatever they could, but nothing could be done."

"You and Chick were soul mates," I said. "A lot of people use that term loosely, but you truly were."

Marge didn't want to dwell any longer on the life they had had together. She wanted to talk about what else she had written down. *Jerry West must have a clock in his head. Chick called it "Jerry's Nervous Time."*

"I'll tell you what that was in reference to. It was like I had a twenty-four-second clock in my head. I would go to practice a little earlier than most people to shoot around, and I used to turn my back to the basket and I would start. I'd say, 'Four seconds—a thousand one, a thousand two, a thousand three, shoot it,' always giving myself enough time to take maybe one or two little dribbles to get somebody leaning."

"Chick never stopped talking about the time you hit that sixty-three-foot shot against the Knicks in the 1970 Finals."

"Yeah, nobody does," I said, "and that's the problem. What they don't talk about is that the shot only tied the score and we lost in overtime, and we lost the series. There was no three-point line back then."

I scored 25,192 points in my fourteen-year career with the Lakers (the most ever, until Kobe Bryant surpassed that record in 2010) and I was the third player in NBA history to reach that plateau. Injuries caused me to miss about two and a half full seasons. Had there been a three-point shot, not only would I have had a lot more points, but perhaps my ability to hit a shot in the closing seconds would have decided more games. The league didn't begin to record steals until the year before I retired, and I would love to have known how many I might have had if figures had been kept of that particular skill throughout my career. There also used to be hand-checking when I played, and games were extremely physical; there is no hand-checking now.

You played within the rules that you had at the time.

One steal in particular will always stand out, the one I mentioned much earlier. We were playing the Celtics in the 1962 Finals. It was Game Three and there were three seconds left and we were home at the Sports Arena. The score was tied at 115, Celtics' ball. Sam Jones was trying to throw the ball in to Bob Cousy, but somehow I got my hand on it and deflected it, on the run, toward the Celtics' basket. But instead of pulling up for a jump shot, as our bench was apparently yelling for me to do, which I never heard, I sped to the basket and was able to lay it in as the buzzer sounded. Instinctively, I just knew I would have enough time. Before I even realized what was happening, I was up on my teammates' shoulders and being carried out of the arena as if I were some sort of hero, a role I was never comfortable playing, and a view of myself I stubbornly refuse to share.

12

Dream Game

Madison Square Garden, in New York City

S leep is difficult for me even at the best of times, but when I am unable to find it, my vivid imagination often takes over and keeps me happily engaged. Why, I wondered, had Rick Barry come to mind on my way to see Pete Newell that November day, and my thinking he might have been just as great as Larry Bird? Or John Stockton, and how undervalued I felt he was? I can't say for sure, except that the game of basketball, and everyone associated with it, is something that is nearly always in my thoughts, something I seem to be constantly obsessing about.

Both the days and the nights after Pete's death were extremely hard for me. The one thing I have always known, that I never kid myself about, is that you can't redo time, that no day ever comes back. So I was grateful for one particular night when I was able to temporarily relieve the pain I felt over Pete's passing, one night when I was able to fantasize what a perfect game of basketball might look like, much in the way I imagined games I would play in as I practiced alone on my makeshift court in Chelyan, way back when. (In reality, of course, the only sports in which you can have a perfect game are bowling and baseball, but this was not reality.) Maybe I was motivated by Bill Russell's eloquent description of what his perfect game would look like, but his was much more focused on how he would perform individually and under what circumstances. Or maybe it was my on-again, off-again search for a box score someone had sent me once, of a game in about 1967 or 1968 in which I missed maybe one shot from the field, hit all my free throws, had thirteen or so rebounds and as many assists. The idea of anyone having a game like that is ridiculous. In any case, what I imagined was different from what Bill had, and it was more specific.

The setting is Madison Square Garden, my favorite arena, and it's playoff time, the time I live for. There is a slight chill in the air even though it is spring, a Sunday in May. People are filing into the Garden for this special game, a game to be played at the highest level by players in their prime. Tipoff is set for 2:30 p.m., and this game, which may or may not be a Game Seven, is one that everyone wants to see and that has been sold out for months (though that doesn't prevent the scalpers from furiously plying their trade up and down Seventh Avenue). The electricity outside the Garden as fans head toward the arena is different than anywhere else, just as New York is. I am staying at a hotel close by, mainly because I don't want anything to interfere with my routine of preparation, and because if for some reason I got lost on my way to the Garden, it would sap me of energy and might cause me to lose my focus.

Jack Nicholson has flown in from Los Angeles and is sitting court-side with Sean Connery — my two favorite actors — and Jack is telling Spike Lee and Snoop Dogg how he used to play basketball for his New Jersey high school and how the "little bit of radio coverage" the team received made him feel like a performer as much as a ball player. Dustin Hoffman, Warren Beatty, and Denzel Washington are sitting close by, laughing and cutting up. Frank Sinatra, whom I first met in Palm Springs, is there, and he is with Sandy Koufax (the Dodgers are in New York for a series with the Mets) and Don Drysdale (whom I had a summer camp with). Sam Huff (who had played football at West Virginia and with the New York Giants) has come too, along with Jim Brown, Joe Louis, and Sugar Ray Robinson, who pulled up in his pink Cadillac and caused a stir. Monet and Picasso have, somehow, magically found their way from their studios to the Garden, and they sit next to Stevie

Wonder, who has no trouble visualizing the scene. Bob Short, Jack Kent Cooke, and Jerry Buss decided to sit together. Pete Newell and John Wooden (despite his aversion to pro basketball) are two rows over. My high school friend Kenny Billow, who used to drive me all around Kanawha County, has come from West Virginia, and he has brought my sisters Patricia and Hannah, as well as Betty Underwood, my high school English teacher. Ann Dinardi and Willie Akers have come together, as have Presidents Obama and Clinton, who decide to sit next to George W. Bush—three very different individuals, all of whom love sports. Hell, even that couple who were certain I would never amount to anything have found their way to New York from their porch in Chelyan to see what all the fuss is about.

I am wondering who the best referees for this game of games would be, refs who were fair and with whom you could interact, refs who were not affected by star power, and suddenly Mendy Rudolph, Joe Gushue, and Richie Powers appear near the scorer's table. (I plan to ref too when I am not actually playing.) The game is going to be subject to the rules that were in effect when I played and that ended around the time the Detroit Pistons won two consecutive championships in the late eighties (the NBA was tired of the decline in scoring and how ugly it felt the games had gotten):

- *hand-checking is permitted (unlike today, where the offensive player is at a distinct advantage)*
- *no traveling (unlike today, where two and a half steps is considered acceptable)*
- *no carrying or palming of the ball (your hand has to stay on top of the ball, not on its side)*
- *an assist will be credited only as a result of a pass that leads directly to a basket*

I can hear the squawking that there won't be as many crossover or change-of-pace dribbles, that there will be too many fights, too much grabbing and clutching and holding, that the game overall won't be as fun or exciting to watch, but trust me, when you see the rosters, you will realize there is nothing to worry about.

I see Chick Hearn and I see Johnny Most and I am glad they are here to do the play-by-play. In fact, I feel certain that the game will be so spectacular that Chick will come up with some new Chickisms and that Johnny will actually be able to identify each player by name. (I think back to the time I watched the Celtics play the Yugoslavian national team with Vlade Divac, and heard Johnny, in his wonderfully gravelly voice, intone that "a tall guy with a beard passed to another guy with long arms," and how I laughed my ass off.) At the press table are writers who focus on the game that is being played far more than the personalities who are playing it: Mal Florence and Bill Dwyre and Dan Hafner and Jim Murray of the Los Angeles Times; *the Vecsey brothers, George and Pete, Frank Deford, Dave Anderson, Jimmy Breslin, Red Smith, Doug Krikorian, Joe McDonnell; Mickey Furfari and Bill Smith and A. L. "Shorty" Hardman from West Virginia; and Gay Talese and David Halberstam and David Remnick and John McPhee, writers who don't make their living writing about sports but who write beautifully and insightfully about them just the same.*

Beyond the officiating rules, these are the other conditions that are in place, and the public has been informed of them:

- *each and every player has had the benefit of the best strength and conditioning techniques available, the best doctors, trainers, nutritionists and massage therapists, and state-of-the-art practice facilities*
- *each player is in his prime, somewhere between twenty-six and twenty-nine*

- players travel coach, not on charter planes, and are responsible for their own bags and uniforms; they each have only one pair of sneakers (not a new pair for every game)
- players must travel alone—no entourage, no bodyguards, no publicists, no Twittering—just the player, his teammates, and his coaches, a contained band of brothers

And who might they be? It is 1:45, and I walk down the corridor and straight into the East locker room (which belongs to the Knicks and where I would never go were it not for the fact that this is my dream and I can go wherever I want). I see some of the players reading the rosters for both teams, which I managed to post on the wall hours before anyone got there. They are written by hand, the way I always prefer to do things:

My Dream Game

EAST

Kobe Bryant
Julius Erving
Dwayne Wade
Larry Bird
Oscar Robertson
Bill Russell
Wilt Chamberlain
Tim Duncan
Dennis Rodman
Steve Nash
Charles Barkley

COACH: Red Auerbach
ASST: Phil Jackson

WEST

Michael Jordan
Elgin Baylor
LeBron James
Rick Barry
Magic Johnson
Shaquille O'Neal
Kareem Abdol-Jabbar
Karl Malone
Hakeem Olajuwon
John Stockton
Jerry West

COACH: Pat Riley
ASST: Gregg Popovich

I wrestled back and forth, tossed and turned, before coming up with this list for this game I both wanted to watch and dreamed about being part of. Because I love mystery, I decide that the only thing each player will know beforehand is that he is supposed to arrive at the Garden by 1:00 p.m. and that someone will take him straight to his assigned locker room; then, and only then, will the player find out who else is on his team.

I also thought long and hard about the players whose games I particularly admired and whose contributions I personally felt were undervalued, underappreciated, underrated, or all three. Some of them are on the list above — Duncan, Olajuwon (who is forgotten today as a player although he was a nightmare matchup and his footwork was as graceful as Baryshnikov's), Barry, Stockton, and Rodman. The others are:

Walt Frazier
Dick Barnett
George Gervin
Clyde Drexler
Scottie Pippen
James Worthy
Moses Malone
Robert Horry
Kevin Garnett
Paul Pierce
Dominique Wilkins
Bill Walton
John Havlicek
David Thompson
Gary Payton
Grant Hill
Kevin McHale
Nate Thurmond

I have always wondered—honestly, what player hasn't?—what it would be like to play with or against players from a different era. For me, in particular, I've always wanted to play against Michael Jordan or Kobe Bryant—to find out what they are made of. I know them both as people, but the hard truth is you don't really know what players are made of until you are standing across from them, ready to compete. I could see their determination and intensity in their body language; with me, it was always centered in my eyes. I knew that in the brief period of time that Michael and Kobe had overlapped, they would practically beat each other with sticks to see who would survive, be the last man standing. So in the game this day—after Dave Zinkoff announces the roster for the East and John Ramsey for the West, the only background sound coming from an organ when each player takes the floor—Pat puts me in after five minutes, and I am competing against Kobe. As he crosses halfcourt with the ball, I try to shade him to his left—even though he's great going to his left, I want to limit him to one side of the court and force him to the sideline, want to basically divide the court in two and keep him contained there. (All players today are such accomplished ball handlers—including Kobe—but I honestly feel there is too much dribbling altogether. I know how important it is to remember all the things Kobe, or any player, likes to do best. So if I can force Kobe to think about his options, as opposed to the very thing in that instant he might be determined to do, perhaps I can steal the ball from him a few times and break his concentration.) But if my team, when we are on offense, takes too many quick shots and has too many turnovers, Kobe will get into the open court and take full advantage of that. If Kobe finds his rhythm, I know that I will have to shift my strategy, will have to then do whatever I can offensively, not defensively, to get him to make a mistake. When a player like Kobe or Michael (and everything I have said about Kobe not only applies to Michael, but is raised a notch because Michael was the best defensive player ever at his position) has the ability to score fifty points when he's going good, the only thing you can do is put pressure on them to make them guard you, force them to expend energy and focus on something other than their offense, try to make them respect you to such a degree that they will accept they are in for a long and grueling night. The essence of mano a mano. I know I can get shots off against either Kobe or Michael; that is not the issue. But can I get quality shots off? Against players like that, I have to be more precise, have to get into certain areas that they want to keep me out of. The one significant advantage I have — as did many players of my era, but of course Kobe and Michael have it too — is my ability to shoot the ball deeply, from range.

Even though this appears to be an All-Star Game by the way it is divided, it is not; those games are playground games, farces, whereas this has all the intensity of a playoff game. But in a game like this, where every player is going all out, you have to watch your intensity level. If you are too intense, have too much adrenaline flowing, you can't play your best. You have to find the right balance of physical and mental energy, of heart and head.

I go back to the bench and watch some of these players go at one another. You can have all the talent in the world and yet be a very poor basketball player. Not these guys; these guys have done it, have performed consistently at the highest level. Each one of them has the ability to take over a game, to get to the free-throw line often (one mark of a great player), and to make very few mistakes when a game, particularly a closely contested one, nears its end. Whatever the potential someone saw in each of them has been far exceeded over time. Having one spectacular year is not a measure of a player's greatness, not even close.

I see Kareem out there against Russell (who retired just a few months before Kareem began his career), two centers who rely on finesse more than power, and I wonder how Bill is going to defend against the Sky

Hook. And when Shaquille and Wilt are out there, power against power, I wonder how Shaquille will stop Wilt's fadeaway jump shot. With all the lobs and plays designed just for Wilt, how will Shaquille stop him? And yet, I remind myself that while Wilt was the strongest player in the league when he played, that he just intimidated and scared the hell out of people, Shaquille was in another category altogether; he was so powerful it was ridiculous. He would absolutely destroy other teams, mentally destroy them so that they were beat before the game even started.

And now, in my mind, I switch them around, and Russell is defending Shaquille, and Wilt is playing against Kareem, which of course actually happened, as they overlapped for four years. A couple of minutes later, Wilt is playing Olajuwon and is struggling to combat his quickness, especially how quickly he could jump. (When Olajuwon actually played, a young Shaquille couldn't stop him. Nor could David Robinson or Patrick Ewing. The essence of a great player is his footwork, particularly a great post player.)

In the backcourt, Oscar and Magic are playing each other, and Magic is having a little trouble containing him. As great as Magic was as a team defender, he wasn't quite quick enough to be a great individual defender. He had trouble with Michael and he would have had trouble with an athletic two-guard such as Kobe, or maybe even me. But he had the greatest size advantage of any NBA player at his position and a skill level that was unbelievable. With the ball in his hands, there was no one better. No one. And he made everyone around him better, and now he is doing that out there on the court.

LeBron is going against Dwayne Wade, but he is struggling with his footwork and not playing with the confidence in his shooting that he should have. Five minutes later, though, LeBron gets going, and once that happens, no one can stop him. No one.

Karl Malone is battling with Tim Duncan, but without John Stockton in the game, Karl is not faring well. He knows how to use his body as well as almost any player I can think of, but he is struggling to create things off the dribble. And then when Stockton gets into the game, he creates all sorts of problems for Steve Nash.

Larry Bird is discovering how good Rick Barry actually is (and that even Larry's legendary trash-talking isn't bothering Rick), but it is the battle between Elgin Baylor and Julius Erving that is getting the most oohs and aahs from the crowd. I feel certain that Julius studied Elgin when he played, and now he has a chance to show his teacher what he learned. I love seeing Elgin back in the Garden (and jawing with Spike Lee); fans who never got a chance to see him in person will not forget the dazzling show he is putting on this afternoon.

Red and Pat are coaching their hearts out, Phil and Gregg are constantly in their ears, and all of them have their hands full because not one of these twenty-two players wants to sit — every player wants to be part of this game for as long as it lasts. But sacrifices will have to be made; certain players will have to yield to others, and I wonder who they will be. I also wonder which players will actually be more effective if they play less.

In the stands I notice that Monet and Picasso have pulled out sketchbooks and are drawing what they see, no doubt trying to capture every nuance and marveling at how coordinated everything is on the floor — a beautiful tug-of-war, a combination of precise passing, great shooting, superb defense (so many contested shots!), clever thinking, subtle finesse, and impressive power. Basketball as a perfectly choreographed ballet. (I would give anything to leave the arena and spend days with them afterward, excited to see what their paintings ultimately revealed.) It is really a simple game, you know, this game of basketball. Problems arise when players and coaches try to complicate it.

There are five seconds left and the score is tied at 105 and everyone in the Garden is standing. Red cannot yet light his cigar and Pat looks frenzied, and both Gregg and Phil are doing their best to settle their players down. In both huddles during what will be the last timeout, the discussion is heated and everyone is bickering and jawing about the only thing that matters now: who is calm and determined and confident enough to decide the outcome of a game where amazing has already happened. Kobe is making his argument to Red and Phil that Bird is tired and it has to be him. Wilt wants the ball inside. Kareem quietly reminds Pat that New York is his home and that he wants the play to be drawn up for him and Magic. LeBron wants to take on Kobe in the worst way. And then there is Michael, staring, not talking, certain it will all come down to him.

Finally, I step forward and speak up. "I'm taking it," I say firmly. "I want Shaquille to come out and set a pick on Kobe. Everyone will expect it to be Michael, but I live for this and damn it, I have some seniority here."

Ten players return to the floor and Magic inbounds to me and suddenly the clock starts going off in my head: Five, four—I begin moving to the right, near the top of the key, ready to take the final dribble and get the ball where I want it—three, two—I extend, Shaquille has gotten Kobe off stride—one, and I rise up and release the ball a moment before the buzzer sounds.

Do I make it, or do we go to overtime?

You decide.

13
Seeking David

Paying my respects, South Korea, 2010

In 2008, when the Lakers played the Celtics in the NBA Finals, no one dreaded the series more than Karen. She dreaded it because she knew I would be asked, yet again, to relive some of the worst moments of my life, and she feared the effect it would have on me. I was officially a year out of basketball at that point, but it didn't matter. Reporters were calling at all times of the day and night, wanting to know my thoughts about the rivalry that has defined professional basketball, the rivalry that underscored, at least in my demon-filled mind, the sense that I would always be thought of as a prince but never a king.

I was in Morgantown, West Virginia, at the beginning of the series and everywhere I went people asked me about it. I was surprised that the Lakers were favored because I knew that a number of people had doubts about Pau Gasol's toughness, about how he was going to fare against Boston's front line. Pau had come to the Lakers a few months earlier in a deal that everyone was convinced I had somehow engineered, and I was sick and tired of hearing about it. Mike Heisley had been looking to save money in Memphis and everyone knew that. When I was still with the Grizzlies I had told Mitch that Pau might be available. End of story. But somehow everyone—and I mean *everyone*—was still certain that I had delivered a gift to the Lakers. Such is the nature of rumor and innuendo in pro basketball.

The Lakers wound up going down in six games, and the final game, in Boston, was a drubbing. They lost by a humiliating thirty-nine points, and their bus was rocked by fans afterward, just as it had been in 1984 when the Celtics won the Finals at home. It was a very difficult series for Kobe, who had won the MVP Award for the regular season and had asked me to come to the ceremony. He had trouble getting untracked in the series against Boston's relentless defense. I only went to one home game during the series, as I much prefer watching at home on television. When the Lakers won the Western Conference final two weeks earlier, I was asked by the NBA to present the trophy. Even though I found the invitation flattering, I agreed to do it with mixed emotions. Because of my non-relationship with Phil Jackson, I felt certain that he probably wouldn't want me to be there.

In 2010, the Lakers, who had beaten Orlando for the championship in 2009, played the Celtics again. And once again the press couldn't write enough about the rivalry. I had made some comments the year before about Kobe and LeBron James, about how I felt that LeBron had surpassed Kobe as a player but that Kobe was still the best closer in the game. The press chose to focus on the first part only, and while Kobe professed not to care, I am sure he did. I sensed that Kobe didn't fully realize how difficult the Lakers' quest for a title was going to be, despite their great regular season. Knowing him as well as I do, knowing the depth of his pride, I both felt and hoped my comments would be an enormous motivator, would stoke his considerable competitive fires a little bit. As it happened, the Lakers went on to win the championship, and LeBron, who won the MVP Award for the regular season, went home.

In 2010 LeBron was MVP again but his team went down once more. The Lakers-Celtics series went seven games—only the second time since 1994 a Finals had gone that far—and Kobe was spectacular. Even though he had a subpar seventh game, he won the Finals MVP for a second straight year. Even before the Lakers won the title and Kobe got his fifth ring, matching Magic Johnson and Kareem (who had gotten one earlier with Milwaukee), I made a comment that I thought Kobe had become the greatest Laker ever—and he told everyone that he thought I was. (I thought this was strange; it felt almost obligatory, given that he had refused every opportunity to sit down in person and be interviewed for this book. I was not sure whether the decision was Kobe's or that of his agent, Rob Pelinka, but in any case, I was shocked Kobe would not be willing to contribute his thoughts to a book that would deal in part with our relationship over the years, especially since he knows how I feel about him.)

I left the Staples Center with about a minute or so to go in Game Seven and listened to the rest on the radio; afterward, I was pleased for the players and pleased for the ownership and pleased for the city of Los Angeles, to whom it means so much.

At the beginning of the series, John Wooden died, and I was again reminded of the visit I had made to him that Saturday morning in 2008, of how he had counseled me about putting those losses to the Celtics to rest. And now, two days after the series ended, Karen and I were leaving for South Korea, where I would face head-on the death of my brother David, whose loss, and all the ways it has affected my life, continues to haunt me. I had received an invitation to come to Korea from the chairman of the Poongsan Corporation, Jin Roy Ryu, whom I had met in my new role as the executive director of the PGA's Northern Trust Open. Roy wanted me to have, among other things, the opportunity to visit the area where David had fallen, but I held off on accepting his invitation for the longest time. I had visited the memorial to the Korean War in Washington a number of years ago and I will never forget the eerie, reverent silence as I walked around, almost on tiptoe. Every year on Memorial Day I drive past the intersection of Wilshire and Sepulveda, not far from my house, and can hardly bear to look at the flags that are everywhere. In fact, I don't look. I look away. But I decided that it might be cathartic for me to go to Korea and confront this for myself.

I was glad I did. The trip, during the commemoration of the sixtieth anniversary of the beginning of the war, turned out to be the trip of my—and Karen's—lifetime. I played golf with George W. Bush, a close friend of Roy's, and I gave a basketball clinic for the servicemen and women at the DMZ, and we were treated like foreign dignitaries. The centerpiece of it all, though, was my emotional visit to the place where David fell, a rough, hilly terrain so reminiscent of the area of West Virginia where I grew up that it was both comforting and unsettling. In my mind's eye, I could envision David there, a world away from home, giving his all, struggling with hepatitis and trying to help everyone he could, guided by his enduring belief in the grace and goodness of God. Seeing his name on a wall with those of other West Virginians who had given their lives in battle was a sobering, searing moment for me.

On the day after our return, I went to a memorial service for John Wooden at UCLA's Pauley Pavilion, where the court itself is named after him. More than four thousand people were there, and many of his former players spoke, guys I had either played with or coached, Kareem, Jamaal Wilkes, Keith Erickson, and Gail Goodrich among them. I hadn't seen Stumpy, my backcourt mate, in quite some time, and naturally I thought of the year we won the 1972 championship, a season when each of us averaged more than twenty-five points a game.

Sitting there, I chuckled to myself when I recalled that the real reason John never wanted his players to attend Lakers games was that he thought they would pick up bad habits by watching the pros. I remembered the wonderful story John told of reluctantly going with Fred Schaus to Jack Kent Cooke's home to discuss his possibly coaching the Lakers and then being told by Cooke to "get the hell out" when he maintained the position he always had—that he had no interest in coaching professional basketball—and insisted no coach was possibly worth the money Cooke was offering. He, like Pete Newell, loved to teach, and he was sure pros couldn't be taught anything, especially since money and individual statistics were more important to them than winning; he didn't want to be involved with anything where money came first (he himself only made $32,500 in 1975, his last year at UCLA). I remembered how, beneath his outward appearance of polite formality, there was a fierce competitor, a coach who was always working the referees and opposing players with comments he would utter through his famous rolled-up program. He was one of the coaches I would have loved to play for, and I had told him that (the others, besides Red Auerbach and Pat Riley, whom I've already mentioned, were Bobby Knight, Gregg Popovich, Red Holzman, and, strangely enough, Phil Jackson). John had his own notions of how things should be done—even down to the way a player should wear his socks—and though his players often rolled their eyes behind his back, they got an education in life far beyond the court, and they pretty much conformed. (Even Bill Walton, his biggest nonconformist, who used to severely test John's patience, especially the time he lay down in the middle of Wilshire Boulevard to protest the Vietnam War.) But John, to his credit, had the ability to change. He used to require his players to be on time, wear coats and ties when traveling, and never fool around at practice. If they failed to abide by these rules, he would tell them that the plane for the away game would be leaving without them. He had always run a high-post offense until Kareem (as Lew

Alcindor) came to UCLA, and then he switched to a low-post game because the presence of Alcindor—and later Walton— dictated he do so. When one of his players informed him that even the university chancellor was coming to work in a turtleneck or an open-collared shirt, he decided he would relax his insistence on coats and ties as long as they looked neat.

I smiled as I recalled him telling me that he never smoked or drank—except for the one time he got sick on home brew, when he played at Purdue—and my telling him that I once got so ill my freshman year at West Virginia that it cured me of drinking any- thing for a long time to come. (Even today, I rarely touch hard liquor, preferring wine, which I enjoy collecting.)

But it was trading stories with him about coaches (two in par- ticular stand out) who are barely remembered today—coaches who were real characters, something so lacking in the current ranks—that made time spent with him so enjoyable. We talked about Abe Lemons, who used to coach at Oklahoma City Univer- sity and later at Texas. Abe's ancestry was mostly Native Ameri- can, and one time in Akron, Ohio, he and some other coaches went out to eat, and one of the coaches told the waitress that he would give her fifty bucks if she asked Abe to dance. So she did, and Abe said that he was flattered but warned her that the last time he'd danced, it rained for thirty days. Then at Texas, Abe's team won twenty games a year for three straight years, but he got himself fired. At the press conference, he was asked what he was going to do next. He said he was going to go right out and buy a new car, one with a glass bottom. Everyone was puzzled by Abe's response and asked him, Why a glass-bottomed car? "Because I want to see the look on the athletic director's face when I run over his ass." The athletic director had been a track coach, and before Abe departed, he gave him this piece of advice: "Coach track.

Because all you have to do is tell them to stay left and get back as soon as they can." John then told his own story about Abe, and this also had to do with a waitress in a restaurant. She asked Abe if she could get him something and he said yes, but it wasn't food. "If you pull up another chair and sit beside me and just nag, nag, nag my ass out for the next ten minutes, it would be of great help. I'm going home to my wife after I leave here and I haven't been home for several days, and this will sort of ease it up."

Our all-time favorite, though, was Bones McKinney, the coach at Wake Forest and someone who was part of a basketball camp that I ran at the Virginia Military Institute (and before that at the Miller School outside Charlottesville). Bones's team was playing down at Kentucky, and he wore loose-fitting loafers and pants wherever he went. He usually placed a seat belt around his chair and wore it in order to restrain himself if he got too excited. But on this occasion, Bones had forgotten his seat belt, and so when the ref missed a call, Bones kicked one of his shoes onto the court and then went running out there to retrieve it. As he bent over, all this stuff—pencils and pens and God knows what— came falling out of his pockets. The ref asked him what in the hell he was doing, and Bones said, crouching down in the same way he had taught his players to do, that he thought he would help his team out by playing a little defense. Needless to say, he got a technical.

Abe and Bones are gone now, and as I sat there at Pauley, I couldn't help but wonder when I would be too. Experiencing what I had in Korea made me feel that David's death, in certain respects, had not been in vain. Because the South Korean people sixty years later are still so grateful for our help during that conflict and for the freedom and democracy that they now tenuously enjoy, I find myself feeling free too. Free, for the most part, of the pain and anguish that his death caused our family. Free, to some extent, of the sick drive and need to be perfect in everything I do, spurred by my crazed efforts to somehow compensate for David's terrible loss at such a young and tender age, his whole life ahead of him, a life he never got a chance to live.

The journey I have made, from a home I never wanted to be in to a life that has been richer than I ever could have imagined, is one that I still have trouble grasping, one that I still can't entirely convince myself I have been worthy of and am entitled to. I am still uncomfortable when people praise me because the one person I wanted praise from—my father—I never got, and I will spend the rest of my life never fully understanding why, and why he felt it was okay to physically abuse me in the way that he did. But nothing will change that now and I know it, even if I don't accept it. Time and time again, I think back to a movie I saw once, with Melvyn Douglas and Gene Hackman, a movie that came out a few years after my father's death. It was called *I Never Sang for My Father,* and the lines in it I will never forget are these: *Death ends a life, but it does not end a relationship, which struggles on in the survivor's mind toward some resolution which it may never find.* As with my father, but in a slightly different vein, I know that nothing will ever erase the pain—the deep emotional scars—of losing to the Boston Celtics all those times and feeling I could have done something more, John Wooden's sage advice to me notwithstanding. What I finally realize, though, is that when we lost and I chastised myself, always asking, *What more could I have done?,* I wasn't asking the right question. The real, and even more painful, question was this: *What more could I have done to win my father's love?*

Aside from the days when my depression hobbles me and sinks me into the darkest places, the good news is that I get up every day and, fueled by my vivid imagination and endless curiosity, remain determined to stick around, to be vibrant and active and to give of my time and considerable energy to help others, to live long enough to see how it is all going to work out.

That doesn't mean that I have stopped looking for the nearest exit wherever I go, or am any less tempted to disappear. But what it does mean is that I, Jerry West, have found, at long last, what everyone I know has been convinced, and worried for years, would always elude me—some weird and tenuous semblance of peace.

Epilogue

February 17, 2011

In August of 2010, I returned to Springfield and the Hall of Fame and brought Jonnie and Ryan with me. Not only was my 1960 Olympic team being inducted but Jerry Buss was being inducted as well and I had been asked to be one of his presenters, as I had been for Pat Riley two years earlier.

But not long before the ceremony began, I discovered that my name had somehow been left off the list of presenters. I told the producer for NBA TV that there must have been some mistake, but I didn't press the issue. I was not only at a loss to understand how this could have happened, but I felt embarrassed; many people asked me after the ceremony why I wasn't up there and I didn't know what to say. For much of the weekend I simply stayed in my room and wouldn't answer the phone. Earlier that summer, Jerry and I had had lunch, and I had reluctantly asked him about something that I had heard from more than one person: that Jerry felt I had taken sole credit for things that Bill Sharman was as much responsible for as I had been. Even though I was informed that Bill and Jerry had talked and Bill had told Jerry that he had never felt this way, I needed to ask Jerry about this myself. I brought up something similar in the course of this book, at the end of chapter 6, but that had to do with Jerry and me, and the period when I was still with the organization. The possibility that Jerry Buss still harbored negative feelings toward me years later was very upsetting, and so I did the one thing it has always been a struggle for me to do — confronted someone about something uncomfortable.

Jerry absolutely denied it, which helped relieve any awkward feelings I had and any hurt that I felt, but when I learned that my name was not on the list to present him (initially, Earvin Johnson and I were supposed to be the presenters, but then Jerry asked if everyone who had been enshrined in the Hall during the time he had owned the team could come up), I was perplexed and angry all over again. I do know, *now*, that had I picked up the phone in my room in Springfield, I would have learned that neither the Lakers nor Jerry Buss had anything to do with the mix-up, that it was an honest error on the part of NBA TV and the Hall of Fame, and that everyone felt terrible about it. But I didn't pick up the phone, and as a result, it took me days to get over it; it ruined my time there, and my sons were incredibly upset with me.

What I will treasure from that weekend, though, was the opportunity to reunite with that marvelous Olympic team, all of whom were there except for my roommate, Les Lane, who had died years earlier, at the age of forty-one, and of course Pete Newell. I do think that every one of their names should have been spoken aloud when we were on stage, not just mine and Oscar Robertson's, but the Hall was in charge of the evening, not me. I do know that that will almost certainly be the last time we will ever be assembled in one place, and the last time I will see many of them.

I am not retired. That is not really part of my DNA. I am in the midst of my third year as executive director of the Northern Trust Open, which takes place at the Riviera Country Club each February. In 2010, despite a terrible economy, we raised $1.5 million, which went toward deserving nonprofits in the Los Angeles area, something I am as proud of as anything I have ever accomplished, and more gratifying to me than anything I have ever done. In 2011, we did even better, and I was particularly pleased by the ongoing existence of a Patriots Outpost, right by the tenth hole. It began as a PGA initiative to honor veterans, including my brother

David, and it continues to be there because of the generous support of the Annenberg Foundation. And since 2009, I have been an active spokesperson about the many dangers of atrial fibrillation, spreading awareness to Congress and other groups about the condition I have suffered from for years.

Most of all, though, I continue to do the things that I love, with my boyish enthusiasm and fervor. I love standing under the big, silent oak trees of my friend Jim Justice's property in West Virginia and I love going turkey hunting with him and my son David and my friends Richard Aide and Peck Dorsey. To wake at four thirty in the morning and crouch quietly in the dark woods in camouflage, waiting patiently for the bird's feathers to slowly unfurl, is one of the most beautiful things I have ever experienced, one of my personal Seven Wonders of the World. Even though patience of any kind with anything will always elude me, turkey hunting is an exception. In 2008 and 2010, I wasn't successful at all in this pursuit, and in 2011 I didn't even get off a single shot, but still I persevere.

Jim bought the Greenbrier in 2009 and became a local hero at the eleventh hour, as the failing resort, which is across the street from my home in White Sulphur Springs and to which I have been going for many years, was about to be purchased by the Marriott Corporation. Not long afterward, he told me he wanted to have a new restaurant there filled with my memorabilia. I am still stunned and humbled by his desire to honor me in this way.

Prime 44 West opened in October of that year, and the menu includes some of Karen's recipes. Everything Jim does is first class, and the restaurant is no exception. When he is not overseeing his many businesses and coaching both a girls' and a boys' high school basketball team, he is on the golf course, gearing up for the next time we play. Jim is very competitive — he had a golf scholarship to the University of Tennessee — and the camaraderie we share is so meaningful to us both. But when we play, I am also determined that he not beat me. Old habits, I guess, really do die hard.

On February 17, 2011, a statue of me was unveiled outside the Staples Center in Los Angeles at the beginning of the NBA's All-Star Weekend. This was not something I sought, nor was recognition of this kind ever the reason I played. I felt that if this was what the Lakers wanted to do, then Elgin Baylor should have a statue as well, right next to mine. It was extremely awkward for me, and even more so when Elgin was gracious enough to come and sit next to me on the dais and deliver his own touching remarks. From the time I first got to Los Angeles, he got right on me, razzing me about everything imaginable, especially the part of the world I came from. It took me a little while, but once I understood that, for Elgin, teasing was the ultimate form of affection, I knew we would be friends for life, the bond between us unbreakable, and we have been. Bill Russell was there, just as he was on Jerry West Night forty years earlier, and he told the audience that he had originally put on a green shirt that morning but then realized that it might be better to change to a blue one, that he didn't want to upset me unnecessarily, and then he cackled, of course. Bill also said that "to us, Jerry was not a silhouette. To us, he was a man with a soul." I was beginning to feel very uncomfortable as I sat up there, all of it a bit too much. Kareem spoke, Earvin spoke, Mitch spoke, Pat Riley spoke, and then Jerry Buss slowly made his way to the lectern.

"How many people ever get a statue?" he wondered aloud. "One in a million? Well" — he paused, then said — "Jerry West is one in a million." I was too overwhelmed at the time to fully absorb what Jerry had said. It was only later that I realized how deeply touched I was by the genuineness and sincerity of his words. But sitting there at that moment, all I knew was that I wanted the ceremony to end as soon as possible. If Chick Hearn had been alive, he would have helped me figure out an easy, inconspicuous way to escape. But he is a statue too, not far from mine.

In the audience, Shaquille O'Neal, at the time a member of the Boston Celtics, if you can believe it, mouthed the words *I love you,* and I did the same in response. That he came meant as much, if not more, to me than anything.

But it was the comments from two of my sons that meant the most. Jonnie was in West Virginia and his team was playing the next night, so he sent a videotaped message; in it he said he was sorry he couldn't be there, but "I am doing what you would want me to be doing, Dad—representing the state of West Virginia." And then David, my oldest, came up. He turned to Bill Russell and he reminded him of what Bill already knew but probably hadn't thought about in terms of my first three boys. "I would like to thank Bill Russell for ruining my and my brothers' childhood," he said good-naturedly. Everyone laughed, particularly Bill, because everyone knew there was, unfortunately, a great deal of truth to what David said.

As soon as I pulled the cord that dropped the curtain and unveiled the statue, I immediately looked away. The statue is not only something that means a great deal to my family, it also means I will be around for quite some time, long after I am gone.

Afterword

Much to my surprise, two months after the statue dedication, I was approached by Joe Lacob and Peter Guber, who had become the new owners of the Golden State Warriors in 2010. They wanted to know if I had any interest in joining the team as an adviser and a member of the executive board. My first instinct was that I didn't. But, on some level, I was kidding myself. My passionate love of the game was still fiercely there and I was pretty sure I still had things to offer. I wasn't unhappy with the life I was leading, not at all, but the desire for a new challenge, as it often is for me, was apparently lying dormant somewhere, just waiting to be ignited. Joe and Peter's enthusiasm for what they were hoping to achieve was contagious, and I knew that the Bay Area fan base had always been supportive. The Warriors had been to the playoffs only once since 1994, and I had some ideas as to how I might help them return there. I told Joe and Peter I would come on board if we were all clear about one major thing: I would offer my opinions, but would not assume a decision-making role. I didn't want anyone to feel I was coming there to usurp their authority. I was adamant about that.

After a month of meetings and dinners and all of us getting to know one another, I agreed to join the Warriors in May of 2011. And so a new chapter begins....

Miscellany

What My Body Says

Since injuries are a fact in any athlete's career, I thought it only right for me to allow my body—the instrument and machine I depended on for so many years—to tell its own particular tale. The story begins in 1964, because I don't have the medical records before then. My main injury prior to that time was a severe hamstring pull that occurred during the 1962–63 season, as well as many, many ankle sprains. As I mentioned in the book, I broke my nose nine times in all; twice in college, and seven times as a professional. The floors and surfaces I played on were so much different than those today. As a result, and also because players of my era didn't enjoy the sophisticated training that players do now, hamstring pulls are not as common.

1/27/64	Fracture of right thumb, splinted
2/12/64	Sprain of left ankle
10/12/64	Left knee injury (apparently not major, no specific notes)
12/13/64	Contusion to left hip
12/15/64	Back injury, injected (strain)
1/18/65	Nose fracture
2/8/65	Back strain again

3/10/65   Left knee again, injected, medication

3/15/65   Another left knee injury, treated conservatively on several occasions

11/10/65   Right hip injured, injected

12/21/65   Left knee injured again, contusion, sprain, conservative rx

1/28/66   Right middle finger sprain; left thigh contused

3/25/66   Left foot injured in practice, injected

3/29/66   Jammed thumb, left hand

4/22/66   Right ring finger injured

10/6/66   Left foot again, "possible rupture of ligament," crutches/cast

10/25/66   Left foot reinjured in practice

11/23/66   Left thigh contused

1/3/67   Contusion of right foot

1/16/67   Left ankle strain

2/1/67   Right thumb jammed, sprain

3/2/67   Right hamstring pull (eyelid sutured too); Left shoulder contusion, same game

3/7/67   Fracture of nose

3/17/67   Left ankle sprain again

3/26/67   Left ring finger fractured

9/13/67   Strain of right ankle

11/6/67   Right thigh contusion

12/25/67   Right groin strain

4/26/68   Back injured while passenger in cab (strain upper/lower back)

5/1/68   Left ankle again

10/24/68   Right groin again injured

11/2/68   Hematoma of thigh, treated at emergency room after game

11/11/68	Right foot tendinitis
1/7/69	Left groin injured in game
1/30/69	Left hamstring pulled
2/7/69	Left ankle sprain again
3/13/69	Right elbow contused
3/24/69	Contusion of left foot
4/14/69	Right elbow again
5/13/69	Right hand injured
11/17/69	Left eyelid sutured
11/20/69	Right groin again, pulled
11/27/69	Right ankle sprain again
12/3/69	Right groin again
12/17/69	Left hand injured in practice, contusion, no fracture
2/23/70	Left hamstring pull
4/30/70	Left thumb injury, no fracture
5/6/70	Right hand contusion with some neuritis (ulnar nerve)
12/28/70	Left ankle injury again
1/26/71	Traumatic bursitis, left great toe
3/2/71	Right knee injury in game at Buffalo (torn medial collateral ligament, surgery on 3/3)
10/21/71	Severe sprain, left ankle, casted few days
11/16/71	Right ankle and foot sprain
2/21/72	Contusion, left hand, elbow & shoulder
3/6/72	Muscle spasm after injury to low back in game
11/27/72	Pulled right hamstring; hip pointer, right
12/18/72	Right hamstring pull again
2/23/73	Pulled right hamstring again
3/22/73	Back strain again
4/11/73	Muscle spasm, lower back again, after new injury

9/21/73   Right ankle sprain

10/29/73   Right ankle aggravated, jammed

11/13/73   Left groin strain (rectus abdominis muscle), treated with several injections, different anti-inflammatory medications. Missed about 6 wks. of playing during this period.

2/6/74   Left groin aggravation again

My Playing Career in Numbers

Jerry West

Jerry Alan West (Mr. Clutch, Zeke from Cabin Creek)

Position: Guard • **Height:** 6-2 • **Weight:** 175 lbs.
Born: May 28, 1938, in Chelyan, West Virginia
High School: East Bank in East Bank, West Virginia
College: West Virginia University
Draft: Los Angeles Lakers, 1st round (2nd pick, 2nd overall), 1960 NBA Draft
NBA Debut: October 19, 1960
Hall of Fame: Inducted as Player in 1980
As Coach: 3 Yrs, 145-101, .589 W-L%
As Executive: LAL/MEM franchises, 1982–2007

Statistics courtesy of Basketball-Reference.com

Totals

Season	Age	Tm	Lg	G	GS	MP	FG	FGA	FG%	3P	3PA	3P%	FT	FTA	FT%	ORB	DRB	TRB	AST	STL	BLK	TOV	PF	PTS
1960-61	22	LAL	NBA	79		2797	529	1264	.419				331	497	.666			611	333				213	1389
1961-62	23	LAL	NBA	75		3087	799	1795	.445				712	926	.769			591	402				173	2310
1962-63	24	LAL	NBA	55		2163	559	1213	.461				371	477	.778			384	307				150	1489
1963-64	25	LAL	NBA	72		2906	740	1529	.484				584	702	.832			433	403				200	2064
1964-65	26	LAL	NBA	74		3066	822	1655	.497				648	789	.821			447	364				221	2292
1965-66	27	LAL	NBA	79		3218	818	1731	.473				840	977	.860			562	480				243	2476
1966-67	28	LAL	NBA	66		2670	645	1389	.464				602	686	.878			392	447				160	1892
1967-68	29	LAL	NBA	51		1919	476	926	.514				391	482	.811			294	310				152	1343
1968-69	30	LAL	NBA	61		2394	545	1156	.471				490	597	.821			262	423				156	1580
1969-70	31	LAL	NBA	74		3106	831	1673	.497				647	785	.824			338	554				160	2309
1970-71	32	LAL	NBA	69		2845	667	1351	.494				525	631	.832			320	655				180	1859
1971-72	33	LAL	NBA	77		2973	735	1540	.477				515	633	.814			327	747				209	1985
1972-73	34	LAL	NBA	69		2460	618	1291	.479				339	421	.805			289	607				138	1575
1973-74	35	LAL	NBA	31		967	232	519	.447				165	198	.833	30	86	116	206	81	23		80	629
Career			NBA	932		36571	9016	19032	.474				7160	8801	.814	30	86	5366	6238	81	23		2435	25192

Per Game

Season	Age	Tm	Lg	G	GS	MP	FG	FGA	FG%	3P	3PA	3P%	FT	FTA	FT%	ORB	DRB	TRB	AST	STL	BLK	TOV	PF	PTS
1960-61	22	LAL	NBA	79		35.4	6.7	16.0	.419				4.2	6.3	.666			7.7	4.2				2.7	17.6
1961-62	23	LAL	NBA	75		41.2	10.7	23.9	.445				9.5	12.3	.769			7.9	5.4				2.3	30.8
1962-63	24	LAL	NBA	55		39.3	10.2	22.1	.461				6.7	8.7	.778			7.0	5.6				2.7	27.1
1963-64	25	LAL	NBA	72		40.4	10.3	21.2	.484				8.1	9.8	.832			6.0	5.6				2.8	28.7
1964-65	26	LAL	NBA	74		41.4	11.1	22.4	.497				8.8	10.7	.821			6.0	4.9				3.0	31.0
1965-66	27	LAL	NBA	79		40.7	10.4	21.9	.473				10.6	12.4	.860			7.1	6.1				3.1	31.3
1966-67	28	LAL	NBA	66		40.5	9.8	21.0	.464				9.1	10.4	.878			5.9	6.8				2.4	28.7
1967-68	29	LAL	NBA	51		37.6	9.3	18.2	.514				7.7	9.5	.811			5.8	6.1				3.0	26.3
1968-69	30	LAL	NBA	61		39.2	8.9	19.0	.471				8.0	9.8	.821			4.3	6.9				2.6	25.9
1969-70	31	LAL	NBA	74		42.0	11.2	22.6	.497				8.7	10.6	.824			4.6	7.5				2.2	31.2
1970-71	32	LAL	NBA	69		41.2	9.7	19.6	.494				7.6	9.1	.832			4.6	9.5				2.6	26.9
1971-72	33	LAL	NBA	77		38.6	9.5	20.0	.477				6.7	8.2	.814			4.2	9.7				2.7	25.8
1972-73	34	LAL	NBA	69		35.7	9.0	18.7	.479				4.9	6.1	.805			4.2	8.8				2.0	22.8
1973-74	35	LAL	NBA	31		31.2	7.5	16.7	.447				5.3	6.4	.833	1.0	2.8	3.7	6.6	2.6	0.7			2.6	20.3
Career			NBA	932		39.2	9.7	20.4	.474				7.7	9.4	.814	1.0	2.8	5.8	6.7	2.6	0.7			2.6	27.0

Per 36 Minutes

Season	Age	Tm	Lg	G	GS	MP	FG	FGA	FG%	3P	3PA	3P%	FT	FTA	FT%	ORB	DRB	TRB	AST	STL	BLK	TOV	PF	PTS
1960-61	22	LAL	NBA	79		2797	6.8	16.3	.419				4.3	6.4	.666			7.9	4.3				2.7	17.9
1961-62	23	LAL	NBA	75		3087	9.3	20.9	.445				8.3	10.8	.769			6.9	4.7				2.0	26.9
1962-63	24	LAL	NBA	55		2163	9.3	20.2	.461				6.2	7.9	.778			6.4	5.1				2.5	24.8
1963-64	25	LAL	NBA	72		2906	9.2	18.9	.484				7.2	8.7	.832			5.4	5.0				2.5	25.6
1964-65	26	LAL	NBA	74		3066	9.7	19.4	.497				7.6	9.3	.821			5.2	4.3				2.6	26.9
1965-66	27	LAL	NBA	79		3218	9.2	19.4	.473				9.4	10.9	.860			6.3	5.4				2.7	27.7
1966-67	28	LAL	NBA	66		2670	8.7	18.7	.464				8.1	9.2	.878			5.3	6.0				2.2	25.5
1967-68	29	LAL	NBA	51		1919	8.9	17.4	.514				7.3	9.0	.811			5.5	5.8				2.9	25.2
1968-69	30	LAL	NBA	61		2394	8.2	17.4	.471				7.4	9.0	.821			3.9	6.4				2.3	23.8
1969-70	31	LAL	NBA	74		3106	9.6	19.4	.497				7.5	9.1	.824			3.9	6.4				1.9	26.8
1970-71	32	LAL	NBA	69		2845	8.4	17.1	.494				6.6	8.0	.832			4.0	8.3				2.3	23.5
1971-72	33	LAL	NBA	77		2973	8.9	18.6	.477				6.2	7.7	.814			4.0	9.0				2.5	24.0
1972-73	34	LAL	NBA	69		2460	9.0	18.9	.479				5.0	6.2	.805			4.2	8.9				2.0	23.0
1973-74	35	LAL	NBA	31		967	8.6	19.3	.447			/	6.1	7.4	.833	1.1	3.2	4.3	7.7	3.0	0.9		3.0	23.4
Career			NBA	932		36571	8.9	18.7	.474				7.0	8.7	.814	1.1	3.2	5.3	6.1	3.0	0.9		2.4	24.8

Advanced

Season	Age	Tm	Lg	G	MP	PER	TS%	eFG%	ORB%	DRB%	TRB%	AST%	STL%	BLK%	TOV%	USG%	ORtg	DRtg	OWS	DWS	WS	WS/48
1960-61	22	LAL	NBA	79	2797	16.0	.468	.419											3.1	3.5	6.6	0.113
1961-62	23	LAL	NBA	75	3087	22.6	.524	.445											9.8	3.1	12.9	0.201
1962-63	24	LAL	NBA	55	2163	21.9	.523	.461											5.5	2.6	8.1	0.180
1963-64	25	LAL	NBA	72	2906	24.2	.562	.484											12.2	1.8	14.0	0.232
1964-65	26	LAL	NBA	74	3066	25.0	.572	.497				20.0							14.8	1.9	16.7	0.261
1965-66	27	LAL	NBA	79	3218	24.6	.573	.473				21.9							14.4	2.7	17.1	0.256
1966-67	28	LAL	NBA	66	2670	22.7	.559	.464				23.1							9.4	2.3	11.7	0.210
1967-68	29	LAL	NBA	51	1919	23.2	.590	.514				22.6							8.0	1.6	9.6	0.241
1968-69	30	LAL	NBA	61	2394	22.3	.557	.471				26.4							8.6	2.1	10.8	0.216
1969-70	31	LAL	NBA	74	3106	24.6	.572	.497				27.1							11.5	3.7	15.2	0.234
1970-71	32	LAL	NBA	69	2845	23.5	.571	.494			5.0	32.3							10.2	2.5	12.8	0.215
1971-72	33	LAL	NBA	77	2973	23.1	.546	.477			4.9	33.7							8.4	4.9	13.3	0.216
1972-73	34	LAL	NBA	69	2460	23.2	.533	.479			5.4	35.5							6.7	3.8	10.6	0.206
1973-74	35	LAL	NBA	31	967	22.4	.519	.447	3.0	7.8	5.5	32.5	3.6	1.1				95	1.9	1.3	3.2	0.159
Career			NBA	932	36571	22.9	.550	.474	3.0	7.8	5.1	27.1	3.6	1.1				95	124.6	37.9	162.6	0.213

Playoffs

Season	Age	Tm	Lg	Totals																Shooting			Per Game			
				G	MP	FG	FGA	3P	3PA	FT	FTA	ORB	TRB	AST	STL	BLK	TOV	PF	PTS	FG%	3P%	FT%	MP	PTS	TRB	AST
1960-61	22	LAL	NBA	12	461	99	202			77	106		104	63				39	275	.490		.726	38.4	22.9	8.7	5.3
1961-62	23	LAL	NBA	13	557	144	310			121	150		88	57				38	409	.465		.807	42.8	31.5	6.8	4.4
1962-63	24	LAL	NBA	13	538	144	286			74	100		106	61				34	362	.503		.740	41.4	27.8	8.2	4.7
1963-64	25	LAL	NBA	5	206	57	115			42	53		36	17				20	156	.496		.792	41.2	31.2	7.2	3.4
1964-65	26	LAL	NBA	11	470	155	351			137	154		63	58				37	447	.442		.890	42.7	40.6	5.7	5.3
1965-66	27	LAL	NBA	14	619	185	357			109	125		88	79				40	479	.518		.872	44.2	34.2	6.3	5.6
1966-67	28	LAL	NBA	1	1	0	0			0	0		1	0				0	0				1.0	0.0	1.0	0.0
1967-68	29	LAL	NBA	15	622	165	313			132	169		81	82				47	462	.527		.781	41.5	30.8	5.4	5.5
1968-69	30	LAL	NBA	18	757	196	423			164	204		71	135				52	556	.463		.804	42.1	30.9	3.9	7.5
1969-70	31	LAL	NBA	18	830	196	418			170	212		66	151				55	562	.469		.802	46.1	31.2	3.7	8.4
1971-72	33	LAL	NBA	15	608	128	340			88	106		73	134				39	344	.376		.830	40.5	22.9	4.9	8.9
1972-73	34	LAL	NBA	17	638	151	336			99	127		76	132				49	401	.449		.780	37.5	23.6	4.5	7.8
1973-74	35	LAL	NBA	1	14	2	9			0	0	0	2	1	0	0		1	4	.222			14.0	4.0	2.0	1.0
Career			NBA	153	6321	1622	3460			1213	1506	0	855	970	0	0		451	4457	.469		.805	41.3	29.1	5.6	6.3

Playoffs Advanced

Season	Age	Tm	Lg	G	MP	PER	TS%	eFG%	ORB%	DRB%	TRB%	AST%	STL%	BLK%	TOV%	USG%	ORtg	DRtg	OWS	DWS	WS	WS/48
1960-61	22	LAL	NBA	**12**	461	21.3	.553	.490				19.8							1.7	0.3	1.9	0.203
1961-62	23	LAL	NBA	13	557	22.2	.544	.465				16.6							**2.2**	0.2	2.4	0.209
1962-63	24	LAL	NBA	**13**	538	23.1	.548	.503				19.2							1.7	0.4	2.1	0.188
1963-64	25	LAL	NBA	5	206	25.1	.564	.496				17.3							1.0	-0.1	0.9	0.210
1964-65	26	LAL	NBA	11	470	26.7	.534	.442				22.6							**1.9**	0.0	1.9	0.189
1965-66	27	LAL	NBA	14	619	24.7	**.581**	.518				20.1							2.7	0.4	3.1	**0.237**
1966-67	28	LAL	NBA	1	1	18.1						0.0							0.0	0.0	0.0	0.010
1967-68	29	LAL	NBA	15	622	**25.1**	.596	.527				20.2							3.1	0.5	3.6	**0.278**
1968-69	30	LAL	NBA	**18**	757	**25.2**	.542	.463				31.6							**3.2**	1.1	**4.3**	**0.274**
1969-70	31	LAL	NBA	18	830	21.1	.550	.469				26.7							2.6	0.6	**3.2**	0.184
1971-72	33	LAL	NBA	15	608	18.8	.445	.376			5.4	**35.1**							-0.2	1.2	1.0	0.078
1972-73	34	LAL	NBA	**17**	638	**22.7**	.512	.449			5.4	33.6							1.5	0.9	2.4	0.184
1973-74	35	LAL	NBA	1	14	-1.6	.222	.222	0.0	15.0	6.8	11.5	0.0	0.0				106	-0.1	0.0	-0.1	-0.302
Career			NBA	153	6321	23.1	.541	.469	0.0	15.0	5.4	24.8	0.0	0.0				106	21.3	5.4	26.7	0.203

All-Star Games

Season	Age	Tm	Lg	G	GS	MP	FG	FGA	FG%	3P	3PA	3P%	FT	FTA	FT%	ORB	TRB	AST	STL	BLK	TOV	PF	PTS
1960-61	22	LAL	NBA	1	0	25	2	8	.250				5	6	.833		2	4				3	9
1961-62	23	LAL	NBA	1	1	31	7	14	.500				4	6	.667		3	1				2	18
1962-63	24	LAL	NBA	1	1	32	5	15	.333				3	4	.750		7	5				1	13
1963-64	25	LAL	NBA	1	1	42	8	20	.400				1	1	1.000		4	5				3	17
1964-65	26	LAL	NBA	1	1	40	8	16	.500				4	6	.667		5	6				2	20
1965-66	27	LAL	NBA	1	1	11	1	5	.200				2	2	1.000		1	0				2	4
1966-67	28	LAL	NBA	1	1	30	6	11	.545				4	4	1.000		3	6				3	16
1967-68	29	LAL	NBA	1	1	32	7	17	.412				3	4	.750		6	6				4	17
1968-69	30	LAL	NBA																				
1969-70	31	LAL	NBA	1	1	31	7	12	.583				8	12	.667		5	5				3	22
1970-71	32	LAL	NBA	1	1	20	2	4	.500				1	3	.333		1	9				1	5
1971-72	33	LAL	NBA	1	1	27	6	9	.667				1	2	.500		6	5				2	13
1972-73	34	LAL	NBA	1	1	20	3	6	.500				0	0			4	3				2	6
1973-74	35	LAL	NBA																				
Career			NBA	12	11	341	62	137	.453				36	50	.720		47	55				28	160

College

			Totals																Shooting			Per Game			
Season	Age	College	G	MP	FG	FGA	3P	3PA	FT	FTA	ORB	TRB	AST	STL	BLK	TOV	PF	PTS	FG%	3P%	FT%	MP	PTS	TRB	AST
1957-58	19	WVIRGINIA	28	799	178	359			142	194		311	41					498	.496		.732	28.5	17.8	11.1	1.5
1958-59	20	WVIRGINIA	34	1210	340	656			223	320		419	86					903	.518		.697	35.6	26.6	12.3	2.5
1959-60	21	WVIRGINIA	31	1129	325	645			258	337		510	134					908	.504		.766	36.4	29.3	16.5	4.3
Career			93	3138	843	1660			623	851		1240	261					2309	.508		.732	33.7	24.8	13.3	2.8

Appearances on Leaderboards, Awards, and Honors

All-Star Games	Awards	Honors	MVP Award Shares
1961 NBA	1958-59 NCAA Final Four Most Outstanding Player	1957-58 NCAA AP All-America (3rd)	1960-61 NBA 0.013 (11)
1962 NBA	1968-69 NBA Finals MVP	1958-59 NCAA AP All-America (1st)	1961-62 NBA 0.141 (5)
1963 NBA	1971-72 NBA All-Star Game MVP	1959-60 NCAA AP All-America (1st)	1962-63 NBA 0.040 (5)
1964 NBA		1961-62 NBA All-NBA (1st)	1963-64 NBA 0.081 (5)
1965 NBA		1962-63 NBA All-NBA (1st)	1964-65 NBA 0.202 (3)
1966 NBA		1963-64 NBA All-NBA (1st)	1965-66 NBA 0.227 (2)
1967 NBA		1964-65 NBA All-NBA (1st)	1969-70 NBA 0.609 (2)
1968 NBA		1965-66 NBA All-NBA (1st)	1970-71 NBA 0.217 (2)
1969 NBA		1966-67 NBA All-NBA (1st)	1971-72 NBA 0.479 (2)
1970 NBA		1967-68 NBA All-Defensive (2nd)	1972-73 NBA 0.080 (6)
1971 NBA		1968-69 NBA All-NBA (2nd)	Career 2.090 (20)
1972 NBA		1969-70 NBA All-Defensive (1st)	
1973 NBA		1969-70 NBA All-NBA (1st)	
1974 NBA		1970-71 NBA All-Defensive (1st)	
		1970-71 NBA All-NBA (1st)	
		1971-72 NBA All-Defensive (1st)	
		1971-72 NBA All-NBA (1st)	
		1972-73 NBA All-Defensive (1st)	
		1972-73 NBA All-NBA (1st)	

Appearances on Leaderboards, Awards, and Honors

Championships
(Minimum 1 playoff game)

1972 Los Angeles Lakers (NBA)

Games

1960-61 NBA 79 (1)

Minutes Played

1961-62 NBA 3087 (8)
1964-65 NBA 3066 (6)
1965-66 NBA 3218 (7)
Career NBA 36571 (43)
Career 36571 (47)

Field Goals

1961-62 NBA 799 (6)
1963-64 NBA 740 (6)
1964-65 NBA 822 (2)
1965-66 NBA 818 (2)
1966-67 NBA 645 (8)
1969-70 NBA 831 (3)
1971-72 NBA 735 (10)
Career NBA 9016 (17)
Career 9016 (22)

Field Goal Attempts

1961-62 NBA 1795 (7)
1963-64 NBA 1529 (8)
1964-65 NBA 1655 (5)
1965-66 NBA 1731 (2)
1966-67 NBA 1389 (8)
1969-70 NBA 1673 (5)
1971-72 NBA 1540 (10)
Career NBA 19032 (17)
Career 19032 (21)

Field Goal Pct

1963-64 NBA .484 (6)
1964-65 NBA .497 (4)
1965-66 NBA .473 (10)
1967-68 NBA .514 (4)

Free Throws

1961-62 NBA 712 (2)
1962-63 NBA 371 (9)
1963-64 NBA 584 (3)
1964-65 NBA 648 (2)
1965-66 NBA 840 (1)
1966-67 NBA 602 (3)
1968-69 NBA 490 (5)
1969-70 NBA 647 (1)
1970-71 NBA 525 (4)
1971-72 NBA 515 (3)
Career NBA 7160 (5)
Career 7160 (5)

Free Throw Attempts

1961-62 NBA 926 (2)
1963-64 NBA 702 (5)
1964-65 NBA 789 (3)
1965-66 NBA 977 (1)
1966-67 NBA 686 (4)
1969-70 NBA 785 (1)
1970-71 NBA 631 (8)
1971-72 NBA 633 (4)
Career NBA 8801 (7)
Career 8801 (7)

Free Throw Pct	Assists	Points	Minutes Per Game
1963-64 NBA .832 (2)	1961-62 NBA 402 (6)	1961-62 NBA 2310 (5)	1961-62 NBA 41.2 (7)
1964-65 NBA .821 (5)	1963-64 NBA 403 (4)	1963-64 NBA 2064 (5)	1963-64 NBA 40.4 (8)
1965-66 NBA .860 (4)	1964-65 NBA 364 (6)	1964-65 NBA 2292 (2)	1964-65 NBA 41.4 (5)
1966-67 NBA .878 (3)	1965-66 NBA 480 (4)	1965-66 NBA 2476 (2)	1965-66 NBA 40.7 (7)
1967-68 NBA .811 (9)	1966-67 NBA 447 (5)	1966-67 NBA 1892 (4)	1966-67 NBA 40.5 (7)
1968-69 NBA .821 (8)	1968-69 NBA 423 (10)	1969-70 NBA 2309 (2)	1969-70 NBA 42.0 (3)
1969-70 NBA .824 (8)	1969-70 NBA 554 (7)	1970-71 NBA 1859 (10)	Career NBA 39.2 (7)
1970-71 NBA .832 (7)	1970-71 NBA 655 (3)	1971-72 NBA 1985 (9)	Career 39.2 (7)
	1971-72 NBA 747 (2)	Career NBA 25192 (15)	
	1972-73 NBA 607 (4)	Career 25192 (19)	
	Career NBA 6238 (25)		
	Career 6238 (25)		

Points Per Game	Assists Per Game	Player Efficiency Rating	True Shooting Pct
1961-62 NBA 30.8 (4)	1961-62 NBA 5.4 (7)	1961-62 NBA 22.6 (6)	1961-62 NBA .524 (7)
1963-64 NBA 28.7 (3)	1963-64 NBA 5.6 (3)	1962-63 NBA 21.9 (6)	1963-64 NBA .561 (4)
1964-65 NBA 31.0 (2)	1964-65 NBA 4.9 (6)	1963-64 NBA 24.2 (3)	1964-65 NBA .572 (2)
1965-66 NBA 31.3 (2)	1965-66 NBA 6.1 (5)	1964-65 NBA 25.0 (3)	**1965-66 NBA .573 (1)**
1966-67 NBA 28.7 (3)	1966-67 NBA 6.8 (4)	1965-66 NBA 24.6 (3)	1966-67 NBA .559 (4)
1969-70 NBA 31.2 (1)	1969-70 NBA 7.5 (4)	1966-67 NBA 22.7 (4)	**1967-68 NBA .590 (1)**
1971-72 NBA 25.8 (7)	**1971-72 NBA 9.7 (1)**	**1968-69 NBA 22.3 (1)**	1968-69 NBA .557 (6)
Career NBA 27.0 (5)	Career NBA 6.7 (35)	**1969-70 NBA 24.6 (1)**	1969-70 NBA .572 (6)
Career 27.0 (5)	Career 6.7 (35)	1970-71 NBA 23.5 (2)	1970-71 NBA .571 (5)
		1971-72 NBA 23.1 (3)	
		1972-73 NBA 23.2 (3)	
		Career NBA 22.9 (22)	
		Career 22.9 (23)	

Appearances on Leaderboards, Awards, and Honors

Effective Field Goal Pct	Assist Pct	Offensive Win Shares	Defensive Win Shares
1963-64 NBA .484 (6)	1964-65 NBA 20.0 (5)	1961-62 NBA 9.8 (4)	Career NBA 37.9 (91)
1964-65 NBA .497 (4)	1965-66 NBA 21.9 (6)	1963-64 NBA 12.2 (3)	Career 37.9 (98)
1965-66 NBA .473 (10)	1966-67 NBA 23.1 (4)	**1964-65 NBA 14.8 (1)**	
1967-68 NBA .514 (4)	1968-69 NBA 26.4 (6)	1965-66 NBA 14.4 (1)	
	1969-70 NBA 27.1 (5)	1966-67 NBA 9.4 (4)	
	1970-71 NBA 32.3 (2)	1967-68 NBA 8.0 (5)	
	1971-72 NBA 33.7 (2)	1968-69 NBA 8.6 (4)	
	1972-73 NBA 35.5 (2)	**1969-70 NBA 11.5 (1)**	
	Career NBA 27.1 (83)	1970-71 NBA 10.2 (2)	
	Career 27.1 (84)	1971-72 NBA 8.4 (6)	
		Career NBA 124.6 (8)	
		Career 124.6 (8)	

Win Shares	Win Shares Per 48 Minutes	Hall of Fame Probability	
1961-62 NBA 12.9 (5)	1961-62 NBA 0.201 (5)	Career 1.000 (11)	
1963-64 NBA 14.0 (6)	1963-64 NBA 0.232 (4)		
1964-65 NBA 16.7 (3)	**1964-65 NBA 0.261 (1)**		
1965-66 NBA 17.1 (2)	1965-66 NBA 0.256 (2)		
1966-67 NBA 11.7 (6)	1966-67 NBA 0.210 (5)		
1968-69 NBA 10.8 (9)	1969-70 NBA 0.234 (2)		
1969-70 NBA 15.2 (1)	1971-72 NBA 0.216 (6)		
1970-71 NBA 12.8 (3)	Career NBA 0.213 (13)		
1971-72 NBA 13.3 (5)	Career 0.213 (13)		
Career NBA 162.6 (16)			
Career 162.6 (18)			

Transactions

April 11, 1960: Drafted by the Minneapolis Lakers in the 1st round (2nd pick) of the 1960 NBA Draft.

Authors' Note

When I decided in early 2008 that I wanted to write my autobiography, an idea I had been wrestling with for years, I knew that I wanted to work with someone who had a deep appreciation for the game of basketball but who did not make his or her living writing about it. That is not meant to disparage many members of the press whose work I greatly admire. It is simply to say that I envisioned a book that would be about far more than my life in basketball. I needed to work with someone who would be strong enough to push and probe and challenge and help me gain a richer, if incredibly painful, understanding of all I had faced and endured in my journey from the little burg of Chelyan, West Virginia, until now.

That someone turned out to be Jonathan Coleman. I had read one of his books—*Long Way to Go: Black and White in America*—because the subject of race was of great interest to me. Since my playing career had spanned the civil rights movement and I had been particularly close to my black teammates, I was very curious to learn what it was that motivated Jonathan, and gave him the courage, to take on such a difficult subject.

We met for dinner one night in April, near my home in West Virginia, and again for breakfast the next morning, and it didn't take long for me to know that Jonathan was not only someone I could trust but someone who shared both my curiosity and intensity, someone who could empathize because he was no stranger to some of the things I was talking about, someone who could help me unearth a lifetime of unsettling memories and feelings that I had always done my best to hide, that lay painfully beneath the surface.

When I mentioned in an early chapter that even the writing of this book became another form of competition for me, what I meant was that I told Jonathan, over and over again, that my story was too convoluted for him to ever get out of me, and even if he did, he would never fully understand it in any coherent way.

I didn't make it easy for him, trust me. But on the journey we embarked on together, he never backed down and he never backed up. That is not in his nature, and it is normally not in mine. But there were many times — more than he knew about, until we were done — that I felt it would have been much easier to simply give up and walk away, to not have to relive such personal memories and so many crushing disappointments, let alone share them with someone else.

In my humble opinion, Jonathan was able, through my voice and thoughts and his words, to capture a very complex person, one driven by a compulsive desire to excel. As I said in the prologue, I hope the experience of reading this book, and, perhaps, absorbing the life lessons I have learned along the way, will enable readers to find parallels in their own lives, enable them to find a better place for themselves.

It will ultimately fall to you to determine how well we have done.

—*J.W.*

In all my years as an author I had never collaborated before, nor had I wanted to. My agent, Owen Laster, always felt I lacked the temperament for it, and I am still not sure I have it now. But when Ian Kleinert, who had worked for Owen at one time, phoned me out of the blue and asked if I might have an interest in working with Jerry West, I found myself saying yes, without being entirely conscious of why. All Ian knew at that point was that Jerry emphatically did not want to write a sports book glorifying his accomplishments in a transparently self-serving way. What he wanted was the opposite: a book that would illuminate and reveal a very flawed, extremely hard on himself, humble individual, that would take the reader deep into his life while he explored his demons and hopefully succeeded in making sense of the difficult, improbable road he had traveled—the personal adversity he had faced and the choices he had made along the way. And he apparently wanted a coauthor whom he did not know, someone who was not so close to the game that he or she might not be able to see him clearly, to view beyond him as a basketball player.

When Jerry and I first spoke on the phone, in April of 2008, I was surprised when he said that he was in West Virginia hunting. "Hunting season is in November," I blithely said, even though I am not a hunter. "I am not hunting deer," he said, laughing. "Hell, you don't know *anything* about hunting. If you did, you'd know it was turkey season." I can't say for sure why I immediately knew the game had begun, but I did. I also sensed an instant rapport, one of those intangible things you just know and never question. (By the next time we spoke, five hours later, I had boned up on every aspect of turkey hunting known to man.)

After he talked for a bit about what he wanted to accomplish and why he hoped I could help, I stopped him and said, half seriously, "Jerry, there's one thing you need to know. I grew up a Celtics fan, and, frankly, it might be very hard for me to do this book with you."

There was a long silence on the line before he said, "Oh, don't worry, you'll get over it."

It didn't take me long to realize that Jerry never had. What took me longer to realize was the real reason I said I was interested in the first place. Whenever I watched the Lakers and the Celtics wage their epic battles, Jerry's face was the one I found most inscrutable, the one that interested me the most. Even as a teenager, I was intent on figuring people out; with Jerry, all I could see was the passion and sniper-like intensity with which he played, passion and intensity second to no one's. I had no clue what he was thinking, or who he really was. So, for me, this was an opportunity to peel back the onion, layer by layer, to try and get at, by whatever means necessary, the riddle and enigma that Jerry West had always represented to me (and, I had no doubt, to many, many others). That he has been the silhouetted figure of the NBA logo for more than forty years only furthered my determination to unravel the mystery.

The journey Jerry invited me on and that we took together has been the ride of my life. My previous three books tested me in a variety of ways, but working with Jerry belongs in a separate category. Trust me (as he loves to say). And the trust he had in me, allowing me, quite reluctantly at first, to go wherever I felt I needed to go and to talk to whomever I felt I needed to talk to in order to get as close to the whole story as possible (which I absolutely knew I could never get from him alone; it's human nature after all to leave things out), is something I will always cherish and be grateful to him for.

We are both strong-willed individuals and we are both a little crazy, but in my opinion, it is only because we each care enormously about what we do in our different spheres. We locked horns plenty, but we both knew we were after the same thing. Jerry is the most impatient human being I have ever met, but I have never known anyone who works harder and is more dedicated. Had he not been fully committed to doing this book in a full-on way, I would never have agreed to it. Never. He often threatened that he "could lose interest in doing this in five minutes," but somehow he never did. In Jerry's ideal world, the book would have been published two months after we signed the contract and he could never understand "why it's taking you so damn long." Well, I could never understand, I told him, why it took four years for Shaquille and Kobe to bring the Lakers a championship.

What I do understand, though, and understand beyond measure from having worked with Jerry, is this—all that it takes to endure a seven-game NBA Finals. That, and that alone, is something I would never have experienced otherwise.

—*J.C.*

Acknowledgments

Many, many people contributed to the making of this book and we want to thank them—not only for the generous giving of their time, but for sharing their considerable insight and knowledge, which enriched every page: Kareem Abdul-Jabbar, Mitchell "J.J." Anderson, John Antonik, Willie and Linda Akers, Al Attles, Tony Barone Jr., Tony Barone Sr., Gene Bartow, Elgin Baylor, Mary Belton, Trudy Belton, Bill Bertka, Delania Bierer, John Black, Hannah West Bowman, Thomas Bowman, Sen. Bill Bradley, Joe and Susan Bua, Jeanie Buss, Jerry Buss, Jim Brown, Geoff Calkins, Dyan Cannon, Cedric Ceballos, Charlie Chico, Sam Chico, Jim Cleamons, Jerry Colangelo, Gary Colson, Karen West Comfort, Michael Cooper, Jimmy Cross, Mike Curtis, Adrian Dantley, Marty and Ruth Danzig, Dana Davis, Julie Dawson, Sylvester Dinardi, Keith Erickson, Dan Fegan, Rick Fox, Walt Frazier, Bobby Freedman, Rudy Gay, Laura Glankler, Gail Goodrich, A. C. Green, Willie Gregory, Dave Griffin, Ronnie Grisanti, John Havlicek, Del Harris, Tommy Hawkins, Marge Hearn, Tom Heinsohn, Michael Heisley, Willie Herenton, Jim Hill, Barron Hilton, Lionel Hollins, Rod Hundley, Pitt Hyde, Darrall Imhoff, Phil Jackson, Steve Jackson, Earvin Johnson, Dahntay Jones, Ken Jones, Michael Jordan, Fran Judkins, Mitch Kupchak, Ronnie

329

Lester, Barbara Chamberlain Lewis, Tim Leiweke, Mary Lou Liebich, Bill Lucchesi, Nancy Pat Maloney, Dr. Jimmie Mancell, Bob McAdoo, Joan McLaughlin, Jim McLean, David Miller, Jane West Montgomery, Lee Moore, Jack Nicholson, Billy Noel, Patricia West Noel, Micki Nolan, Shaquille O'Neal, Frank O'Neill, Barry Parkhill, Jim Perzik, Randy Pfund, Buddy Quertinmont, Kurt Rambis, Glen Rice, Pat Riley, Oscar Robertson, Lon Rosen, Claire Rothman, Bill Russell, Fred and Barbara Schaus, Byron Scott, Bill Sharman, Brian Shaw, Earl and Karen Shultz, Adrian Smith, Joe Smith, Sonny Smith, Wendy Smith, Zelda Spoelstra, Bob Steiner, David Stern, Monte Stewart, Bill Strickland, Charles Sweeney, Arn and Nancy Tellem, Mychal Thompson, Ron Tillery, Rod Thorn, Gene "Bumper" Tormohlen, Jack Twyman, Kiki Vandeweghe, Gary Vitti, Chris Wallace, Donnie Walsh, Hakim Warrick, Van Weinberg, Barbara West, Charlie West, David West, Jonnie West, Karen West, Kim West, Mark West, Michael West, Ryan West, Jamaal Wilkes, Matt Winick, John Wooden, James Worthy.

Our deepest thanks to the six individuals who not only patiently transcribed all the interviews but also took the time to share their own good thoughts along the way: Emily Barker, Jack Murray, Sarah van Steenburg, Lauren Ulmer, and, especially, Wistar Murray (the first) and Laila Getachew (the last and longest). Because they understood the sensitive, intimate nature of what they were listening to, they agreed not to discuss the interviews with anyone, and, to the best of our knowledge, they never did.

The West Virginia and Regional History Collection is the division of the West Virginia University Libraries where all of the materials related to the research and writing of this book will find their permanent home. John Cuthbert, the curator and director, and associate curators Kevin Fredette, Harold Forbes, Michael Ridderbusch, and Anna Schein welcomed us warmly and did whatever they could to be of help, as did WVU Libraries dean Frances O'Brien and associate dean Myra Lowe. (At one point, in a meeting we had there in September of 2008, I lamented the fact that I had been gone from the state for long periods of time, to which Myra Lowe responded: "Don't worry, Jerry, we never let go of you, and we never will.") Kevin Fredette deserves added thanks because he suggested that Dennis Bidwell, a former prison warden, would be a good man to help with anything and everything West Virginian. Dennis wasn't just good, he was great, in every conceivable way.

We would like to thank our agent, Ian Kleinert of Objective Entertainment, who, with an assist from Jordan Bazant and Jon Salant from the Agency Sports, not only brought the two of us together but found a first-rate publisher in Little, Brown, where we have been fortunate to work with Geoff Shandler (who acquired the book and became its editor), Liese Mayer, Michael Pietsch (the imprint's wry publisher), Nicole Dewey, Michelle Aielli, and Laura Keefe from publicity, Heather Fain, Amanda Tobier, and Anna Balasi from marketing, Craig Young from sales, and Nancy Wiese, Amanda Brown, and Tracy Williams from subsidiary rights. I would put this team on the court with anybody.

Since this is a memoir, not a scholarly work of history, we felt that it was unnecessary to have a formal notes section and bibliography. Though interviews were the primary source material, there was, for context, perspective, and a variety of other reasons, much reliance on magazine and newspaper articles, school newspapers and yearbooks, letters, contracts, game programs, scrapbooks, scribbled musings, advertisements, media guides, miscellaneous pieces of local history and lore, countless videotapes, audio recordings, photographs, and other books. These are some, but by no means all, of the writings that were especially helpful: *The Hero with a Thousand Faces* by Joseph Campbell; *Unholy Ghost: Writers on Depression*, edited by Nell Casey; *Wilt* by Wilt Chamberlain and David Shaw; *The White Album* and *The Year of Magical Thinking* by Joan Didion; *The Punch* by John Feinstein; *Blink, Outliers*, and *The Tipping Point*, by Malcolm Gladwell; *The Coldest Winter* and *Playing for Keeps* by David Halberstam; *A Good Man: The Pete Newell Story* by Bruce Jenkins; *Rome 1960* by David Maraniss; *A Sense of Where You Are* by John McPhee; *The Big O* by Oscar Robertson; *Second Wind: The Memoirs of an Opinionated Man* by Bill Russell and Taylor Branch; *The Los Angeles Times Encyclopedia of the Lakers* by Steve Springer; *Darkness Visible* by William Styron; *The Gay Talese Reader* by Gay Talese; *The Rivalry* by John Taylor.

I (Jonathan) would especially like to thank the following people, people who helped in many and different ways to make the whole process of working on this book less arduous and less lonely: Gib and Liz Akin, Bill Balcke, Jane Barnes, Ann Beattie, Sydney Blair, Alyssa Brandt, Sara Bullard, Robert Byron, Ben Coleman, Michael Coleman, Camille Cooper, Kathryn Court, Sam Crosby, Jan Drolshagen, Robert Emery, Michael Fried, Russ Gallop, Tom Gilroy, Susan Harris, Steve Heim, Alan Kotz, Kathy Krometis, Avery Lawrence, Tan Lin, Bruce and Jane Littlejohn, Susan McCabe, Sarah McConnell, John McDonnell, Barry Parkhill, Nita Reigle, Ken Rivkind, Charles Roumeliotes, Elisabeth Seldes, Andy Selfridge, Loren Shetler, Gabe Silverman, Barbara Smith, Michael Stephenson, Gay and Nan Talese, Jay Stowe, Jonnie Zion, Tobi Zion, Tony Zullo.

Four people in particular need to be singled out: Jerry Lakoff, Bob Lindsey, David Morris, and Ryan West. All of them had an unwavering belief in this book that others might have considered beyond reason, and all of them never ceased to be supportive (especially Ryan, when his dad was driving me crazy). David also offered countless rides to the airport and "things to consider," for which I will always be appreciative.

I would especially like to thank Karen West for allowing me to enter her and Jerry's marriage over the course of three years. She is as strong-willed as Jerry and I are, and theirs is one of the most interesting marriages I have ever been around. I am sure I wore out my welcome many times, but somehow, some way, it all came together. Karen played many roles, wore many hats, during the entire intense process of doing this book and it could not have reached completion without her. Thanks, Karen. (By the way, we still need to have our third and deciding tennis match.)

Around the time the first words of this book made their way onto paper, Kristi Rose materialized from nowhere and made her way into my life. She sat quietly in a darkened study one Sunday evening in September, two days after we met, listening intently to the beginning. Ever after, D always wanted me to read to her. We talked, and we laughed, about everything, and we took it all in. Her presence, these days, continues to be felt in the form of her absence.

My daughter, Logan, continues to be the light of my life. She is a trailblazer for her generation, and she never questions the importance of social justice, of doing good work, of being of service to others, and of always remaining humble. I am her father, so I can say these things. Being her father has been the best—and hardest—job I have ever had.

During the course of this book, I lost three people who were very important to me, yet I feel them with me every day: Tom Buckley, David S. Broder, and Owen Laster (the last two on the same day). Each was self-effacing and self-deprecating, and they carried themselves with dignity. All of them, each in his own way, helped me become a better man.

I (Jerry) would first like to thank all of my teammates — living or deceased, from Chelyan Junior High onward — but in particular Willie Akers, for all the reasons I wrote in the book but that only scratch the surface, and Elgin Baylor, who took me under his wing when I first got to Los Angeles and showed me what it meant to be a professional basketball player. Thanks, Elg.

To all my coaches, from Duke Shaver to Fred Schaus to my favorite, Bill Sharman, I am grateful for both your guidance and your patience.

To the players I coached and the players whom I was responsible for as general manager of the Lakers and president of the Grizzlies, I know I struck many of you as hard to please. I cared about each and every one of you, even if I had a strange way of showing it at times.

To the four owners I played and worked for — Bob Short, Jack Kent Cooke, Jerry Buss, Mike Heisley — I hope you feel that your belief and investment in me reaped the benefits you hoped for. To Jerry in particular, the conversations we would have late into the night are easily among the best memories of my life.

I always tried to meet the high standards of the three women I worked for on the Lakers: Joan McLaughlin, Claire Rothman, and my irreplaceable assistant, the late Mary Lou Liebich. And when I didn't, which was often, they let me know about it. I appreciate the fact that all three of you always reminded me where the bar was set. And a big thank-you to the rest of the Lakers family — especially Tania Jolly, who became a star in her own right — and to the Grizzlies family as well. I couldn't be happier for the success the team and the city of Memphis enjoyed in the 2010–11 season.

A big thanks to everyone in the media who ever covered me as a player or an executive — especially Doug Krikorian, Joe McDonnell, Mal Florence, Scott Ostler, Ted Green, Rich Levin, Jim

Murray, Mickey Furfari, A. L. "Shorty" Hardman, Bill Smith, Tony Constantine, Pete Vecsey, Frank Deford, Aileen Vosin, Mitch Chortkoff, T. J. Simers, Bill Dwyre, Bill Plaschke, Bud Furillo, Dan Hafner, Jim Gray, and my great friend Jim Hill. All of you challenged me and, often, made me bigger than I was, or ever deserved to be.

An assortment of people who fit no particular category but whom I want to acknowledge and thank: John Hosford, a Los Angeles fireman; Jess "Waddy the Body" Watson; Hollis Johnson, for all the lunches and for all the good times we had on our fishing trips; Charlie Rosenzweig and Zelda Spoelstra of the NBA; and Dana Davis, who, among other things, allowed Jonathan to stay with him for seven nights in Memphis, which Dana continues to insist was six too many. In Memphis as well there is John Stokes, whom I hunted with numerous times, and Brent Ross, Steve Blagburn, and Keith Burnett, who uncomplainingly converted an inestimable number of videotapes into DVDs.

To my surrogate mother, Ann Dinardi, who understood me and what I needed. And to my mentor, Pete Newell, my thanks for never giving up on me and taking me with you to Rome. I am sorry I didn't get there in time that day, Pete, to talk with you once more. You meant the world to me and I hope you knew that.

A special debt of gratitude to Chick Hearn who, with his wife, Marge, will always be family to me. The same goes for Dr. Robert Kerlan, Bob Falkenberg, Richard Collis, Tom Polich, Gary Colson, Ken Jones, Bobby Freedman, Lon Rosen (who has been devoted to every member of my family for as long as I can remember; I often give Lon a hard time, but he knows how I feel about him), Arn and Nancy Tellem, Steve and Ellen Jackson (my wonderful neighbors up the street with whom Karen and I spend many quiet evenings, having dinner and watching movies), and Jerry and Margie Perenchio. I have never met a woman who is funnier, or more at home with men, than Margie. She keeps me loose.

Tommy and Estela Sagubo, who have been an integral part of the West household for years, are family too. If you ever come to my house in California and hear someone on the basketball court out back, it's almost certain to be Tommy, knocking down shot after shot.

To those who are family by blood, the Wests: I hope that after reading this my four siblings will better understand their brother, flaws and all, will better understand why I had to write this, and will forgive me for any pain that it might have caused you in the process. I wish the same for my five sons — that perhaps they will see their father in a different light. I know it hasn't been easy at times, having me as your dad, but I love you all very much. At some point, my three grandchildren may get around to reading this, and even, I hope, get something out of it.

I want my nephew Kim West, who is also my lawyer and who never complains about anything (at least that I am aware of) to know this: I view you as a son, Kim.

As I wrote earlier, Karen's family, the Buas (including her late father, Bennie) embraced me at a time in my life when I was lost and needed embracing. I love having them over, on Sunday nights especially and on holidays, and even though I don't stay at the dinner table for as long as they love to, my feelings for Trudy (my mother-in-law), Karen's sister Mary, her brother Joe and his wife, Susan, and their children run both true and deep.

And finally, to my wife, Karen, to whom I have been married for thirty-three years (and counting), all the things that words cannot begin to convey. It has not always been smooth, I know that, but I am grateful that you stayed in the game.

About the Authors

Jerry West was born in 1938 in Chelyan, West Virginia. He was an All-American at West Virginia University, won a Gold Medal with his Olympic team in 1960, and played professional basketball for the Los Angeles Lakers from 1960 to 1974. During that time, he was selected to the All-Star team every year and the All-Pro first team in ten of those years, and his team won one championship, in 1972. He is the only professional player from a losing team ever to be given the MVP Award in the playoffs. When he retired, he was the third-highest scorer in NBA history. From 1976 to 1979, he coached the Lakers and guided them to the playoffs all three seasons; from 1979 to 1982, he was a special consultant to the team; and from 1982 to 2000, he was the general manager, then head of basketball operations. During that time, the Lakers won six championships. From 2002 until 2007, he was the president and head of basketball operations for the Memphis Grizzlies, who reached the playoffs in three of those years. In 2011, he became an adviser to the Golden State Warriors and a member of their Executive Board.

Mr. West has five sons—David, Michael, Mark, Ryan, and Jonnie—and lives with his wife, Karen, in both California and West Virginia.

*   *   *

Jonathan Coleman was born in 1951 in Allentown, Pennsylvania. A graduate of the University of Virginia, he is a former journalist with CBS News. He is the author of three critically acclaimed books (two of which were *New York Times* bestsellers): *At Mother's Request* ("A masterwork of reporting"—*Washington Post Book World*); *Exit the Rainmaker* ("A fascinating, symbolic statement of the American psyche"—*Los Angeles Times Book Review*); *Long Way to Go: Black and White in America* ("A stunner...Coleman's narrative technique is superb...a brilliant work"—*Library Journal*). He has contributed to *The New Yorker, Time, Newsweek,* and *New York* magazine, among other publications, has taught literary nonfiction writing at Virginia, and lectures at universities around the country.

Mr. Coleman has a daughter, Logan, and lives in Charlottesville, Virginia.